India's National Income, 1950-1980

India's National Income, 1950-1980

AN ANALYSIS OF ECONOMIC GROWTH AND CHANGE

V.K.R.V. Rao

SAGE PUBLICATIONS
New Delhi/Beverly Hills/London

First published in 1983 by

Sage Publications India Pvt Ltd
C-236 Defence Colony
New Delhi 110 024, India

Sage Publications Inc
275 South Beverly Drive
Beverly Hills, California 90212

Sage Publications Ltd
28 Banner Street
London EC1Y 8QE, England

Published by Tejeshwar Singh for Sage Publications India Pvt Ltd, phototypeset at The Word, Nehru Place and printed at Pearl Offset Press, Kirti Nagar, New Delhi.

Library of Congress Cataloguing in Publication Data

Rao, V.K.R.V. (Vijayendra Kasturi Ranga Varadaraja),
1908—
India's national income, 1950-1980
Bibliography: p.
1. National income—India. I. Title.

HC440. I5R32 1983 339.354 82-22972
ISBN 0-8039-1950-6
ISBN 0-8039-1951-4 (pbk.)

Contents

List of Tables

Preface

It was more than four decades ago that I first ventured into the field of research on India's national income. My first book on this subject — *An Essay on India's National Income – 1925-29* — was published by Allen and Unwin in 1936 and my second book — *The National Income of British India, 1931-32* — by Macmillan in 1940. The first book discussed the history of previous estimates and dealt with India's national income from 1925 to 1929. My second study was primarily an estimational analysis and was based on published and unpublished data and special investigations which I had undertaken.

My interest in national income continued even after 1940, but I could find no time to study it seriously because of my involvement in various activities which included teaching, research on current problems, administration, membership of numerous committees and commissions, a ministerial interlude, and the founding of several institutions for teaching and research in economics and allied social sciences. A generous offer of a National Fellowship by the Indian Council of Social Science Research in June 1977 enabled me to return to my first academic love. However, this time I was was not interested in estimational analysis or in proferring suggestions for estimational improvements. The intervening period of approximately forty years had seen an immense addition to the statistical and other material relating to various aspects of the country's national income. At the same time, during this period I had many opportunities to delve deep into the problems of the Indian economy both as a Professor and a man of public affairs engaged in economic planning and decision-making. It was, therefore, possible for me to take up a long-term study of India's national income after independence and use national accounts data for an economic analysis of growth and change covering a period of thirty years from 1950-51 to 1979-80.

My thanks are due to my colleague Dr V.G. Rao at the Institute for Social and Economic Change, Bangalore, for assisting me in supervising and checking the statistical data involved and for acting as a sounding board for my ideas. My thanks are also due to Mr Nagabhushana for helping me with the laborious statistical work and for suffering with patience the irritating extra work involved by the many changes in the tables, calculations and data which I continued to make till just before finalising the book. I am also grateful to Mr Ramachandran and Mr Krishnamurthy for typing the numerous drafts of the manuscript, and to Mr B.M. Veerabhadraiah and Miss Shreedevi for comparing the drafts of the typescripts innumerable times. I am indebted to the Indian Council for Social Science Research and its then Member-Secretary, the late Mr J.P. Naik, for offering me a National Fellowship; to the Institute of Economic Growth and its Chief Accounts Officer, Mr T.C. Sharma, for administering it; and to Mr Y.V. Chandan for looking after my typing and other requirements during my periodic visits to the Institute. My thanks are also due to the Institute for Social and Economic Change, Bangalore, where I spent most of my time while working on this study. Last, but not least, my thanks are due to the CSO, its Director-General, Dr B.N. Seal, its Additional Director, Miss Uma Datta Roy Choudhury, and its Joint Director, Mr Jagdish Kumar, for their prompt compliance with the author's requests for data; similarly to Mr S.B. Gotheskar of the National Income Unit of the Reserve Bank of India, and similarly to the Directors of the State Statistical Bureaus.

In returning to a serious study of India's national income after a lapse of four decades and completing this work, I had the satisfaction of fulfilling a long cherished dream. I only hope that its results may prove of some interest, if not value, to fellow-workers in national income and to policy-makers in planning and economic growth in this country.

Bangalore V.K.R.V. RAO
December 1982.

Introduction

This book deals with the growth of India's national income over a period of thirty years (1950-51 to 1979-80). It is primarily based on the national accounts data published by the Central Statistical Organisation of the Government of India in their annual White Papers. In addition, relevant data available in the Reserve Bank of India publications, the National Sample Survey and other statistical data published by the Government have also been used.

The object of this study is to analyse the growth and change in the Indian economy over a period of thirty years, primarily on the basis of the national accounts data covering this period. It also includes projections of growth and change in the last two decades of the century and presents alternative scenarios of India's national income in 2001 AD.

The first chapter discusses the concept of national income and its limitations; the second the data base and methodology used for the study, which is followed by a description and analysis of the different aspects of India's economic growth and change as seen through national income data. The third chapter deals with the growth of the national income in nominal and real terms, the base year used for the constant price series being 1960-61 rather than 1970-71 which has been used in the official discussions on the subject. The effects of the growth of money income on the distribution of real income among the different sectors of the economy has also been assessed.

The fourth chapter deals with the changes that have taken place in the organisational pattern of the economy in terms of the public sector, the organised private sector, the unorganised or unincorporated and individual-based private sector, and the mixed incomes of the self-employed. This chapter also deals with the changing shares of the primary, secondary and tertiary sectors and their sub-sectors in the NDP and links the sectoral changes in the NDP with changes in the occupational structure of the work-force. The fifth chapter deals with changes in the product-mix of the national income by commodities and sectors of industrial origin, and comments on significant aspects of this change.

The sixth chapter deals with changes in the quantum and composition of consumption and its distribution by rural and urban sectors as well as by expenditure decile groups.

Chapter 7 makes use of the data available on state domestic products to analyse inter-state variations in growth and national shares, changes in ranking, and the extent to which inter-state inequality has undergone a change. Chapter 8 considers the question of factor shares, the data available confining the study to about two-thirds of the national domestic product. Chapter 9 deals with the growth and composition of savings by the public sector, private corporate sector and the household sector. The causes behind the secular growth in the savings rate are explained and the savers are identified by classes and by sectors.

Chapter 10 deals with the growth and changes in the volume and composition of capital formation and highlights the increasing share of the public sector in capital formation. An analysis is also made of changing shares in capital formation in construction, machinery and equipment, and stocks. Capital-output ratios are examined on both a macro and a sectoral basis and the sharp increase in this ratio over this period is analysed. Chapter 11 focuses on productivity and growth by taking up labour productivity, capital productivity, land productivity and management productivity and the relation of these four factors of production to the growth of the national product. The growth rate and changes in productivity by sectors of industrial origin are also considered. Chapter 12 presents alternative projections of India's national income in 2001 AD on the basis of observed trend-growth rates during the twelve years 1968-69 to 1979-80 in the net domestic product as a whole, and by industrial origin and state domestic products. This chapter also itemises some of the policy implications that emerge from this study which, if implemented, could go a long way towards increasing economic growth and improving the distribution of the fruits of such growth during the concluding decades of the century.

The Concept and its Limitations

1

Till the development of the national income concept, economic analysts used to rely largely on indicators — such as indices of sectoral production and money supply — to represent the economic activity of a country. Because these measures cover only some segments or assets of an economy, they cannot be considered as representative of the overall economic activity of a country. Conceptually, national income is nothing more than a simple linear aggregation of income accruing to the factors of production, supplied by the normal residents of the country in question.

Though national income is a conceptually simple and satisfactory index of overall economic activity, given the heterogeneous nature of goods and services that a country encompasses, the measurement of national income is not that simple. The circular nature of all economic activities suggests that the index can be measured in three ways — at the point of production, after the point of flow of income, and at the point of final utilisation. In literature these measures are referred to as the product, income, and expenditure methods respectively.

In the production method, because the physical units of production of different commodities cannot be totalled, a common denominator, such as value, is essential. Under this approach, depending upon the final use of the estimate, an economy is divided into different industries or final uses, and the outputs of these industrial groups are converted into money terms and added up to arrive at the estimate of national income.

The implicit assumption behind this exercise is the identification of relative prices with corresponding differences in relative utilities and scarcities. This is what is supposed to happen under market prices, but even here it is income distribution which determines market demand and not relative utilities to consumers with equal incomes; while scarcities could be due not only to the market allocation of productive resources but also to mistaken utilisation or under-utilisation of productive capacities, lack of flexibility to price response in the production mechanism, deliberate restrictions on production, and random fluctuations in the natural phenomena which affect production.

When both prices and production are controlled or regulated, prices become more a reflection of public policy than of producer or consumer choice and can no longer be fully identified with relative utilities and scarcities that are supposed to be functions of a system of market prices. When national expenditure exceeds the value of the output of goods and services at a given price level, there is a tendency for all prices to rise which is termed inflation; but this general rise is not uniform for all commodities and services so that a new element is now introduced into relative prices. Inflation thus results not only in a rise in the general level of prices but also differential rises in individual prices of both production and consumption goods and services, so that changes in the value of money differ from different producers and different consumers, with prices ceasing to reflect either the pre-inflation or the non-inflation correspondence with relative utilities and scarcities. The deflation of money national income by the observed change in the general level of prices does not capture this differential change in price relations.

The use of national income as a macro-economic indicator of economic well-being is thus subject to even conceptual limitations by the fact that it can only be expressed in money terms. These limitations have been discussed at length in the literature on the international comparability of national income magnitudes but have not been taken sufficiently into account in the discussions of the magnitude of a given national income or changes in this magnitude over a period of time. The difficulties created by having a deemed rate of capital consumption are resolved only by using the gross domestic product (GDP) in place of the net domestic product (NDP) and gross domestic capital formation (GDCF) in place of net domestic capital formation (NDCF). However, it is only the NDP which is available for consumption and investment or additions to NDCF which, along with other factors like technical development and size and quality of the labour force, determines the growth of the NDP.

The effect of changes in the general level of prices on the magnitude of the national product is taken care of by the use of deflators, though this does not bring out the changes in the product-mix caused by the decline of old commodities and the emergence of new commodities, nor the changes in relative price over the base period. No attempt is made to weigh the national income time series by changes in its consumption by income groups (a suggestion to this effect was put forward some time ago by McNamara during the later years of his stewardship of the World Bank), or by its relation to the production of the population below the poverty line, or attention given to changes in its total magnitude. Similarly, no deduction is made in the national accounts data for the increased costs resulting from urbanisation and industrialisation — though the former has been conceputally recognised, while the latter is beginning to be recognised in terms of ecological damage, but not yet in terms of psychological damage to the quality of life. It is also not clear whether the deduction for capital consumption in the form of depreciation allowance for replacement includes obsolescence or any allowance for the depletion of non-renewable resources and their replacement by alternative resources; but from available data, it appears that this takes the form of fresh captial formation from current resources rather than from depreciation funds earmarked for that purpose.

The national income concept also does not take account of variations in the purchasing power of the unit in which it is expressed for different income groups, for different regions in the country concerned, and for urban-urban and urban-rural dichotomies. Nor has any satisfactory answer been found to the vexing problem of the changes in real national income behind changes in the output of the government sector in areas outside the scope of private activity, such as the maintenance of law and order and national security. If national income goes up as a result of an increase in employees' compensation in the realm of law and order and defence, even if it is deflated to take account of a rise in the cost of living, does it mean a real rise in national income? How far is an increase in the expenditure of the government on law and order and defence an indicator of better economic well-being or should it be regarded as an increase in the cost of producing the national income and therefore deducted from the GDP for arriving at the NDP? What is the opportunity cost of increasing employment in this sector of the government? Is there a norm for the proportion of such expenditure to the NDP above which it ceases to be an addition to real income? What is the effect of the purchasing power created by this additional employment on increasing the domestic output of goods and services? Then, again, what would be the effect on the alternatives in production and employment if the purchasing power which is taken away from the tax-payer is left with him as his personal disposable income which he can use either for consumption or capital formation?

These are questions which cannot be dealt with on purely economic grounds, but which do have economic consequences, and which affect the competence of a national income series as a macro-indicator of economic betterment. There is also the question whether one should treat the economic services rendered by the government in different sectors as an expense which should be deducted from the gross value added to arrive at the net value added or the NDP. Apart from this sector of government expenditure, the output of the public sector under government administration is an important part of the NDP; but it is valued on the basis of administered prices which do not compare with similar prices in the non-government sector. A conceptual solution has not yet been found for the government sector in national income analysis.

The national income concept does not, of course, take account of such imponderables as the state of public contentment, sense of national security, alienation, psychological tensions, domestic law and order, family ties, problems of the aged and the retired, and all the incidental social, cultural and political changes which accompany and effect the growth of the national income.

The foregoing delineation of the conceptual limitations of national income as a macro-indicator of the level and changes in economic well-being does not mean, however, that the measure should not be used as a macro-indicator of economic gowth and change. But these limitations should always be kept in mind when using national income results, and allowance made, to the extent possible, for these factors which do not get included in the national income concept, whether for practical or other reasons.

Apart from its conceptual limitations, national accounts data also suffer from the limitations that emerge in its measurement. Ideally, the value of output can be measured by a census of production of all goods and services valued at current prices. Deducting from it the cost of inputs, one can arrive at the GDP, and then at the NDP by deducting the estimated consumption of capital used in production. Yet, it is not possible to undertake such a complete census and cover all self-employed or family enterprises, small and tiny enterprises and many services in the non-salary and non-wage sectors. As a result, one has to resort to sample surveys, indicators for moving from bench-mark surveys, and other kinds of estimation. The more the economy is organised in corporate, or incorporate but otherwise organised units, the greater will be the coverage of the census and the less the error, excepting for deliberate or involuntary mistakes in returns.

The difficulty of course will arise in calculating the rate of capital consumption in different units and sectors; also in estimating changes in stocks and their valuation. The pricing of goods and quality differentiation will also present problems. But, on the whole, to the extent that commodity production data and prices can be directly obtained from producing units, it is possible to obtain a large measure of accuracy in national income estimation. However, there will be difficulties when one takes up the service industries in the census, especially in the private sector, but these can be overcome by adopting suitable norms. There could be greater uncertainty in the net value added by the service industries as compared to the commodity industries. When prices are administered or regulated and transactions take place outside the limits they set, there will be some error in estimation of net value added, both in the case of the commodity and the service sectors. Because of the better organisation of economic activity, developed countries can get better results from a census of production than the less developed ones.

Where the bulk of the producers pay income-tax and the rest of the workers make a regular payment which is linked with their income, the income method can give fairly accurate results, except of course for evasion or under-reporting of income. This method will not cover the incomes of the self-employed who do not pay any income-tax or make social security payments, nor of wage earners or other service workers whose incomes are below the exemption limit. But in developed countries, where income tax or social security payments cover the bulk of the population, a large measure of accuracy can be obtained by employing the income method. By combining the income method with the census of production method, developed industrial countries, where only a small proportion of the labour force is employed in agriculture, can turn out far more accurate national accounts data than the developing countries with a high proportion of the labour force involved in agriculture, the dominance of small and unregistered units in both the commodity and service sectors, the low coverage of income tax, and the lack of accounts of expenditure and returns on the part of the bulk of the producers.

In India, the estimation of national income and related aggregates is undertaken by the Central Statistical Organisation (CSO) attached to the Ministry of Planning, Government of India. The estimates are published annually as the *National Accounts Statistics* (NAS). The estimates prepared annually use the latest available data collected from different sources. To ensure the use of the most recent information it becomes necessary, from time to time, to introduce minor revisions in the method of estimation. Such chages are generally indicated in the annual NAS, as and when they are introduced. Besides, the CSO tries to revise its annual estimates periodically and retrospectively, may be on account of the latest available information. These continuous changes, however, caution the user to opt for the latest available NAS. Otherwise, inferences are susceptible to measurement errors. This is quite clear, for example, from the five different estimates given for the 1975-76 NDP by successive NAS publications — while the 1978 NAS places this figure at Rs 60,851 crores, the 1979 NAS estimates it at Rs 61,864 crores, the 1980 NAS gives it as Rs 61,899 crores, the 1981 NAS puts it as Rs 62,394 crores and the latest (1982) NAS gives it as Rs 62,324 crores.

The method of estimation of national income adopted by the CSO is a combination of the product and income approaches. The estimate of national income for a particular year is obtained by aggregating the contributions to NDP by a number of industrial sectors and then adjusting the total for net factor income flows from abroad. For this purpose, the economy is initially divided into fifteen industrial sectors. While the contributions of six industrial sectors — namely, agriculture, forestry and logging, fishing, mining and quarrying, manufacturing, and construction — are estimated through the product approach, the contribution of the remaining are calculated through the income approach. An examination of the sector-wise estimates indicates that only about 60 per cent of the estimate of NDP for a particular year depends on direct information relating to that year, the estimate for the remaining 40 per cent is obtained through indirect approaches, involving intrapolations of bench-mark information. Table 1.1 gives an idea about the current data base used for estimating the national income of 1976-77. The estimates of net factor income from abroad are based on exchange control data compiled by the Balance of Payments Division of the Economic Department, Reserve Bank of India. Though the limitations of this data from the national income point of view are well known, the distortions brought forward by these limitations are not. At the same time, since this item constitutes a very negligible share in the national income of any given year, it should not cause undue worry.

Turning to other aggregates, while estimation of private final consumption expenditures and captial formation is approached through the commodity flow method, estimates of savings and factor shares are based on independent direct data sets. In India, because of the existence of unincorporated en-

Table 1.1

Share of the Estimate of NDP Based on Direct Current Data, 1976-77

Industry	Share in NDP	Per cent of Estimate Based on Current Data		
		Output	Input	Value Added
Agriculture	39.8	67.6	21.5	58.2
Forestry	1.2	59.7	—	56.9
Fishing	0.9	96.2	—	83.9
Mining & quarrying	1.3	100.0	97.6	99.4
Registered manufacturing	9.9	100.0	100.0	100.0
Unregistered manufacturing	5.8	—	—	26.1
Construction	5.8	48.6	50.7	49.3
Electricity, gas, etc.	1.3	—	—	100.00
Railways	1.5	—	—	100.0
Other transport	2.8	—	—	33.3
Communication	0.7	—	—	100.0
Trade, hotels, etc.	13.1	—	—	6.4
Banking & insurance	3.1	—	—	94.6
Real estate, etc.	2.6	—	—	50.8
Public administration	5.1	—	—	92.5
Other services	5.1	—	—	64.2
TOTAL	100.0	—	—	59.6

Source: CSO, *National Accounts Statistics — Source and Methods,* April 1980.

terprises and household industries which either do not maintain accounts or are wholly managed by self-employed workers, factor incomes generated cannot always be separated between income from labour and other factors. To accommodate this, factor incomes are categorised under five heads — compensation of employees, rent, interest, profit and mixed income. Mixed income covers the total income of own account workers as well as the profits generated in unincorporated enterprises. Savings represent the excess of current income over current expenditure. Accordingly, they represent balancing items on the income and outlay accounts of producing enterprises and households, government administration and other final consumers. Keeping this in view, for the purpose of the estimation of savings the economy is divided into three broad constituent sectors — households, private corporate and public. Household savings are divided into financial and physical savings, and the latter are obtained as residuals — from the aggregate estimates obtained for the economy, those corresponding to the private corporate sector and the public sector and obtained on a commodity flow approach are deducted to give the household sector's contribution to savings in the form of physical assets. The private corporate sector estimates are based on an analysis of sample companies undertaken by the Reserve Bank of India (RBI) and blown up on the basis of the ratio of paid-up capital of the sample companies to all total companies. Implicit in this is the assumption that savings are linearly related to paid-up capital, while the savings of the public sector are obtained directly from budgetary accounts and the balance sheets of public enterprises.

It must be added that the CSO has been making available, over an increasing area, desegregated data on the major items constituting the national income, and also publishing as appendices to the NAS special time series on some items or missing segments in the time series, all of which enable an interested researcher to use the NAS more effectively for an analysis of growth and change in the economy. Further, the National Sample Survey Organisation and the Research Cells in the RBI and State Income Units in the State Statistical Organisations have been publishing data which constitute a useful supplement to the NAS and aid an analysis of growth and change in the economy. Altogether, to one who has dealt with national income data before the advent of independence, when it consisted largely of making bricks without straw,[1] the position is very different today with the abundance of data available and the extensive field they cover of different sectors or aspects of the national economy. They may not all be equal in accuracy, element of guess work or estimational efficiency, but they do provide a lot of useful material. And it is this which makes possible this attempt to look at the economy as a whole and trace its growth over the years.

Reference

1. V.K.R.V. Rao, *National Income of British India, 1931-32*, London, Macmillan, 1940.

Data Base and Methodology 2

When discussing the various aspects of national income and its reflection of and impact on the domestic economy, it is customary to deal with GDP and NDP rather than GNP and NNP, as it is difficult to identify income from abroad by the different categories of industrial origin or factors of production. Moreover, in India, this factor constitutes a negligible portion of national income and can be dealt with separately (see Appendix 1). As depreciation or capital consumption, which differentiates GDP from NDP, is based on conceptual terms rather than on detailed statistical calculations, it also needs to be considered separately (see Appendix 2). The major subject of this work is, therefore, the net domestic product (NDP) of the Indian economy and its desegregated data.

The NDP should be equal to the sum of the net product of all industrial sectors of the economy (industrial, in this context, means all economic activity, not only manufacturing). It should also correspond to net domestic income or the total of all factor payments. It should also be equal to the sum of final consumption and net saving in the economy. These identities make a study of the NDP interesting, not merely as an overall aggregate of the national economic condition but as an indicator of the working of the economy, its growth, its distribution among different categories of economic activity, different factors of production, different organisational patterns, and between the public sector and private sector, its consumption-mix and capital formation, and its distribution by income groups and impact on poverty. It should be possible not only to study the past and the trends it reveals, but also to make projections of the future either by extrapolation or on the basis of defined changes in the parameters that determine production, distribution and utilisation of the national product. To the extent possible, and subject to all the conceptual and data limitations inherent in the subject, the NDP will be viewed from this broad angle and the working of the Indian economy as reflected in the NDP data will be analysed.

Given the revisions that the NAS has undergone with the availability of more recent information, the data are collected from the latest NAS accounts for a given period. While the October 1964 *White Paper* is used to obtain information relating to the period covering 1950-51 to 1960-61, October 1976 is used for information from 1960-61 to 1970-71, and February 1982 for data relating to 1970-71 to 1979-80. At present, only 'Quick Estimates' are available for 1980-81; these are still tentative and are likely to be changed considerably. Therefore, this study is confined to the thirty year period from 1950-51 to 1979-80.

To identify the changes in the real NDP and its related aggregates, it is necessary to use a constant price time series. The NAS documents present three such series, one with 1948-49 as the base for the earlier period, another with 1960-61 as the base for a later period, and finally one with 1970-71 as the base for the entire period. It is not desirable to use all three series, as the wide differences they make for in absolute figures of the NDP for individual years would only cause confusion and may lead to misleading inferences by an unwary use of individual absolute figures, though the growth rates shown by the different series do not show much difference. Table 2.1 illustrates the wide differences that result in calculating absolute figures for individual years by using these alternative bases for the constant price time series.

Table 2.1

Growth in NDP at Three Different Bases (Rs Crores)

Year	*1948-49 Base*	*1960-61 Base*	*1970-71 Base*
1950-51	8870	9122	16798
1951-52	9120	9306	17128
1955-56	10480	10870	19969
1960-61	12619	13335	24360
1965-66	14416	15234	27335
1970-71	18129	19158	34519
1975-76	21213	22417	40170
1978-79	24706	26150	46713

The differences are widest between the figures based on 1948-49 and those which use 1970-71 as the base (which has now been adopted by the CSO for estimating changes in the real NDP over the entire period). These differences can partly be attributed to the absolute differences in the price levels of the two years. Part of the gap is also because of the differences in the weighting diagrams adopted by these two price series, as can be seen from Table 2.2.

It must also be noted that the index of wholesale prices, which includes the effect of the increasing quantity of money as also the changes in the weighting pattern, rose from 95.39 per cent in 1950-51 to 181.1 per cent in 1970-71.

Because of these differences between 1950-51 and 1970-71, using absolute figures based on 1970-71 for any purpose other than calculating the rate of growth would lead to absurd results, which is evident if any key item is taken.

Table 2.2

Weights Used for Price Index Calculations

Items	*1950-51 Base*	*1970-71 Base*
I Food articles	504	431.21
II Fuel, power, light & lubricants	30	84.59
III Industrial raw materials	155	118.68
IV Manufactures	311	365.52

For example, let us take capital formation in 1950-51 at current prices and 1970-71 prices — the 1970-71 base would show capital formation at Rs 1641 crores, while its estimated value at current prices is only Rs 630 crores. This would apply to practically all the items constituting the NDP, as the price level in 1970-71 was much higher than in 1950-51, apart from significant changes in commodity weights and individual price relatives. In fact, the constant price figure for the NDP for 1950-51 would only be 92.9 per cent of the current price figure for that year on the 1948-49 base and 95.5 per cent on the 1960-61 base, while it would be as much as 175.9 per cent on the 1970-71 base.

Using the 1970-71 price figure is also open to the serious objection that when one is compiling a time series on the basis of constant prices, it is not desirable to make backward projections; and if one has to do it, the period over which the backward projections are made should be short rather than long. Taking 1970-71 as the base for calculating the NDP at constant price from 1950-51 is too long a period for a meaningful interpretation of the reality of the change that has taken place since then.

Therefore, this study will not use the 1970-71 based time series in the ensuing discussion of the NDP and related figures. The choice of the base, then, lies between 1948-49 and 1960-61. The 1948-49 base is not acceptable not only because it is so far removed from 1978-79 in terms of the structure of the economy but also because it only marks the beginning of Indian independence and Indian planning and cannot cover many of the changes that have taken place since then. The 1960-61 base comes nearest to the 1948-49 base in price terms and to that of 1970-71 in commodity weight terms, while the series based on 1948-49 and 1970-71 are the farthest removed from each other in terms of both price and commodity. Under the circumstances, the time series based on 1960-61 prices will be used for identifying and analysing changes in India's real NDP during this period and for interpreting the economic development that has taken place in the light of national accounts data.

Growth is measured in two alternate forms in this analysis. First, wherever comparisons are attempted in terms of magnitude, growth is measured on the basis of three-year averages related to the end points. This is rationalised in terms of the economy's heavy dependence on agriculture which is known for frequent annual fluctuations resulting from weather and other climatic factors. Second, wherever growth rates are compared, the rate is measured in terms of a compound growth rate, annual observations being the bases for such calculations.

The work-force data are collected from the four annual censuses that cover the period under review. Employment and related data are drawn from labour statistics and the labour yearbooks published by the Ministry of Labour. The state domestic products (SDPs) and their distribution are taken from the RBI bulletins of April 1978, July 1979 and September 1981. The data required for international comparisons are taken from the UN yearbooks.

The NAS has classified the organisational pattern of the economy under two heads — the organised and unorganised sectors. The organised sector is defined as

> generally all enterprises which are either registered or come under the purview of the Indian Factories Act, 1948, Mines and Minerals (Regulation and Development) Act, 1957, the Company Law, the Central/State Sales Tax Acts, and the Shops and Establishment Acts of the State Governments. Also included are all government companies, departmental enterprises as well as public sector corporations, forestry, irrigation works and plantations. The organised sector includes all the activities coming under the industrial heads of Electricity, Gas and Water Supply, Railways, Passenger Transport by tramways and buses, Freight Transport by road in the public sector, Ports and Pilotage, Lighthouses and Light Ships, Air Transportation, Flying and Gliding Clubs, Airports, Warehousing Corporations, Cold Storage, Registered Trade, Hotels and Restaurants, Banking and Insurance other than those relating to money lenders and pawn brokers, Joint Stock Companies engaged in real estate business and other business services, public administration and defence, community and personal services operated by recognised educational institutions, public sector medical and health services, sanitary services, research and scientific services and joint stock companies.

The unorganised sector consists of the rest of the economy and includes unincorporated enterprises and household industries which maintain accounts or do not do so or are wholly managed by self-employed workers. As the income generated in the latter two categories cannot always be separated into factor incomes, they have termed their NDP as 'the mixed income of the self-employed'. Thus the economy can be classified into three sectors with reference to the identifiability of their respective NDPs by factor incomes — the organised, unorganised, and self-employed.

Data on all the four types of factor incomes — namely, compensation of employees, rent, interest and profits (including dividends) — are furnished for the organised sector. For the unorganised sector, data is available for compensation of employees, rent and interest, but not for profits and dividends, since these have been included in the mixed income of the self-employed. It is, therefore, necessary to make an estimate of the profits and dividends that accrue to the unorganised sector in order to bring them on par with the organised sector in respect of all the four categories of factor payments. A corresponding deduction has also to be made from the mixed income of the self-employed so as to make it truly representative of the income of the self-employed that cannot be broken up into factor shares. To do this, one assumes that the relation of profits and dividends to the total of the three other factor incomes (for which data are available) in the unorganised sector is the same as in the case of the organised private sector for which full data is available.* By adding these estimates of profits to the three other categories of factor income of the unorganised sector we are able to obtain the total factor income in that sector. The balance constitutes the incomes not identifiable by factor break up in the unorganised sector and constitutes the mixed incomes of the self-employed. Thus, in this study, the organisational pattern of the economy has been divided initially under two broad heads; namely, one whose NDP can be broken into factor shares and the other whose NDP is a mixture of factor incomes and cannot be divided into factor shares. These are referred to as the 'modern' and the 'traditional' sectors respectively.

Two sources of data are available for expenditure on private final consumption. One is the CSO *White Paper on National Accounts* where the estimates are in terms of national aggregates. The other is in the NSS data on final consumption expenditure of sample households by per capita monthly expenditure classes for urban and rural areas. The CSO data give a time series of private final consumption expenditure from 1950-51 to 1978-79 at constant prices (base 1970-71) but only from 1960-61 at current prices. No similar time series is available in the NSS data. The consumption expenditure data derived from the NSS data are not comparable with those given in the CSO data even for common years, as there are discrepancies between them in their individual and overall totals, and the differences are not of the same order of magnitude. The difference between these alternative estimates of consumption expenditure has been dealt with in detail in many of the papers that are concerned with consumer behaviour.

There is some controversy on the view that the NSS estimates are superior to the NAS estimates. This discussion is of no immediate relevance for our study. However, there is no doubt that the NSS data do show the pattern of distribution of consumption both by expenditure classes and by rural/urban areas, which can be used with credibility. In fact, they have been widely used for this purpose, both by official agencies and by individual scholars, for, among others, studies on the incidence of indirect taxation, distribution of

* Some support for this assumption can be had from the Reserve Bank survey on small scale industries for 1977-78. This indicates that the wage component of gross value added by small scale units (mostly unregistered) is, on an average, 49.1 per cent, while the corresponding figure for a registered manufacturing unit was 51.9 per cent or practically the same as in the small scale units. *Reserve Bank Occasional Paper*, 1980, p. 158.

income, level of poverty, and formulation of elasticities of demand by commodities. But to view the broad subject of growth and change in the country's private final consumption expenditure, NAS data are preferred not only because they give a time series for the entire period under review but also because our analysis of growth and change in the Indian economy is basically a study of national accounts data from this angle.

Though this study prefers to use the 1960-61 base series for all requisite comparisons, this is not possible in the case of consumption expenditure analysis. This is because, till today, the CSO has not published, along with its 1960-61 and 1970-71 base estimates of consumption, a corresponding current price series for the period 1950-51 to 1960-61. These data do not facilitate converting the 1970-71 base estimates given for 1950-51 to 1960-61 into 1960-61 base estimates, and the CSO has not provided such data. Accordingly, in the discussion relating to consumption expenditure, the estimates used are 1970-71 base figures. This should not affect the inferences drawn, for the analysis has avoided the use of magnitudes of the estimates.

It would be interesting to find out what happened over this period to the distribution of private final consumption between rural and urban areas in the country, between expenditure groups of ascending size in the population, and between inter-state population groups. The NAS data give only national totals of private final consumption expenditure. Assuming that the distribution pattern indicated by the NSS data is realistic, NAS consumption data can be apportioned to different states. This assumption is to be supplemented with an additional estimate which follows from the fact that NAS estimates are available for the period 1956-57 to 1973-74 only. The NSS round covering data relating to 1978-79 is completed but the results are yet to be published. Therefore, this study purposes to use the simple linear trend extrapolation to obtain estimates for the years not covered by NSS rounds.

The CSO has recently started compiling SDPs. Though the data are used in this study, they do not contain details of industry-wise distribution. However, such information is given in some RBI bulletins. Normally, the constant base series are used to gain an understanding of growth and distribution; but the use of real SDPs provided by the RBI gives rise to certain problems. Apart from the fact that the RBI gives the SDPs of some states at 1970-71 prices and others at 1960-61 prices, the deflators used are not uniform for all the states, nor are they identical with the deflator used for the NDP. Thus, according to the RBI data, whereas the average annual increase in the NDP deflator between 1970-71 and 1977-78 is 8.40 per cent, some of the SDP deflators are above this figure (Madhya Pradesh 9.50, Kerala 8.80, Bihar and Gujarat 8.50), while many of the state deflators are below this figure (Jammu and Kashmir 6.50, Karnataka 7.00, Punjab 7.10 and West Bengal, Tamil Nadu and Himachal Pradesh 7.30). The range of the average annual increase between 1970-71 and 1977-78 in SDP deflators is from 6.50 to 9.50 per cent. If the rise in the SDP deflators is viewed from 1960-61 to 1977-78, they range from 2.28 to 3.37 per cent. Under these data constraints, this study proposes to discuss geographical distribution in terms of current prices.

It is customary for analysts of national income data to identify the shares of the factors of production in the national product and the changes, if any, in these shares over a given period for which a time series data is available. The traditionally accepted factors of production are four — namely, land, labour, capital and enterprise — and their shares are described as rent, wages and salaries or employees' compensation, interest, and profits. The *UN Yearbook of National Accounts, 1979,* which is the latest available edition, does not go into the details of these four categories of factor incomes, but groups them under two heads, viz., employee compensation and operational surplus. Operational surplus is a catch-all which remains after deducting employees' compensation from the NDP or, if GDP is used, after deducting from it, besides employee compensation, indirect taxes minus subsidies and consumption of fixed capital. Table 2.3 gives a consolidated picture of the data contained in these tables on the share of employees' compensation in the NDP and GDP of India.

Table 2.3

Share of Employee Compensation (Percentage)

Year	*Share in NDP*	*Share in GDP*
1970	84.7	73.0
1971	63.6	72.0
1972	83.7	72.0
1973	85.8	74.0
1974	85.5	73.0
1975	84.5	71.0
1976	82.7	69.0
1977	83.1	70.0

The UN tables give a misleading picture of the share of employee compensation in the national product, making it much higher than that of any other country listed in its yearbook. This is because of the inclusion of the mixed income of the self-employed in the Indian national product in the UN tabulation of the share of employee compensation. In actual fact, the mixed income of the self-employed includes payment for all the four factors of production; but as it is not possible to segregate them and as they all accrue to the self-employed, they have been lumped together under the head 'mixed income of the self-employed'. It is simply not possible to segregate the whole of the Indian national product, net or gross, into its constituent factor shares; and to do so would only yield a misleading picture of the Indian economy. It is, however, possible to identify the shares of the different factors of production in the national product if the share of the mixed income of the self-employed is excluded. To do this some adjustments, like the one proposed earlier, have to be adopted.

There are two official rates of estimation for savings — one prepared by the RBI and the other constructed by the CSO. In addition, the National Council of Applied Economic Research (NCAER) also constructs its own estimate of savings, but the objective in this case is to gather information on the motivational and behavioural aspects of household saving. Continuous time series are not compiled by the NCAER. Further, the household sector used by the NCAER has a different coverage from those of the RBI and the CSO. While an institutional approach—which equates the household sector with individuals, non-corporate business and non-profit private institutions—is adopted by the RBI and the CSO, the NCAER identifies it with change in earned surplus.

The first set of RBI estimates covering the periods 1950-51 to 1957-58 were published in the March 1960 issue of its monthly bulletin. These estimates were partially revised and published along with the 1958-59 estimates in the August 1961 issue of the RBI bulletin. A third study, which appeared in March 1965, further revised the earlier estimates while presenting the estimates for the period 1959-60 to 1962-63. In all these surveys estimates were prepared for physical and financial savings, and were divided into rural and urban sectors. Since the publication of the third study the RBI bulletins have been confined only to the estimation of financial savings and do not provide a rural-urban break up of total savings. The first set of savings estimates prepared by the CSO was published in 1961 and since then the estimates have been made available for the period starting with 1950-51. At present, the estimates are available for the entire thirty-year period covering 1950-51 to 1979-80. These are available at current prices and no sectoral break up is provided.

An examination of the RBI and the CSO estimates shows considerable differences in the magnitude of estimates. Both the series indicate similar trends and fluctuations. Since this study is aimed at examining the growth and changes indicated by national income accounts, the CSO estimates are preferred. However, to examine the differential growth attributed to rural-urban sectors, the trends indicated by the RBI are superimposed on the CSO estimates. The share of the rural sector's savings in total savings for the period 1950-51 to 1962-63 has indicated rather stable proportions with small fluctuations. Hence, for the purpose of this study, while 1950-62 aggregate savings estimates given by the CSO are divided into rural and urban, using the shares of corresponding years as indicated by RBI estimates, the average rate indicated for the period 1950-63 is applied uniformly for all the post-1962-63 years to arrive at a rural-urban break down.

An alternative is to estimate rural savings through the familiar regression approaches using total savings and rural savings given by the RBI for the period 1950-63 as the data base. Of these two alternative estimates, the estimates given by the constant ratio method are preferred, because they appear more realistic on *a priori* grounds.

Regarding capital formation, the NAS has started publishing these series since 1961 and the latest publications carry the series covering the period starting with 1950-51. These estimates are prepared separately for construction, machinery and equipment, and change in stocks. The commodity flow approach is used for preparing these estimates. Accordingly, the estimates are made available for the private and public sectors individually, but not for each industrial category. The estimates are constructed at both current and constant prices. The latter series are obtained through a mix of a variety of deflators.

Estimates of capital formation for the entire period are available in the NAS, but these are given in terms of gross capital formation, as capital consumption is not available for individual sectors of industrial origin. Nor is any break down available of changes in stocks in terms of raw materials, semi-finished goods, and finished goods or by producer and consumer goods. A break down of capital formation by construction, machinery and equipment, and changes in stocks are available for the economy as a whole, and for the public and private sectors separately; but industry-wise data are not available though the NAS does give figures for the break down of total capital formation by industrial origin. There are also other limitations on the use of capital formation data which are referred to in the relevant chapters. As the NAS gives only figures of annual additions to gross capital formation and not of capital stock, this study has used the capital stock estimates given by Uma Roy Choudhury[1] for 1950-51 and built its own capital stock estimates for the period, using the additions to capital formation given in the NAS data.

For the purpose of this study, productivity is measured under three heads—labour productivity, capital productivity and land productivity. The data required for the third measure are taken from *Estimates of Area and Production of Principal Crops* published by the Ministry of Agriculture, while figures for the first two are estimated from the NAS data. Finally, projections for the year 2000 AD make use of the trend rates of growth during the period under review, compiled from the NAS data.

Reference

1. Uma Datta Roy Choudhury, 'Industrial Break-down of Capital Stock in India,' *Income and Wealth,* IARNIW, April 1977.

Growth of Real and Nominal NDP 3

NDP represents the unduplicated value of all goods and services produced in the economy at a given period of time, net of the depreciation in the use of the equipment used for the purpose. This aggregate is measured either at constant or current prices. When it is measured at current prices the value of the NDP is determined both by the quantum of output and the changing prices at which they are valued from year to year.

In an inflationary period, much of the increase in theNDP will only represent the rise in prices. To determine the change in real output, adjustments will have to be made for the illusory change resulting from the price rise. To make this adjustment, the value of each component of the aggregate output in each year is expressed in terms of the price prevalent in one single base year, and the results give a time series of NDP values at constant prices or of changes in real output. It is obviously necessary to use this series when dealing with real output. For the purposes of economic analysis of national accounts data it may be sufficient to use the NDP and its components at current prices. As indicated earlier, the constant price series used in this study is 1960-61 unlike the CSO which uses 1970-71 as the base for its constant price series of national accounts data.

Table 3.1 gives the average levels of NDP achieved at both current and constant prices by the ten three-year sub-periods that cover the thirty year period running from 1950-51 to 1979-80.

It is evident from this Table that the NDP at current prices has grown by 732 per cent during the period under review—from Rs 29,370 crores in 1950-52 to Rs 244,500 crores in 1977-79. Much of the increase, however, has taken place in the post-1961 period. Thus, during the first decennial period, the rise in nominal NDP was only 38 per cent, whereas during the second decennial period it was 136 per cent and during the third period 157 per cent.

It is obvious that the 732 per cent increase shown in money national income over the thirty year period is illusory. Column 3 of the Table indicates that the growth in real terms was only 169 per cent. It is also clear from this Table

Table 3.1

Growth of Nominal and Real NDP (Rs Crores)

Period	At Current Prices	At 1960-61 Prices	Divergence	Per Capita NDP	
				Nominal	Real
1950-52	29370	28040	0.9547	267.97	255.84
1953-55	30070	31600	1.0509	259.67	272.88
1956-58	35320	34955	0.9897	287.62	284.65
1959-61	40400	39619	0.9807	309.82	303.83
1962-64	52140	45013	0.8633	374.57	323.37
1965-67	73191	47242	0.6455	492.54	315.91
1968-70	95258	54462	0.5717	599.86	342.96
1971-73	128185	58945	0.4598	754.47	346.94
1974-76	189377	65628	0.3465	1042.25	361.19
1977-79	244500	75415	0.3084	1257.07	387.74

that while in the first decade the real increase in the NDP was practically the same as its increase in nominal or money terms, the next two decades saw a growth in nominal income that was almost four times that of the real income. While the divergence between the nominal and real NDP was of the order of 1: 0.98 in 1958-61 and 1: 0.57 in 1968-70, it became 1: 0.31 in 1977-79. The inflationary effect of the price rise has been sharpest in the post-1970 period.

The difference in the NDP at current and constant prices is due to a number of reasons. In the case of both commodities and services, the current price constitutes the price paid (or imputed) in the case of commodities, and remuneration paid in the case of services. The price of commodities is determined by both supply and demand factors — shortages leading to an increase in price which does not come down proportionately when the supply increases. This is partly because of the secular rise in demand due to the increase in population and economic growth, but it is due even more to the increase in demand that takes place as a result of the compensatory rise (to the extent achieved) in the remuneration of the employee sector. It is also due to the rise in money demand resulting from inflationary financing, length of the gestation period for investments to turn into production, and unfruitful investment.

Another factor that affects the value of the commodity sector at current prices is state regulation of prices of defined commodities, and governmental fixing of the prices of commodities produced by the public sector. A further factor relating to the commodity sector is the price-stickiness of some agricultural commodities when their prices rise due to temporary shortages. A similar stickiness is found in non-agricultural commodities due to a formal or informal understanding on the part of their producers or stockists or both. In the case of the employee sector, the rise in remuneration usually follows the rise in commodity prices and then becomes a sustaining factor for a further rise in commodity prices. Not all constituents of the employee sector get an equal rise in remuneration, nor in fact do all commodities experience an equivalent rise in prices. The struggle which usually precedes a rise in the remuneration of the employee sector often causes disruption in production and functions as a supply factor for sustaining the rise in price.

The accelerated divergence in nominal and real NDPs is explained by the fact that the implicit NDP deflator has risen from 1.000 in 1960-61 to 1.7513 in 1970-71 and to 3.5226 in 1979-80. The acceleration in the price deflator is not peculiar to the Indian economy alone. Table 3.2 shows that the rate of inflation recorded by the Indian economy falls on the lower side of the inflation ratio indicated by a good number of developing economies.

Table 3.2

Rates of Inflation of Selected Economies

Inflation Rate (Internal)	*No. of Countries*	
	1960-70	*1970-77*
-0.50 – 2.00	25	–
2.10 – 4.00	39	3
4.10 – 6.00	20	2
6.10 – 8.00	8	15
8.10 – 10.00	1	22
10.10 – 12.00	2	12
12.10 – 14.00	2	14
Above 14.00	8	37
TOTAL	105	105

Though India's inflationary record does not compare badly with that of other developing countries and, more recently, with that of developed countries as well, the effect of inflation has been felt far more severely in our country. This is partly because of the low per capita income base in India as compared to other countries, and the large proportion of its population which lives below the poverty line. The situation has been aggravated by the fact that during the last two decades of the period, which were inflationary, the population has grown at a rate of about 2.5 per cent a year, as against 1.2 per cent in the non-inflationary decade which preceded it. Per capita income in real terms has gone up during these thirty years by only about 52 per cent as against the rise in nominal terms of 369 per cent. The money illusion is evident in the phenomenal growth in both NDP and per capita NDP at current prices witnessed during the last two decades of the period.

The higher growth observed by the nominal NDP is not uniformly transmitted over all the functional sectors of the economy. While the overall NDP implicit price deflator had an annual compound growth rate of 5.00 per cent over the whole period 1950-51 to 1979-80, it was 5.90 for the primary sector, 4.60 for the secondary sector and 3.50 for the tertiary sector. This means that the money value of output as compared to its quantum grew fastest for the primary sector, less for the secondary sector, and least for the tertiary sector.

As the rise in the implicit price deflator for the primary sector was higher than that for the NDP as a whole while the rise in those of the secondary and tertiary sectors were lower, the primary sector got a differential advantage over the other two sectors and absorbed a larger share of the NDP at current prices than was justified by its contribution to the NDP at constant prices. In contrast to this, the secondary sector got a smaller share of the NDP at current prices than its contribution at constant prices, and the tertiary sector a still smaller share. As it is the NDP at current prices which matters, as far as purchasing power in money terms is concerned, it is the primary sector which has gained the most (or lost the least) from the inflation that has accompanied the growth of the real NDP during this period. Simultaneously, the secondary and tertiary sectors have lost, the latter in a larger measure than the former.

This finding, arising from a sectoral analysis of NDP growth in monetary and real terms on the basis of the national accounts data, is also confirmed by studies which have been made in the net barter and net income terms of trade between the agricultural sector and the non-agricultural sector.[1] For instance, Thamarajakshi, whose study covers the period 1951-52 to 1972-73, states:

'During this period while all prices received by agriculture rose at 5.94 per cent per annum, those paid by agriculture registered an annual rate of increase of 4.45 per cent; consequently, net barter terms of trade improved in favour of agriculture at 1.43 per cent per annum. It is further noteworthy that since 1964-65, net barter terms of trade have been consistently favourable to agriculture, average level of index being over 120 during the 11-year period ending 1974-75. Moreover, the rate of improvement in terms of trade of foodgrains, compared to non-agricultural commodities purchased by agriculture for all uses, is equal to that in the overall terms of which all commodities have been exchanged between the two sectors during this period. What is even more striking is that the prices received by agriculture have risen at a faster rate (5.94 per cent) than those of intermediate products purchased by agriculture from non-agriculture (4.53 per cent). As a result terms of trade of all agricultural products sold to non-agriculture vis-a-vis non-agricultural intermediate products purchased by agriculture have improved in favour of agriculture at a compound rate of 1.34 per cent.

'Compared to this, prices paid by non-agriculture for agricultural raw materials have recorded a faster rate of increase (5.89 per cent) than those paid by agriculture for all non-agricultural products (4.45 per cent). Finally, the index of income terms of trade, which is a true reflector of the economic betterment of the agricultural sector, has grown at as high a rate as 4.53 per cent per annum during this period, thereby showing the increasing capacity of this sector to purchase non-agricultural commodities. Thus, looked at from any angle, the terms at which trade has been transacted between agriculture and non-agriculture have been improving in favour of the former since 1951-52'.[2]

It seems to follow, therefore, that the primary sector, which is predominantly agricultural, has achieved substantial gains at the expense of the secondary and tertiary sectors because of the differential movement of the sectoral implicit price deflators. It must be pointed out, however, that this relates to the period as a whole, and ignores the differences that emerged during its sub-periods including the 1970s, which we shall consider later.

Taking the period as a whole, it would not be correct to assume that the agricultural sector alone has obtained this differential gain at the expense of the other sectors. The primary sector also includes fishing and forestry, the implicit deflators of whose NDPs have risen faster than that of agriculture (5.2 per cent and 3.9 per cent as against 3.2 per cent of agriculture during the period 1960-80). This still leaves the agricultural sector NDP with a higher implicit price deflator than those of the other two sectors over the period 1950-51 to 1979-80. However, the effect of this on the difference between the nominal and real values of its output in terms of purchasing power, affects only its marketed output and cannot cover the agricultural output which is not sold on the market, though an imputed value for this output is included in the money value of the NDP from agriculture.

According to the studies made by Thamarajakshi, Venkataramanan and Prahaladachar, the marketed share of the value of agricultural output was 54 per cent in 1973-74, having risen from about 45 per cent in 1951-52. This, therefore, leaves out a little less than half of the agricultural output from the price effect, and to that extent diminishes the gains attributed earlier to the primary sector from the price effect. Thus, the real gainers were only those in the agricultural sector who sold their output, and only to the extent of the output sold.

In this connection, it is interesting to note that according to Thamarajakshi's latest study on the subject, while the index of agricultural output rose from 68.45 (base 1960-61 = 100) in 1951-52 to 128.14 in 1974-75, that of the marketed surplus of agriculture rose from 66.59 to 150.47. The compound rate of growth in the case of output was 2.53 per cent, while that of marketed surplus was 3.11 per cent. The money effect, therefore, has been increasing in the agricultural sector because of the increasing growth of its marketed surplus as compared to its output.

The marketed output, however, is not distributed proportionately over the different size classes of agricultural holdings. Hence it is important to look at the structure of the agricultural economy from the point of view of its marketing behaviour.

Unfortunately, not many studies of marketed surplus by size class of agricultural holdings, which broadly corresponds to income groups among the cultivators, are available. Generally, non-food crops are usually marketed to the extent of the whole of their production irrespective of the size of holdings. In fact, small holdings do have a significant proportion of their cropped area under non-food crops and are, therefore, linked to the market mechanism and gain or loss by the price effect. It is in respect of foodgrains that there is a large difference in the marketed proportion of production by different size classes of holdings.

Dharam Narain's pioneering study,[3] which included in the marketed surpluses both food and non-food crops, found the marketed proportion of output higher for the smaller holdings. His findings have now been modified by subsequent studies. For example, Utsa Patnaik,[4] using the same methodology as Dharam Narain, shows that the marketed proportion of output rises with an increase in the size of the holding. According to her, the share of the small and medium holdings in the aggregate marketed surplus in 1960-61 was only 33 per cent, the bulk of the surplus being contributed by the large land owners. Following a different methodology, P.S. Sharma[5] found that holdings below five acres had no surplus to sell, while larger holdings of ten acres and above accounted for as much as 91 per cent of the surplus. Based on a sample survey covering 2500 farmers, Satyapriya[6] found that while holdings above five acres account for 92 per cent of the marketed surplus, holdings above ten acres make for as much as 73 per cent of the surplus.

Though there are no macro studies on the subject, there are a few micro studies. One study covering fifteen villages in the Hooghly district of West Bengal for the period 1970-71 to 1972-73[7] shows that the net marketed surplus was actually negative up to 1.7 acres, remained constant at about 5 per cent up to five acres, and increased thereafter with the increase in size of holdings. Another micro study covering North Bihar showed that nearly 80 per cent of the households in the size group below five acres had no surplus to sell. A third study (H. Laxminarayana, unpublished) shows that holdings above 10 acres accounted for 84.9 per cent of the marketed surplus in 1971-72 for a village in Ludhiana district, and 80.8 per cent for a similar sized group in a Hissar village during the same year. A more recent study by M.V. Nadkarni[8] of a millet-growing region in Maharashtra, which covered 143 farm households with varying sizes of holdings spread over fifteen villages in the area, also supports the findings of the other micro studies referred to earlier in regard to the distribution of the marketed surplus. He found that both the marketable surplus and the marketed surplus were negative for jowar and bajra and, for total foodgrains, in the smallest two size classes of below 2 hectares and 2 to 4 hectares, and in the case of jowar, even for the next size class of 4 to 6 hectares. This is well illustrated by Table 3.3 compiled from his figures of the net marketed surplus as a percentage of net available output for cereals and by size class of holdings.

The positive nature of the percentage of net marketed surplus to net available output in the case of wheat is a clear indication of the fact that, in this millet-growing region, wheat is treated as a cash crop even by the smallest size class of agricultural holdings. The fact that 93 out of 143 households have a negative percentage of NAS to NAMS in jowar shows that their price interest in jowar coincides with that of agricultural workers and non-agricultural workers or a vast majority of the rural population. Jowar constitutes nearly 54 per cent of the net available output of all foodgrains. It is obvious that the main beneficiaries of the increasing marketed surplus have been the medium and large holdings. It must be added that these conclusions

Table 3.3

NMS as a Percentage of NAO

Size Class in Hectares (and No. of Households in each Class)		*Jowar*	*Bajra*	*Wheat*	*All Food-grains*
Up to 2	(13)	−31.4	−11.8	28.6	−12.5
2.1 to 4	(25)	−10.0	−31.9	18.1	− 8.5
4.1 to 6	(22)	− 9.4	18.4	37.8	6.8
6.1 to 10	(33)	−11.2	14.7	26.8	15.9
10.1 to 15	(24)	23.4	29.7	47.3	31.0
Above 15	(26)	30.3	30.2	25.5	32.5
ALL CLASSES	(143)	15.7	20.4	30.5	21.4

apply essentially to the producers of foodgrains and not intermediate products, partly because the green revolution has not affected the latter to any significant extent and partly because the small holdings also grow and sell non-food crops.

On the conservative assumption that unirrigated holdings above ten acres (or four hectares) in size and irrigated holdings of above 2.5 acres (or one hectare) are the main contributors to the marketed surplus of foodgrains and, therefore, the beneficiaries from a price rise in foodgrains, we find that they constitute a minority of cultivators according to the agricultural census of 1970-71. Relevant figures are given in Table 3.4.

Table 3.4

Holding-wise Distribution of Irrigated Area

Size Class	*Wholly Irrigated Holdings*		*Wholly Unirrigated Holdings*	
	No. (in 000)	*Per Cent in Total*	*No. (in 000)*	*Per Cent in Total*
Below 2.5 acres	8770	70.5	20805	51.1
Between 2.5 and 10 acres	3036	24.5	13788	33.9
Between 10 and 25 acres	538	4.3	4484	11.0
Between 25 and 50 acres	78	0.6	1230	3.0
Above 50 acres	13	0.1	390	1.0
TOTAL	12435	100.0	40697	100.0

Source: Government of India, *Agricultural Census, 1971*, Ministry of Agriculture, 1975.

There are also 5.3 million partly irrigated holdings, which have, on an average, more than 2.5 acres each. Adding this to the 3.7 million wholly irrigated holdings with more than 2.5 acres, we get a total of nine million which constitutes 30.5 per cent of all holdings that have some irrigated area.

Of the wholly unirrigated holdings, 20 per cent constitute the main contributors to the marketed surplus of foodgrains. This also means that 55.4 million cultivators, whose holdings are either wholly unirrigated or irrigated to the extent of less than 2.5 acres, or 78.6 per cent of the total number of operational holdings in the country, have a negligible share in the marketed output of foodgrains and do not, therefore, benefit significantly from the rise that may take place in foodgrain prices. In fact, some of them would be buyers of foodgrains and to that extent adversely affected by a rise in foodgrain prices.

The obvious conclusion from the above is that the main beneficiaries from the price effect on agriculture have been the cultivators who grow non-food crops and those who, owning bigger sized and or irrigated holdings, grow food crops. These are the Kulak classes who have also benefited from the new agricultural technology and are becoming the major contributors to the increasing marketed surplus of foodgrains. Their gains have been not only at the expense of the non-agricultural sectors of the economy but also at the expense of the weaker sections of rural society.

It must be pointed out that the divergence in the annual compound growth rate of the sectoral implicit price deflators used here is for the period of thirty years from 1950-51 to 1979-80. If this period is broken into three sub-periods —1950-51 to 1960-61, 1960-61 to 1970-71 and 1970-71 to 1979-80—the higher differential growth rate of the implicit price deflator on the primary sector is true only for the first two sub-periods, while for the third sub-period it comes down below the implicit price deflators of both the secondary and tertiary sectors (see Table 3.5).

Table 3.5

Compound Growth Rates of Implicit Price Deflators
(1960-61 Base)

Period	*Primary*	*Secondary*	*Tertiary*	*Total NDP*
1950-51 to 1960-61	0.70	−0.83	−1.51	−0.26
1960-61 to 1970-71	8.60	5.40	6.00	7.10
1970-71 to 1979-80	6.20	9.10	8.40	7.50
1950-51 to 1979-80	5.90	4.60	3.50	4.90

The price premium obtained by the primary sector during the years 1950-51 to 1970-71 was reversed during 1970-71 to 1979-80, which explains the recent and almost spontaneous countrywide agitations by farmers and their political lobbies for higher agricultural prices. It is not surprising that the small and marginal farmers, who do not have much of a marketable surplus, have also joined the agitation because of the effect that the differential rise in the price of non-agricultural products has had on their living standards and even on the small quantum of production inputs used by them.

So far the discussion has been confined mainly to the primary sector. The implicit price deflators of the other two sectors have a lower growth rate than that of the primary sector. For the secondary sector, details of implicit price deflators over the whole period are available only for two sub-sectors — mining and manufacturing; their compound rates of implicit price deflator growth are presented in Table 3.6 at 1960-61 prices.

Table 3.6

Compound Growth Rates of Implicit Price Deflators on the Manufacturing Sector

Period	*Mining & Quarrying*	*Manufacturing*	*Total NDP*
1950-51 to 60-61	2.00	3.50	-0.26
1960-61 to 70-71	5.60	5.00	7.10
1970-71 to 79-80	13.30	8.90	7.50
1950-51 to 79-80	4.70	7.00	4.90

It is seen that the implicit price deflators of both mining and manufacturing have been higher in their rate of growth during the first sub-period (1950-51 to 1960-61) and the third sub-period (1970-71 to 1979-80), while during the second sub-period (1960-61 to 1970-71), they were lower than that of the NDP. One would normally expect, therefore, that the growth of these sub-sectors would be higher during the first and third sub-periods and lower during the second sub-period. In actual fact their growth rates have been higher during the first and second sub-periods and lower during the third sub-period. This seems to show that the growth rates of sectoral output in the secondary sector are not directly connected with its differential price advantage as compared to that of the NDP. Evidently, there are many factors besides differential price advantage that determines the output of individual commodities in the secondary sector.

Data on implicit price deflators in the tertiary sector are available for all its sub-sectors and these show wide variations among the sub-sectors as shown in Table 3.7.

Table 3.7

Compound Growth Rates of Implicit Price Deflators of the Constituents of the Tertiary Sector

Sub-sector	*1950-51 to 60-61*	*1960-61 to 70-71*	*1970-71 to 79-80*	*1950-51 to 79-80*
Railways	–0.16	2.90	4.70	1.10
Other transport	–1.55	6.50	8.40	5.70
Communication	–1.21	6.40	7.70	4.20
Trade, hotels & restaurants	–4.28	7.40	9.60	3.10
Banking & insurance	0.80	8.10	10.00	6.90
Real estate	–1.96	4.20	6.00	1.90
Public administration	–0.05	4.20	5.20	1.50
Other services	0.70	5.50	12.00	5.10
Tertiary sector	–1.51	6.00	8.40	3.50
TOTAL NDP	–0.26	7.10	7.50	4.90

It is not surprising that the sub-sector of the railways shows the least rise in its implicit price deflator over the whole period as also in each of the sub-periods, as the railways are a government monopoly; and its price rise is determined as a part of budgetary policy rather than to keep pace with the general rise in prices. This means, in effect, that its services are cheaper as compared with other goods and services and its contribution to the real NDP is not reflected in its valuation at current prices. In contrast to this, the pricing of communication services, which is also determined by the government, brings it nearer to the price deflator both of the tertiary sector and of the NDP than is the case with the railways.

The pricing of governmental services in terms of public administration is almost at par with that of the railway services, and its implicit price deflator has increased at a much lower rate than either its sectoral or the NDP deflator. While in the case of the railways the under-valuation of its real contribution has led to a neglect of its maintenance and expansion requirements, in the case of public administration it has led to extravagances in its use, a proliferation of poorly paid government servants, and an increase in inefficiency, corruption and industrial unrest over the period. If its price deflator had followed the NDP trend or even the tertiary sectoral trend, it would of course have meant less employment in public administration, but would also have led to a more efficient and honest governmental machinery. Further, it would have restrained the reckless manner in which government regulation and interference with private activity had been proliferating over the period ostensibly in the interests of a socio-economic policy, for which the community is not prepared to pay its economic price.

In contrast to the low growth rate of the implicit price deflator in the case of those services provided by the government sector, the price deflator of the sub-sector comprising banking and insurance stands out sharply by its much higher rate of growth, and provides a startling confirmation of the privileged position this sub-sector and its factors of production occupy in the national economy.

The sub-sector of real estate, which is mainly composed of the rent of residential dwellings, shows a low rate of growth in its price deflator; this is also due to government intervention which, though well intentioned, has had very little connection with tenants' current capacities to pay. This has, in fact, led to a serious shortfall in investment in residential construction. It is no wonder that the housing shortage in urban areas has reached such appalling dimensions and is leading to the growth of slums as well as affecting the mobility of skills so essential for efficient and maximum production.

It is also noteworthy that the sub-sector of trade after 1960-61, or during the second and third sub-periods, shows a higher price deflator than manufacturing or governmental or other non-governmental and non-financial services. In fact, its implicit price deflator would have been even higher, but for the fact that it is an imputed item which is not based on current data. The real losers in this sector have been those with incomes fixed by contract, whether in government or private services.

We will now examine the rising price deflator with regard to its effect on the real value of the rupee for different classes of Indian society.

Table 3.8 presents indices of the cost of living for three section of society,

Table 3.8

Cost of Living Indices

Year	*National Cost of Living Index*	*Cost of Living for*		
		Agricultural Labour	*Industrial Workers*	*Urban Non-manual Employees*
1960-61	100	100	100	100
1961-62	104	103	104	104
1962-63	108	110	108	108
1963-64	116	118	113	113
1964-65	127	143	124	124
1965-66	138	158	132	132
1966-67	156	190	146	146
1967-68	176	206	159	159
1968-69	170	185	161	161
1969-70	178	193	177	167
1970-71	180	192	186	174
1971-72	189	200	192	180
1972-73	208	225	207	192
1973-74	250	283	250	221
1974-75	301	368	317	270
1975-76	285	317	313	277
1976-77	293	302	301	277
1977-78	309	336	324	296
1978-79	319	329	331	306
1979-80	362	344	360	330

namely, agricultural labour, industrial workers, and urban non-manual employees. Similar cost of living indices for other sections of society — such as the better-off classes in rural and urban society — are not available. Column 2 of Table 3.8 gives an estimate of changes in what may be called the national cost of living. The NAS do give data on private final consumption expenditure for the nation as a whole for the period 1960-61 to 1980-81 at current prices; and along with the data on final consumption expenditure at constant prices, it can be used for compiling a broad kind of measure of a national cost of living index covering all sections of society — the poor, the better-off, and the rich.

The overall implicit price indices of net domestic product and private final consumption expenditure have a wider coverage than the wholesale price index of the consumer price indices and may be assumed to present more realistic trends in producer prices and retail prices. In the case of the former, i.e., NDP, the overall implicit price deflator reflects the effect of changes in prices of commodities as well as the cost of services like transport, trade, community and personal services, whereas the wholesale price index covers the price of commodities only. Similarly, the implicit deflator of final consumption expenditure gives an overall measurement of movement of retail prices affecting the standard of living of the total population, whereas the consumer price indices refer to specific groups of employees only. The implicit price indices differ from the independent data on wholesale prices or consumer prices also because these deflators are of Paasches' type, i.e., current weighted indices, whereas the directly available price index numbers are of Laspeyres' type, i.e., base weighted.[9]

What has been termed here the national cost of living index is the implicit price deflator of aggregate private consumption expenditure given by the NSS. This includes the cost of living of all sections of Indian society, including the middle and upper classes, while the other indices refer to the cost of living of specified classes of Indian society none of whom belong to the upper or upper-middle classes.

A comparison of these four cost of living indices show that, taking the period as a whole, they all have a similar upward trend, but there are variations in their comparative degree of rise. The national cost of living index was uniformly higher than that of urban non-manual workers, indicating that the price effect of inflationary development was more unfavourable to the upper and upper-middle classes than to the lower middle classes. It was also uniformly higher than the cost of living index of industrial workers during the earlier part of the period (1960-61 to 1969-70). This trend was reversed during the latter half of the period, indicating that the better-off sections of society suffered a larger price effect during the second half of the period than industrial workers; but they fared better than agricultural labourers throughout the period.

Within the three specified classes, urban non-manual workers whom we have identified with the lower middle class experienced a lower measure of the price effect than industrial workers and a much lower effect than agricultural labourers. The most affected were agricultural labourers whose cost of living index was uniformly higher than that of either industrial workers or non-manual urban workers or the national cost of living index, except during the last two years of the period. Broadly speaking, therefore, it was the working classes, both rural and urban, who suffered most from the price effect on their cost of living.

References

1. (a) R. Thamarajakshi, 'Intersectoral Terms of Trade and Marketed Surplus of Agricultural Produce, 1951-52 to 1965-66,' *EPW*, June 28, 1969.
   (b) L.S. Venkataramanan, and M. Prahaladachar, 'Inter-sectoral Terms of Trade and Marketed Surplus of Agriculture 1964-65 to 1973-74.' Paper presented at the Indo-Hungarian Economists Seminar, Lonavale, February 1979.
2. R. Thamarajakshi, 'Price Incentives and Agricultural Production.' In Douglas Ensinger, ed., *Food Enough for Starving Millions,* New Delhi, Tata McGraw-Hill, 1977.
3. Dharam Narain, *Distribution of Marketed Surplus of Agricultural Produce by Size-level of Holdings in India 1950-51*, Bombay, Asia Publishing House, 1961.
4. Utsa Patnaik, 'Contributions to the Output and Marketable Surplus of Agricultural Products by Cultivating Groups in India, 1960-61,' *EPW*, December 1975.

5. P.S. Sharma, 'Marketable Surplus in Subsistence Crops: A Case Study of a Deficit Village in Rajasthan,' *EPW,* February 1969.
6. V.S. Satyapriya, *Marketing of Paddy: Study Based on Ignatpuri Taluka,* Maharashtra, Gokhale Institute, 1974.
7. Ashoka Hati, 'Non-Linear Marketable Supply Functions,' *EPW,* July 17, 1976.
8. M.V. Nadkarni, *Marketable Surplus and Market Dependence in a Millet Region,* Allied Publishing House, 1980.
9. CSO, 'Brief Analysis of Results.' In *White Paper on National Accounts Statistics, 1970-71 to 1976-77,* p. 10.

Changing Structure of the Economy 4

This chapter deals with the changes in the structure of the economy under three heads namely—fluctuations in year to year growth; sectoral and occupational distribution; and organisational patterns.

Fluctuations in real growth from year to year are common to most countries. The position in India is presented in Table 4.1.

Table 4.1

Annual Rates of Changes in Real NDP

Year	*Rate of Change*	*Year*	*Rate of Change*
1951-52	2.0171	1966-67	0.8599
1952-53	3.2882	1967-68	8.3241
1953-54	6.3150	1968-69	2.8118
1954-55	2.8574	1969-70	6.3698
1955-56	3.4155	1970-71	5.1973
1956-57	5.5847	1971-72	1.7339
1957-58	−1.7257	1972-73	−1.0421
1958-59	8.1568	1973-74	4.7258
1959-60	2.1313	1974-75	1.5207
1960-61	7.0311	1975-76	9.2071
1961-62	3.6745	1976-77	1.6486
1962-63	2.0108	1977-78	8.4744
1963-64	.5.5236	1978-79	5.2960
1964-65	7.7006	1979-80	−4.7564
1965-66	-4.9538		

Table 4.1 shows that while annual fluctuations of a wide order are seen in all the three decades, there seems to be a tendency towards an increase in the element of fluctuation over succeeding decades. Thus, while the standard deviation for the entire period from its trend rate was 0.2333, it was 0.0089 in the first decade, rose to 0.0146 in the second decade and touched 0.0162 in

the third decade. While there was one year of negative change during the first and second decades, there were two negative years during the third decade. The fluctuations during the first decade ranged between −1.7257 to +8.1568; during the second decade from −4.9538 to +8.3241; and during the third decade from −4.7564 to +9.2071. That the green revolution and the significant increase in agricultural productivity it effected has not given more stability to the annual rates of growth of the NDP is clear from this analysis. In fact, the amplitude of the annual fluctuations has increased during the third decade.

Table 4.2 presents the annual rates of changes observed by the three sectors along with those of the real NDP. An examination of this shows that the annual variations are not very specific to the primary sector alone. Fluctuations, though not of the same order of magnitude, are observable in the other two sectors as well.

Table 4.2

Annual Rates of Per Cent Changes in Real Sectoral Income and NDP

Year	*Primary*	*Secondary*	*Tertiary*	*Total NDP*
1951-52	1.5430	0.1906	4.2010	2.0171
1952-53	5.0207	0.1268	1.6996	3.2882
1953-54	7.7839	6.0798	3.3424	6.3150
1954-55	0.2379	8.4179	5.1523	2.8574
1955-56	0.0509	10.1872	6.1159	3.4155
1956-57	4.9644	8.4458	4.8871	5.5847
1957-58	−4.9395	−0.2765	3.6627	−1.7257
1958-59	11.8356	5.5453	4.7427	8.1568
1959-60	−2.3231	6.8301	6.1261	2.1313
1960-61	9.1868	9.9590	6.5533	7.0311
1961-62	6.8491	7.6034	5.9670	3.6745
1962-63	−2.6274	7.0667	6.2979	2.0108
1963-64	2.8324	9.5438	6.8309	5.5236
1964-65	8.9593	7.2947	6.1114	7.7006
1965-66	−13.8105	2.9720	2.7875	−4.9538
1966-67	−1.2041	1.0960	3.3500	0.8599
1967-68	15.2656	3.1749	3.5115	8.3241
1968-69	0.5016	4.3824	4.8467	2.8118
1969-70	6.2449	8.3722	5.0844	6.3698
1970-71	8.5946	−0.8156	5.1599	5.1972
1971-72	−0.6430	2.5354	4.4402	1.7339
1972-73	−6.4125	3.7202	2.6956	−1.0421
1973-74	7.3799	2.4485	3.1498	4.7258
1974-75	−1.9787	2.7044	5.0058	1.5207
1975-76	12.9360	5.1235	7.6550	9.2071
1976-77	−6.5680	9.7282	6.2828	1.6486
1977-78	12.4859	6.5829	5.4803	8.4764
1978-79	1.6504	8.1189	7.5009	5.2960
1979-80	−13.1670	−2.3956	2.6672	−4.7564

While the primary sector shows ten years of negative change over the previous years, the corresponding figure for the secondary sector was three;

for the tertiary sector it was nil. In terms of a significant positive change over the previous year (three or more percentage points) the primary sector had eleven years (of which seven had been preceded by years of negative change), the secondary sector had four such years and the tertiary sector had only one such year. While all the three sectors showed fluctuations in their rates of change over previous years because of the interaction between them, fluctuations were largest in the case of the primary sector, much less in the case of the secondary sector and least in the case of the tertiary sector. But fluctuation from year to year was common to all the sectors, as can be seen in Table 4.2.

The standard deviation from the trend rate for the entire period was 0.0389 for the primary sector, 0.0306 for the secondary sector and 0.0254 for the tertiary sector. A disquieting feature of the growth achieved during this period was the increase in the years of negative change over previous years in the primary sector from two in the first decade to three in the second decade, and five in the third decade. In the secondary sector, it was one in the first decade, nil in the second decade and two in the third decade; while in the tertiary sector, it was nil in all the three decades. These figures suggest that the observed annual fluctuations in the real NDP are not wholly accountable as corollaries of fluctuations in the primary sector. The extent of annual fluctuations in the NDP and its tendency to increase over the period is not a satisfactory accompaniment of the secular rate of growth which has taken place during the thirty years, 1950-1980.

As regards sectoral distribution, Table 4.3 presents annual compound growth rates of real incomes generated by the three sectors as well as of the NDP for the total thirty-year period and for the three ten-year sub-periods.

Table 4.3

Compound Growth Rates

Sector	*50-51 to 60-61*	*60-61 to 70-71*	*70-71 to 79-80*	*50-51 to 79-80*
NDP	3.77	3.39	3.71	3.63
Primary	2.66	1.78	1.69	2.09
Secondary	5.81	4.94	4.84	5.19
Tertiary	4.63	4.76	5.27	4.95

It is evident from Table 4.3 that while the compound rate of growth of the NDP over the whole period is 3.63 per cent, that for the primary sector is 2.09, while for the secondary and tertiary sectors it is 5.19 and 4.95 per cent respectively. The rate of growth of the secondary and tertiary sectors has thus been more than double that of the primary sector, with the secondary sector having an edge over the tertiary sector.

The position in the sub-periods, each of which constitutes a decade, shows that the growth rate has declined in the second decade as compared to the first, both in respect of the NDP as a whole and of its three sectors. However, in the third decade, the growth of the NDP has risen as compared to the second, but still remains below that of the first decade. This is entirely due to the rise in the growth rate of the tertiary sector which was high enough to offset the fall in the growth rates of the secondary and primary sectors.

Another feature of growth highlighted by Table 4.3 is the steady fall in the growth rate of the secondary sector from the first to the second decade, and from the second to the third decade. In comparison, the tertiary sector had a steady increase in its growth rate from the first to the second and from the second to the third decade, in spite of the vastly increased rate of industrialisation during the second and third decades, as compared to the first. This is a clear indication of the slackening of the rate of industrial growth in the second half of the thirty-year period. Nevertheless, taking the period of thirty years as a whole, the secondary sector has risen almost as fast as the tertiary sector, and has contributed significantly to the structural change in the economy, which was evident at the close of the 1970s.

The slackening of the growth of the secondary sector in its NDP contribution, especially during the latter half of the period, seems to indicate some measure of retrogression in the inter-sectoral growth of the Indian economy. If this trend continues into the 1980s, it does not augur well for either the overall growth of the economy or its structural change in the desired direction.

A similar conclusion has been reached by Shetty.[1] He has divided the period 1950-51 to 1976-77 into two sub-periods—namely, 1950-51 to 1964-65 and 1967-68 to 1976-77—and omits from his calculations the two drought years of 1965-66 and 1966-67. The data he adduces certainly supports his findings, but the correctness of the opted procedure of excluding the two drought years from the calculations of the compound rates of growth over this period is not free from certain limitations. Theoretically, when bad years are excluded, bumper years like 1955-56, 1960-61, 1970-71 and 1973-74 should also be excluded from the calculations. After all, agriculture, the dominant component of the primary sector, has a history of constant fluctuations in output, which the application of the new agricultural technology has not yet eliminated. All that the bio-chemical revolution in agriculture has done is to raise the level of both the peaks and troughs in agricultural production. The troughs have not disappeared, as can be seen in 1976-77 and in 1979-80.

If fluctuation is a normal feature of Indian agricultural output and good and bad monsoons a periodic feature, then the proper thing to do is to include all years, whether good or bad, while calculating growth rates, though one must always take cognisance of the character of the agricultural year when comparing the NDP between two individual or terminal years in any given period. Hence, it is better to use triennial averages for compiling annual figures in order to minimise the fluctuation element, which the Ministry of Agriculture does when compiling its indices of agricultural production and productivity.

It was not necessary for Shetty to have excluded from his calculations the two drought years 1965-66 and 1966-67 to formulate his thesis of a structural retrogression in the Indian economy during the latter half of the period. Even if these years are included, and the time series extended to 1979-80, one can find evidence of structural retrogression in the economy, except for the rise in the last triennial period. This is illustrated in Table 4.4.

Table 4.4

Changes in Sectoral Shares

Year	Sectoral Shares			Percentage Change in Sectoral Shares		
	Primary	*Secondary*	*Tertiary*	*Primary*	*Secondary*	*Tertiary*
1950-52	56.27	16.87	26.86	—	—	—
1953-55	55.97	17.38	26.65	−0.53	3.02	−0.78
1956-58	53.27	18.93	27.80	−4.82	8.92	4.32
1958-61	50.87	20.22	28.91	−4.51	6.81	3.99
1962-64	46.92	22.46	30.62	−7.76	11.08	5.91
1965-67	42.88	24.18	32.94	−8.61	7.66	7.58
1968-70	43.78	23.62	32.60	2.10	−2.32	−1.03
1971-73	42.40	23.61	33.99	−3.15	−0.04	4.26
1974-76	40.62	23.92	35.46	−4.20	1.31	4.32
1977-79	38.20	25.05	36.75	−5.96	4.72	3.64
1950-51	56.13	17.25	26.62	—	—	—
1979-80	35.44	25.68	38.88	−36.86	48.87	46.06

Table 4.4 shows a significant difference between the behaviour of the secondary sector and the tertiary sector. While the tertiary sector's gain in percentage terms was less in the first decade than that of the secondary sector and its gain during the second decade over the first was almost the same (13.4 per cent as against 13.57 per cent), its gain in the third decade over its share in the second decade was as much as 18.71 per cent, whereas that of the secondary sector was only 6.78 per cent. Also, the percentage gain in the NDP of the secondary sector shows a consistent fall from decade to decade. In fact, the 5.21 percentage points lost by the primary sector during the third decade becomes the gain of the tertiary sector with 3.77 percentage points, while the percentage gain of the secondary sector was only 1.44 points. Table 4.3 also shows that the growth rate of the secondary sector has been steadily falling over the period—from 5.81 per cent in the first decade to 4.84 per cent in the third decade.

There can be no doubt, however, that in spite of this retrogressive trend in the secondary sector, there has been a significant change in the structure of the economy over this thirty-year period. The primary sector's share has fallen by 36.86 per cent, while those of the secondary and tertiary sectors have increased by 48.87 and 46.06 per cent respectively. The primary sector's share in the NDP in 1979-80 is thus 35.44 per cent, as against 56.13 per cent in 1950-51, while that of the secondary sector is 25.68 per cent as against 17.25

per cent. The share of the tertiary sector is 38.88 per cent as against 26.62 per cent.

It is natural to expect a corresponding change in the occupational distribution of the work-force by these different sectors. This, in fact, has been the experience of newly developed countries. One may, therefore, examine the Indian position from this point of view.

Data on occupational distribution of the work-force are not maintained on an annual basis, and are available only at decennial intervals through census data. We have, therefore, to resort to the Indian censuses of 1951, 1961 and 1971 for getting relevant data on occupational distribution.

It is well known that the occupational data given in these three censuses are not comparable in their original form. The 1951 census classification defines the labour force as consisting of 'self-supporting persons', 'earning dependents', and 'non-earning dependents'. An 'earning dependent' is defined as a person who was in receipt of an income which was not sufficient for his own maintenance. This work-force was then classified under categories of industrial origin.

The 1961 census classified the population into two broad categories of 'workers' and 'non-workers'. The former included not only self-supporting persons and earning dependents of the 1951 census, but also non-earning dependents who were actively participating in economic activity, though without receiving any income either in cash or kind attributable to their work participation.

The 1971 census concentrated only on the main activity of the person enumerated, and classified the population as 'workers' and 'non-workers' as the 1961 census had done. The difference was that a worker was defined as one who engages in a main economic activity, and classified workers according to the main type of activity that the person returns himself as engaged in mostly. This excluded from the category of working persons those who did not have one main activity, though they may have participated in economic activity on a part-time basis or as subsidiary work, with or without receiving any specific return in cash or kind as remuneration for their work.

Hence, the 1971 census left out a large number of workers, mostly the female population who were employed in agricultural work or some household economic activity. This made the 1971 figures of workers not comparable with either the 1961 or the 1951 figures. Most demographers who have written on this subject have used only the figure for male workers for intertemporal comparison, as the definitional difference of a worker between the two censuses did not have much effect on the numbers returned under male workers.

Accordingly, this study has used only the figure of male workers in all the three censuses to compare the changes in their occupational structure. Doing so, we found that the 1951 census of all non-agricultural workers (self-supporting plus earning dependents) was higher than the total of what was given under the detailed occupational categories of that class, being 31.41 million and 30.74 million respectively. We, therefore, decided to distribute pro rata the difference of 0.33 million among the occupational categories of the industrial and service workers with their individual proportions to the total of this class. This makes the total of industrial and service workers equal to the total provided by the census of all non-agricultural workers. The number of male workers returned under 'mining and quarrying' was also transferred to the primary sector to make the data comparable with that of the 1961 census, as the latter gave only a consolidated total of workers in mining and quarrying and activities allied to agriculture. A similar analysis has been done with the 1971 census data. The picture that emerges from these adjustments is presented in Table 4.5.

Table 4.5

Percentage Distribution of Sectoral Male Workers

Sector	*Percentage of Total No. of Workers*		
	1951	*1961*	*1971*
Primary	69.1	68.0	70.4
Secondary	12.6	12.7	11.2
Tertiary	18.3	19.3	18.3
TOTAL	100.0	100.0	100.0

The difference of 0.1 in the total of 1971 is the result of rounding off the individual figures to the first decimal point.

Table 4.5 can be compared with Table 4.6, which gives the sectoral composition of the NDP in three years, 1950-51, 1960-61 and 1970-71. These roughly correspond to the three census years. Table 4.6 gives the relevant data at constant prices on the 1960-61 base.

Table 4.6

Sectoral Share in NDP

Sector	*1950-51*	*1960-61*	*1970-71*
Primary	56.13	51.23	44.67
Secondary	17.25	20.12	22.86
Tertiary	26.62	28.65	32.47

The sectoral distribution of the work-force as given in the census data shows that the primary sector's share recorded a marginal fall in 1961 as compared to 1951, and a marginal rise in 1971 as compared to 1961. The secondary sector shows a marginal rise from 1951 to 1961 and then falls from 1961 to 1971. The tertiary sector rises in 1961 as compared to 1951 but falls to its original 1951 position in 1971. Taking the two end periods, the share of the primary sector in the work-force rises from 69.1 per cent in the 1951 census to

70.4 per cent in 1970-71; the secondary sector's share falls from 12.6 per cent in 1951 to 11.2 per cent in 1971; while the tertiary sector shows no change, being 18.3 per cent both in 1951 and 1971.

Though the occupational change between 1951 and 1961 is in the same direction as the sectoral shares in the NDP in the case of the primary and tertiary sectors, it is not of the same dimension. In the secondary sector, however, the occupational change between 1951 and 1961, while being in the same direction, records only a sub-marginal rise as against a sharp rise in its share of the NDP. Regarding occupational change in the share of the three sectors between 1961 and 1971, it is in the opposite direction to the sectoral NDP shares in the case of all the three sectors.

Taking the period as a whole, the census data show structural retrogression in occupational terms, which is directly at variance with structural progress in terms of the NDP shares of the three sectors. It is this which constitutes both the problem and the paradox of Indian economic development and has led to the current controversy about growth and employment and the disillusion with industrialisation as a means for increasing employment and changing the sectoral composition of the work-force. It also shows that, taking the changes in the sectoral shares of the NDP over the whole period, productivity per worker in the primary sector has not kept pace with that in the secondary sector (and, to a lesser extent, in the tertiary sector) and reinforces the controversy about the link between growth, productivity and employment.

The NAS has given its estimate of the distribution of workers in 1961 and 1971 according to their occupation by industrial origin. This confirms the failure of the occupational structure to keep in line with changes in the structural shares of the NDP. Thus, while the index of growth in the total number of workers between the two census years (with 1961 = 100) was 109.96, that in the primary sector was 109.06. In the tertiary sector it was 109.37, while in the secondary sector it was 107.77. It is a significant fact that exceeding the overall index of growth was the growth in the number of their workers in some of the sub-sectors. Electricity, gas and water supply were at 214.9, banking and insurance at 218.3, public administration and defence at 152.8 and manufacturing at 137.6. Surprisingly, the index of growth in the sub-sector 'real estate' was as high as 224.5, in contrast to its lower growth in the NDP. The only sub-sector showing a decline was community and personal services other than public administration. Its index of growth was only 81 and was in line with its low rate of growth in the NDP during these two years.

It is of historical interest that the thesis of structural retrogression in the Indian economy was put forward by the author[2] more than twenty-seven years ago. He also dealt with the position in the years 1931 and 1951 on the basis of census data for the two years and sectoral income data on the basis of his book *National Income of British India, 1931-32,* (1940), and *Final Report of the National Income Committee* (1950). Table 4.7 summarises the relevant data.

The only difference between the present study and the earlier study is that during the period 1931 and 1951, while there was structural retrogression in

Table 4.7

Percentage Distribution of Work-force and Sectoral Incomes

Sectors	*Working Force*		*Sectoral Income*	
	1931	*1951*	*1931*	*1951*
Primary	71.2	73.0	53.8	52.0
Secondary	16.3	13.0	16.6	15.3
Tertiary	12.5	14.0	29.6	32.7

occupational terms, the change in occupational distribution between the primary, secondary and tertiary sectors was accompanied by a similar change in the sectoral distribution of national income between the two years. However, the change between 1951 and 1971 dealt with here lay in the opposite direction in which the occupational and sectoral income distribution moved during these two years. The lack of correspondence between the two movements represents another paradox of Indian economic development during the post-independence period.

The position, however, seems to have changed and a correspondence re-established between occupational and sectoral income distribution between 1971 and 1981. Paper 3 of the Census of India (which has only just become available) gives provisional population tables by workers and non-workers, but does not give figures by primary, secondary and tertiary sectors, nor by their sub-sectors. It only uses four categories—cultivators, agricultural labourers, household industry and other workers. It is not, therefore, comparable with the data given earlier in this chapter. Further, it provides comparative figures only for 1961, 1971 and not for 1951.

The Census paper also states that the proportion of workers in the population at the 1971 and the 1981 censuses are comparable. However, those recorded at the 1961 census are probably higher because of the question in the 1961 census regarding work participation. Since it gives occupational figures for 1981, though only in terms of four categories, these can be further reduced into the two broad categories of agricultural workers and non-agricultural workers, which can be used to view changes in the occupational structure between 1961 and 1981 in comparison with the changes in the share of agriculture and non-agriculture in 1960-61 and 1980-81 in the NDP at constant prices. The relevant figures are given in Table 4.8.

Though Table 4.8 also confirms the earlier thesis of the occupational structure not responding to the change in sectoral NDP shares between 1961 and 1971, it does indicate that the position altered favourably between 1971 and 1981 and that, finally, the occupational structure has started responding to the change in NDP sectoral shares. Thus, while the share of agriculture in the NDP has declined from 42.76 per cent in 1970-71 to 35.52 per cent in 1980-81, its share in the total number of workers has also declined from 69.78 per cent in 1971 to 66.69 per cent in 1981. This is an indication of economic

Table 4.8

Share of Agriculture and Non-Agriculture in the NDP and in the Work-force

Census Year	*Share of Agriculture (per cent)*		*Share of Non-Agriculture (per cent)*	
	NDP	*Work-force*	*NDP*	*Work-force*
1961	49.34	69.51	50.66	30.44
1971	42.76	69.78	57.24	30.22
1981	35.52	66.69	64.48	33.31

progress in structural change in line with what has taken place in the structure of the economies of the now developed countries, though it has taken India thirty years of economic growth to achieve this breakthrough. If this becomes a trend for the future, then one can look forward to India reaching a more balanced structural position between agriculture and non-agriculture in occupational terms, a narrowing of the difference between income per worker in agriculture and non-agriculture as well as a rise in the income per worker in agriculture more in line with the rise in the NDP.

The NAS has started providing substantial details recently on the organisational patterns of the NDP industrial groups. These data are utilised here to view the change that has taken place in the organisational pattern of the Indian economy. A traditional economy is marked more by self-employment than by employment on wages and salaries; production by unincorporated enterprises, individuals and households whose income from production is an unidentifiable mixture of all categories of factor shares; production for self-consumption or local exchange rather than for the market; a public sector largely concerned with law and order and defence with little involvement in either economic enterprise or social services; and a dominantly rural demographic pattern. Boradly, a traditional economy is identified with a subsistence rather than a market economy; and this was largely the case with India before independence. Marked changes have taken place in all these factors during the period under review with the economy moving away from a traditional towards a modern organisational pattern.

As seen in Chapter 2, the NAS has classified the organisational pattern of the economy under two heads—the organised and the unorganised sectors. The unorganised sector includes 'unincorporated enterprises and household industries which either do or do not maintain accounts or are wholly managed by self-employed workers'. As the income generated from these cannot always be separated into factor incomes, it is termed as 'the mixed income of the self-employed' in the NAS data. But the data also include a break up by wages, interest and rent of part of the production in the unorganised sector. Thus, the economy can be classified into three sectors with reference to identification by factor incomes of their respective NDPs—organised, unorganised and self-employed.

Data on all four types of factor incomes—compensation of employees, rent, interest and profits (including dividends)—are furnished for the organised sector. For the unorganised sector, data is available on compensation of employees, rent and interest, but not on profits and dividends as these have been included in the mixed income of the self-employed. It is, therefore, necessary to make some estimate of the profits and dividends that accrue to the unorganised sector in order to bring them on par with the organised sector for all the four categories of factor payments. A corresponding deduction has also to be made from the mixed income of the self-employed to make it truly representative of the income of the self-employed. To do this, as indicated in Chapter 2, it is assumed that the relation of profits and dividends to the total of the three other factor incomes (for which data are available) in the unorganised sector is the same as in the case of the organised private sector for which data is available on the four categories of factor incomes.* Adding these estimates of profits to the three known categories of factor incomes of the unorganised sector, one can obtain factor-wise incomes in that sector. The balance constitutes the incomes not identifiable by factor break up in the unorganised sector and the mixed income of the self-employed.

The organisational pattern of the economy can now be treated under two broad heads—one whose NDP can be broken up into factor shares and the other whose NDP is a mixture and cannot be broken up into factor shares. The former may be termed as the modern sector in organisational terms and the latter the traditional (or the self-employed) sector. Their NDP contributions have been calculated at constant prices (base 1960-61). These are given in Table 4.9 for quinquennial periods during the years 1960-61 to 1979-80.

It is evident from Table 4.9 that there is a steady increase in the share of the modern sector in terms of the totals for the quinquennial periods, indicating a

Table 4.9

Modern and Traditional Sectors in the Economy — NDP Shares by Quinquennial Totals at Constant Prices

	NDP (in Rs Crores)			*Percentage Share in Total NDP*	
Period	*Identifiable Factor Incomes or Modern Sector*	*Non-identifiable Factor Incomes or Traditional or Self-employed Sector*	*Total*	*Modern Sector*	*Traditional Sector*
60-61 to 64-65	39549	32624	72173	54.79	45.21
65-66 to 69-70	45825	36732	82557	55.51	44.49
70-71 to 74-75	58507	40081	98588	59.34	40.66
75-76 to 79-80	72740	47808	120548	60.34	39.66

* As seen in Chapter 2, this assumption gets some support from the Reserve Bank survey on small scale industries for 1977-78.

trend towards modernisation in the organisational pattern of the economy. The increase in the share of the modern sector in terms of quinquennial data is from an average of 54.79 per cent to 60.34 per cent in the last quinquennial period. If data had been available for the earlier years, this change would have been seen to be sharper. All the same, that nearly 40 per cent of all economic activity still falls in the mixed income of the self-employed shows that the traditional sector continues to play a strong role in the organisational pattern of the Indian economy.

What has been termed the modern sector includes the public sector (which the NAS lists under the organised sector), incorporated and registered enterprises in the private sector (which is also listed by the NAS under the organised sector) and households keeping accounts as well as other unincorporated enterprises (whose income is identifiable by factor shares) which the NAS has listed under the unorganised sector. As the organisational pattern of the first two may be deemed to be superior to that of the third, one may re-classify the data given for the modern sector in Table 4.9 into two categories—the 'organised' to include the first two categories listed above and the 'unorganised' to include the third, which may also be called unincorporated enterprises and households keeping accounts in the private sector.

Table 4.10 gives the shares of these two segments of the modern sector—the organised and unorganised—in the total of all identifiable factor incomes as well as in the NDP as a whole. It is seen in this Table that over a twenty-year period the organised sector has increased its share of the total of factor incomes as well as its share of the NDP. This means that the public sector and the registered and incorporated enterprises in the private sector have been gaining in the modern sector, thus reinforcing the trend towards modernisation in the organisational pattern of the economy.

Table 4.10

Per Cent Shares of Organised and Unorganised Sectors in India

Period	*Percentage Share in Total of Identifiable Factor Incomes*		*Percentage Share in NDP*	
	Organised	*Unorganised*	*Organised*	*Unorganised*
1960-61 to 64-65	51.45	48.55	28.19	26.61
1965-66 to 69-70	56.75	43.25	31.50	24.01
1970-71 to 74-75	54.94	45.06	32.60	26.74
1975-76 to 79-80	58.49	41.51	35.29	25.05

However, it must be noted that this improvement in the role of the organised sector is due wholly to the increasing share of the public sector, both in the income accruing to the organised sector as well as in the NDP (see Table 4.11). This increasing share of the public sector in the NDP from organised economic activity is spread unevenly over different sectors of industrial origin as seen in Table 4.12.

Table 4.11

Percentage Share of Public Sector

Period	*Income Accruing to Organised Sector*	*Total NDP*
1960-61 to 64-65	42.99	12.12
1965-66 to 69-70	48.98	15.43
1970-71 to 74-75	56.22	18.33
1975-76 to 79-80	62.06	21.90

Table 4.12

Percentage Share of Public Sector by Sectors of Industrial Origin in the Income from Organised Economic Activity

Sector of Industrial Origin	*1960-61 to 64-65*	*1965-66 to 69-70*	*1970-71 to 74-75*	*1975-76 to 79-80*
Agriculture	47.51	59.19	64.10	65.24
Forestry	26.26	26.12	31.12	35.87
Mining	13.65	23.96	45.14	83.97
Manufacturing	10.16	14.50	19.55	24.28
Construction	12.98	15.82	18.98	24.24
Electricity, gas & water	69.35	75.00	84.00	88.40
Railways	100.00	100.00	100.00	100.00
Other transport & storage	100.00	100.00	100.00	100.00
Communication	36.44	37.13	67.72	80.62
Trade & hotels	4.93	16.85	34.37	57.19
Banking	41.53	46.24	70.51	80.62
Public administration	100.00	100.00	100.00	100.00
Other services	67.98	79.31	68.28	65.24
TOTAL	42.99	48.98	56.22	62.06

Further, it is clear from Table 4.12 that the public sector has increased its share of organised economic activity in all three sectors — tertiary, secondary and primary. Thus, apart from government irrigation systems, railways, communication and public administration where the public sector enjoys a monopoly, it has increased its share significantly in organised economic activity in other sectors of industrial origin, such as mining, manufacturing, construction, transport other than railways, trading and hotels, banking and insurance, and community and personal services. Whether this means an improvement in the organisational pattern of the economy is debatable; so is the question whether it means an advance towards state capitalism or to socialism. What is clear is the rising role of the public sector in organised economic activity in India after the advent of independence and the attempts at planned development that followed.

This expansion of government activity in the economic sphere has been brought about through departmental and, more important, non-departmental enterprises. This is evidenced by the compound rate of growth of non-departmental enterprises, which has been not only much higher but has been growing faster than public administration. That this is not entirely due to the very low base from which the growth has been calculated is seen from the fact that non-departmental enterprises did have a significant role in the Indian economy even before 1960-61. Departmental enterprises, of course, have had a long and lasting place in the public sector, though their rate of compound growth is less than that of public administration. The relevant figures are provided in Table 4.13.

Table 4.13

Percentage Rates of Annual Compound Growth at 1960-61 Prices

Period	*Public Administration*	*Departmental Enterprises*	*Non-departmental Enterprises*
1960-61 to 70-71	7.50	5.30	17.00
1970-71 to 79-80	7.00	7.10	18.00
1960-61 to 79-80	7.10	5.70	17.70

For the period as a whole, the compound growth rate of public administration is about 25 per cent more than that of departmental enterprises, but it has been only about 40 per cent of the growth rate of non-departmental enterprises. In absolute figures, whereas the NDP value of public administration at constant prices increased from Rs 538 crores in 1960-61 to Rs 1,926 crores in 1978-79, that of the non-departmental enterprises increased from Rs 165 crores to Rs 3,130 crores. Thus, the absolute increase in the contribution of non-departmental public enterprises has been much higher than that of public administration. The increase in public enterprises as a whole over the base year is Rs 1,018 crores, which is still higher than that of public administration, in spite of the lower rate of growth in the contribution of departmental enterprises. The national income data thus clearly indicate the degree of success attained by the official policy of promoting the public sector by setting up non-departmental enterprises and giving the public sector a more prominent place in the organised structure of the Indian economy, though the Indian economy as a whole continues to be dominated by the private sector

Another change of note is the increasing importance in manufacturing of registered enterprises which belong to the organised sector, as compared to the unregistered segment which broadly belongs to the unorganised sector. If we take the changes in the average annual shares by decennial periods of registered and unregistered manufacturing enterprises in their total NDP, we get the results shown in Table 4.14.

The unorganised sector has not only a smaller role in manufacturing but its

Table 4.14

Percentage Distribution of Manufacturing (Value Added)

Period	Percentage Shares in Value Added	
	Registered	*Unregistered*
1950-51 to 1960-61	54.80	45.20
1960-61 to 1970-71	60.40	39.60
1970-71 to 1979-80	62.30	37.70

role has also been declining over the period under review. However, the fact that it still had a share of 37.7 per cent during the latest decade shows that unregistered enterprises, which form a part of the modern sector identifiable by factor incomes and can broadly be identified with the small and tiny sectors in industry, occupy a significant place in Indian industry. The much smaller decline in its role during the third period as compared to the second period shows that the support given to the small and tiny sectors during recent years has had some effect, by arresting the rate of decline of the unorganised sector in industry.

It is interesting to see the variations in the shares of registered and unregistered enterprises by individual industries. Data on this subject is available up to 1979-80 and are presented by selected years in Table 4.15.

As seen in Table 4.15 during 1979-80, the latest year for which a time-series is available by industrial origin, registered enterprises had a dominant share in the value added in chemicals and products, metal manufacturing and engineering, and food, drink and tobacco, and their shares in these groups have been increasing over the period. Unregistered enterprises have, however, had a dominant share in wood products, including furniture and fixtures. As regards textiles, tailoring and leather foot-wear, unregistered enterprises have gained an edge over registered ones over the period. Similarly, in miscellaneous industries, the unregistered sector has gained at the expense of the registered sector. In both cases, the comparative position of unregistered and registered enterprises has been reversed in favour of the former in the final year of the period from that in the initial year.

More detailed data for sectors of industrial origin are available for registered and unregistered manufacturing enterprises for the 1970s which are given in Table 4.16.

Table 4.16 shows that, within the composite category of food, drink and tobacco, it is in food products that registered enterprises have increased their share from 59.29 to 65.63 per cent, while in leather and leather products, unregistered enterprises have the dominant role and have increased their share from 75.35 per cent in 1970-71 to 80.30 per cent in 1979-80. It is only with regard to beverages and tobacco that both registered and unregistered enterprises have a virtually equal role, but registered enterprises have increased their share marginally from 48.77 per cent in 1970-71 to 51.18 per

Table 4.15

Share in the NDP from Each Manufacturing Group (Percentages)

	1951-52		1955-56		1960-61		1965-66		1970-71		1975-76		1979-80	
	Regd.	Unregd.	Regd.	Unregd.	Regd.	Unregd.	Regd.	Unregd.	Regd.	Unregd.	Regd.	Unregd.	Regd.	Unregd.
1. Textiles, tailoring & leather foot-wear	59.54	40.46	55.88	44.12	54.07	45.93	49.91	50.09	49.76	50.24	49.25	50.75	50.28	49.72
2. Wood & wood products, furniture fixtures	4.27	95.73	5.81	94.19	7.88	92.12	11.92	88.08	14.64	85.36	9.26	90.74	13.09	86.91
3. Metal manufacturing & engineering	64.50	35.50	71.71	28.29	74.76	25.24	80.03	19.97	78.75	21.25	79.99	20.01	82.35	17.65
4. Chemicals & products	75.12	24.88	77.46	22.54	81.10	18.90	83.18	16.82	82.20	17.80	81.83	18.17	84.27	15.73
5. Food, drink & tobacco	50.74	49.26	49.51	50.49	54.24	45.76	62.40	37.60	64.46	35.54	59.58	40.42	69.44	30.56
6. Other Industries	59.66	40.34	63.07	36.93	68.34	31.66	72.79	27.21	61.11	38.89	56.01	43.99	44.33	55.67
7. Net value added, less imputed bankcharges	54.11	45.89	55.07	44.93	57.71	42.29	61.99	38.01	61.97	38.03	60.91	39.09	63.19	36.81

Table 4.16

Value Added by Registered and Unregistered Enterprises in Each Manufacturing Group (Percentage)

Industry	Registered		Unregistered	
	1970-71	79-80	1970-71	79-80
1. Food products	59.29	65.53	40.71	34.47
2. Beverages, tobacco & tobacco products	48.77	51.18	51.23	48.77
3. Textiles	57.24	57.36	42.76	42.64
4. Wood and products, furniture & fixtures	12.31	10.97	87.69	89.03
5. Paper, printing	74.55	67.35	25.45	32.65
6. Leather & products	24.65	19.70	75.35	80.30
7. Chemicals & products	86.28	87.94	13.72	12.06
8. Rubber & plastic products	87.63	86.72	12.37	13.28
9. Non-metallic minerals	54.96	48.05	45.04	51.95
10. Basic metals & alloys	98.40	98.71	1.60	1.29
11. Metal products except machinery & equipment	44.54	39.80	55.46	60.20
12. Machinery except electrical machinery	75.25	76.04	24.75	23.96
13. Electrical appliances	83.39	86.09	16.61	13.91
14. Transport equipment	82.03	81.36	17.97	18.64
15. Miscellaneous manufacturing industries	58.45	41.14	41.55	58.86
16. Repair services	32.62	64.00	67.38	36.00
17. Net value added, less imputed bank charges	62.22	63.52	37.78	36.48

cent in 1979-80.

Table 4.16 also shows that in regard to rubber and plastic products, basic metals and alloys, non-electrical machinery, electrical appliances and transport equipment, registered enterprises have the dominant role, with 86.72, 98.71, 76.04, 86.09 and 81.36 per cent respectively of the value added by both registered and unregistered enterprises in these categories. For metal products other than machinery and equipment, however, unregistered enterprises claimed a share of 60.20 per cent in 1979-80. This is also an increase from its share in 1970-71 (55.46 per cent). In non-metallic minerals, unregistered enterprises account for a share of 51.95 per cent in 1979-80, an increase again from its share in 1970-71 which was 45.04 per cent. In the case of textiles, however, unregistered enterprises have not been able to make much headway during the 1970s, their share being only 42.64 per cent in 1979-80 as against 42.76 per cent in 1970-71. Under miscellaneous manufacturing industries, however, unregistered enterprises have recorded a significant advance in their share, from 41.55 per cent in 1970-71 to 58.86 per cent in 1979-80, indicating a certain element of dynamism in their operation.

On the whole, unregistered enterprises, or the unorganised sector in manufacturing, still continue to play an important role in Indian industry, though their share has declined from 45.2 per cent in the first decade to 37.7 per cent in the third decade. It is interesting to note, however, that its rate of decline has fallen sharply in the 1970s, the percentage points lost between 1970-71 and 1979-80 being only 1.90 as compared to 5.60 between 1950-51 and 1960-61, and 3.60 between 1970-71 and 1960-61. This indicates the comparative success of the official industrial policy of promoting the small and tiny manufacturing sectors.

This unorganised private sector, identifiable with factor incomes with the adjustments we have made for the inclusion of its profits, is also a part of the process of modernisation in the economy, looking to the financial assistance it is now getting from the organised banking system. This sector consists of unincorporated enterprises run by partnerships, proprietory concerns, joint families, associations, trusts and individuals; it is not only important in itself but also in comparison with organised corporate enterprises in the private sector. This is clearly seen in Table 4.17. Compiled from Reserve Bank data this Table provides the distribution of outstanding credit of scheduled commercial banks divided between the corporate sector, unincorporated sectors, and individuals in the private sector as in June 1979.

Table 4.17

Distribution of Outstanding Credit (1979) Between Companies, Partnerships and Individuals (Figures in Rs Lakhs)

Occupation	*Public and Private Ltd. Companies*	*Partnership & Proprietory Concerns*	*Individuals*
Agriculture	17865	22051	53182
Industry	529929	233666	8357
Transport operations	9869	8308	35079
Professional services	386	1459	2389
Artisans & craftsmen	427	1461	353
Other services	5491	10965	2654
Trade	28135	111403	6068
Personal loans including consumer durables	5	144	25492
All others	10113	15677	10122
TOTAL	602220	405134	143696

Table 4.17 also shows that unincorporated enterprises have a more important role than corporate enterprises in the private sector with regard to agriculture, services, trade and miscellaneous, while individuals play a more important role than both in agriculture and transport. Corporate enterprises play a dominant role in industry, while individuals, of course, are practically the sole recipients of personal loans which are meant not only for business but for various other purposes, including purchase of consumer durables. Taking the total of all the occupational activities, individuals and unincorporated enterprises claim almost as big a share of bank credit as incorporated enterprises.

As regards the traditional sector, or the self-employed with mixed incomes not separable by factor shares, we have seen earlier that its share in the NDP at constant prices has declined over the period, from 45.20 per cent during the quinquennium 1960-61 – 1964-65 to 39.66 per cent during the quinquennium 1975-76 – 1979-80. This decline has changed the pattern of distribution of the income of the self-employed from the different sources of industrial origin. This can be seen from Table 4.18.

Table 4.18

NDP of the Self-employed by Industrial Origin

Sector of Industrial Origin	*1960-61 to 64-65*	*1965-66 to 69-70*	*1970-71 to 74-75*	*1975-76 to 79-80*
Agriculture	65.39	61.69	75.52	65.10
Fishing	0.11	0.33	0.53	0.62
Mining & quarrying	—	–0.01	0.19	0.16
Manufacturing	7.19	7.27	7.62	8.91
Construction	1.97	2.30	1.03	0.87
Transport other than railways	0.81	1.13	1.80	2.28
Trade, storage & hotels	17.96	20.51	13.15	18.94
Finance	0.06	0.05	0.05	0.07
Real estate	0.08	0.08	0.24	0.34
Other services	6.43	6.65	2.87	2.71
TOTAL	100.00	100.00	100.00	100.00

Between the initial year of the period covered by Table 4.18 (1960-61) and its final year (1979-80) the changes have been as follows: agriculture from 67.37 to 58.33 per cent, fishing from 0.11 to 0.57 per cent, mining from 0.02 to 0.16 per cent, manufacturing from 6.39 to 10.09 per cent, construction from 1.91 to 0.85 per cent, transport other than railways from 0.72 to 2.59 per cent, trade including storage and hotels from 16.79 to 21.37 per cent, finance from 0.07 to 0.09 per cent, real estate from 0.10 to 0.39 per cent, and other services from 6.52 to 4.52 per cent.

The share of the primary sector shows a fall from 67.48 to 59.90 per cent, the secondary sector a rise from 8.32 to 11.11 per cent, and the tertiary sector a rise from 24.20 to 28.99 per cent. Yet if one takes the quinquennial average over the period, the primary sector shows a rise from 65.50 to 66.96 per cent, the secondary sector a rise from 7.19 to 8.76 per cent, while the tertiary sector shows a fall from 25.34 per cent to 23.31 per cent.

It seems clear from these figures that, in the income of the self-employed, some categories of industrial origin—like fishing, quarrying, manufacturing, transport, trade and real estate—have had a significant increase in their shares, while others, like construction and community and personal services, have suffered a significant decline. In the case of the remaining categories of industrial origin, the change has not been of a significant order. Agriculture, trade and manufacturing continue to account for more than 90 per cent of the income o the self-employed with agriculture dominating, followed at a long distance by trade, and at a shorter distance by manufacturing. Surprisingly, community and personal services account for such a small portion of the income of the self-employed and that even their meagre share of 6.52 per cent in 1960-61 should have fallen so drastically to 4.52 per cent in 1979-80.

A complete picture of the organisational pattern of the Indian economy in 1960-61 and in 1979-80 is given in Tables 4.19 and 4.20.

Table 4.19

Percentage Share of Sectors of Different Organisational Patterns in 1960-61 NDP

Industrial Origin	*Public Sector*	*Private Sector*			*Total*
		Incorporated Sector	*Unincorporated Sector*	*Self-employed with Mixed Income*	
Agriculture	0.22	0.37	17.83	30.93	49.35
Forestry & logging	0.36	0.94	—	—	1.30
Fishing	—	—	0.52	0.05	0.57
Mining & quarrying	0.12	0.83	0.04	0.01	1.00
Manufacture	0.61	7.42	2.96	2.93	13.92
Construction	0.32	2.09	1.40	0.88	4.69
Electricity	0.34	0.17	—	—	0.51
Railways	1.89	—	—	—	1.89
Communication	0.47	—	—	—	0.47
Other transport	0.45	0.73	0.45	0.33	1.96
Trade, storage & hotels	0.04	0.84	1.12	7.71	9.71
Finance	0.46	0.72	−0.01	0.03	1.20
Real estate, etc.	—	0.03	2.87	0.04	2.94
Public administration	4.03	—	—	—	4.03
Other services	1.34	0.77	1.36	2.99	6.46
TOTAL	10.65	14.91	28.54	45.90	100.00

The two Tables (4.19 and 4.20) show that while there have been significant changes in the organisational pattern in the different individual sectors of industrial origin, as far as the overall picture of the economy is concerned, the only significant change is the conspicuous increase in the public sector, which has doubled its share, and the conspicuous fall in the share of the self-employed in the private sector with their mixed income. The two other sectors of organisational pattern have not shown any significant change. Incorporated enterprise in the private sector has had a marginal fall in its share from 14.91 to 13.89 per cent, while the unincorporated private sector has had a sharper fall from 28.54 per cent to 23.72 per cent. The public sector's share has increased from 10.65 per cent to 23.55 per cent, while the share of the self-employed in the private sector has fallen from 45.90 per cent to 38.84 per cent. The national accounts data show that, on the whole, the economy is moving from the traditional to the modern pattern in organisational terms, though it is the public sector which has played a major role in this process.

With the change in the organisational pattern, there has been a significant

Table 4.20

Percentage Share of Sectors of Different Organisational Patterns in 1979-80 NDP (at 1960-61 Prices)

Industrial Origin	Public Sector	Private Sector: Incorporated Sector	Private Sector: Unincorporated Sector	Private Sector: Self-employed with Mixed Income	Total
Agriculture	0.51	0.23	10.03	23.06	33.83
Forestry & logging	0.36	0.73	—	—	1.09
Fishing	—	—	0.30	0.22	0.52
Mining & quarrying	0.93	0.08	0.02	0.06	1.09
Manufacture	2.62	8.72	2.94	3.92	18.20
Construction	0.67	1.85	1.99	0.33	4.84
Electricity	1.39	0.16	—	—	1.55
Railways	2.12	—	—	—	2.12
Communication	0.85	—	—	—	0.85
Other transport	0.80	0.20	1.43	1.01	3.44
Trade, storage & hotels	0.66	0.40	3.04	8.31	12.41
Finance	2.06	0.40	0.02	0.04	2.52
Real estate, etc.	—	0.05	3.43	0.15	3.63
Public administration	8.85	—	—	—	–8.85
Other services	1.73	1.07	0.52	1.74	5.06
TOTAL	23.55	13.89	23.72	38.84	100.00

change from a subsistence to a market oriented economy. The change towards market orientation can be seen by the increasing role of trade, transport, communication and banking in the NDP. Table 4.21 gives the relevant data at 1960-61 prices for selected years.

Table 4.21

Index of Growth (1960-61 = 100)

Year	Trade	Transport	Communication	Banking	NDP
1950-51	100.00	100.00	100.00	100.00	100.00
1955-56	125.74	127.41	135.29	151.95	119.16
1960-61	165.90	173.49	185.29	207.79	146.19
1965-66	213.61	237.35	283.35	289.61	167.00
1970-71	269.22	291.87	379.41	407.79	210.02
1975-76	324.53	401.20	544.12	523.38	245.75
1979-80	395.87	460.74	617.65	806.50	271.32

This trend of modernisation is further confirmed by the increasing industrial input that is going into increasing agricultural output during this period. It is reinforced by the increasing share of chemicals, machinery and electrical and transport equipment in the value added from registered manufacturing during this period. Table 4.22 gives the relevant data.

Table 4.22

Share of Modern Inputs of Agriculture and Manufacturing (Percentage)

Year	*Share in Industrial Inputs in Agriculture*	*Share of Chemical, Machinery and Electrical and Transport Equipment in Registered Manufacturing*
1951-52	1.41	17.80
1955-56	2.09	21.67
1960-61	3.97	25.04
1965-66	9.34	32.69
1970-71	20.49	33.67
1975-76	30.75	36.51
1979-80	38.01	37.90

The change which has taken place in the organisational pattern of economic activity and its growing market orientation, both indicating a change from a traditional to a modern economy, is thus confirmed by this analysis of the national accounts data for the period under review.

The changes in the structure of the Indian economy during the thirty-year period have been many. There has been a significant change in the structure of the economy, with the primary sector's share in the NDP at constant prices falling in each of the three sub-periods covered by the years 1950-51 to 1979-80, while that of the tertiary sector has risen during all the sub-periods, and that of the secondary sector has fallen marginally in the first sub-period and risen in the second and third sub-periods. We find that the average annual share of the primary sector in the NDP fell from 56.13 per cent in 1950-51 to 37.02 per cent in 1979-80. The secondary sector increased its share from 17.25 per cent to 24.40 per cent and the tertiary sector from 26.62 per cent to 38.58 per cent. The primary sector's compound rate of growth declined from 2.7 per cent in the first decade to 1.7 per cent in the third decade, while that of the tertiary sector rose from 4.6 per cent during the first decade to 5.3 per cent in the third decade. The secondary sector's growth rate has gone down from 5.80 per cent during the first decade to 4.70 per cent in the third decade. All the same it is clear that, though the rate of growth of the NDP in the third decade was lower than in the first decade, the decline in the rate of growth was much higher for the primary sector as compared to the secondary sector.

Over the period as a whole, the Indian economy became less geared to the primary sector and its dominant component—agriculture—and more attuned to the secondary and tertiary sectors; and, in terms of percentage growth between the two, slightly more to the secondary than to the tertiary sector. This may be regarded from the developmental point of view as a progressive change in the structure of the Indian economy during this period.

However, corresponding changes in the occupational structure of the work-force, which is an allied aspect of the structure of the economy, does not confirm this finding. On the contrary, the primary sector actually showed a marginal increase in the proportion of its working force to the total working force (from 69.1 per cent in 1951 to 70.4 per cent in 1971) while the secondary sector showed a significant fall (from 12.6 per cent to 11.2 per cent), the tertiary sector remaining constant at 18.3 per cent. This indicated a structural regression in occupational terms, which is directly at variance with the structural progress shown by the changes in the share of the NDP of the three sectors. This is what constitutes both the problem and the paradox of Indian economic development. It has also led to the controversy about the linkage between growth and employment and the current disillusionment concerning the effectiveness of the type of industrialisation India has adopted in the context of increasing employment and changing the occupational composition of the work-force by the three sectors. Further, it shows that the productivity per worker in the primary sector has not kept pace with the growth of the NDP, unlike in the secondary and tertiary sectors. However, the preliminary results of the 1981 census on occupational distribution gives evidence of a break away from this trend for the first time.

Thus, while the share of agriculture in the NDP declined from 42.74 per cent in 1970-71 to 35.52 in 1980-81, its share in the total number of workers also declined from 69.78 per cent in 1971 to 66.69 per cent in 1981. If this becomes a trend that continues over the coming decades, India may reach a more balanced occupational structure between agriculture and non-agriculture by the end of the century. It may also lead to a narrowing of the difference in the income per worker in agriculture and non-agriculture that would be more in line with the rise in the NDP.

Another reason for taking a less pessimistic view of the future is the growing share in the NDP of what the NAS terms the organised sector. Unfortunately, data on the NDP contribution of the organised sector is available only from 1960-61. Our observations on this subject are, therefore, confined to the period 1960-61 to 1979-80.

Taking the NAS definition of the organised sector and converting the data given in their reports to constant prices on the base 1960-61, we find that while the unorganised sector grew at the compound rate of 2.9 per cent over the period, the organised sector grew at 4.1 per cent a year; and its share of the NDP grew from 28.2 per cent in the quinquennium 1960-1965 to 35.3 per cent in the quinquennium 1975-80. Within the manufacturing sector, registered enterprises claim the major share of that sector's contribution to the NDP with 54.8 per cent in the first decennial period and 62.4 per cent in the third decennial period, of these thirty years. If we take the first and last year of the period under review, the registered sub-sector of manufacturing increased its share of the NDP from this sector from 54.0 per cent in 1950-51 to 63.74 per cent in 1979-80. The industrial sector of the Indian economy thus presented a marked contrast to the rest of the economy in the role that registered (and therefore organised) enterprises play in its operation. In spite of the rapid growth of the organised sector, the unorganised sector still continues to dominate the Indian economy with two-thirds of the NDP, which is not entirely due to the agricultural sector.

Yet another way of analysing the structural change in the economy is to look at the role of the public sector during this period. Here, again, data is available only from 1960-61. During the nineteen years from 1960-61 to 1979-80, the growth rate of the public sector was 6.0 per cent a year, while that of the private sector was only 2.8 per cent; and its share in the NDP grew from 12.1 per cent in the quinquennium 1960-65 to 21.9 per cent in the quinquennium 1975-80.

Thus, the public sector has nearly doubled its share of the NDP at constant prices during this period, and now accounts for one-fifth of the economy. It may be added that a major portion of the increase in the NDP share of the public sector was due to government enterprises, both departmental and non-departmental, which represent commodity production and marketed services. However, the private sector still continues to dominate the Indian economy, claiming nearly 80 per cent of the NDP at the end of the period—and this is not wholly due to the role of agriculture.

As regards the structural change in the distribution of the NDP between the commodity and non-commodity sector, the latter (which is the same as the tertiary sector) has been growing much faster than the commodity sector during each of the sub-periods, as well as over the period as a whole. This is primarily due to the inadequate growth of the secondary sector, especially manufacturing and construction, rather than the failure of the agricultural sector, where we have done quite well by international standards. It is this which constitutes a major part of the explanation for the growth of poverty and unemployment in the country in spite of our planned efforts to accelerating the country's economic development.

To conclude, our analysis of national income data highlights important structural changes during the period 1950-51 to 1979-80 such as the trend towards modernisation, market orientation and the increasing role of the secondary and tertiary sectors. Nevertheless, the Indian economy continues to be dominated by the primary sector and by unorganised enterprises. The startling feature of the structural change is the failure of the occupational structure to coincide with the sectoral NDP structure during the first two decades of the period under review. But the latest data available from the 1981 census seems to show that the occupational structure is now departing from this trend in the direction of a more balanced response to the changing sectoral structure of the NDP.

References

1. S. Shetty, 'Structural Retrogression in Indian Economy,' *EPW* (Annual), February 1978.
2. V.K.R.V. Rao, 'Changes in India's National Income — A Static Economy in Progress,' *Capital* (Annual), December 1954, pp. 15-17.

NDP by Sub-sectors or the Product Mix

5

In Chapter 4 it was observed that though the occupational structure has not kept pace with the changing inter-sectoral pattern of the NDP, the thirty years under review have witnessed a fall in the primary sector's share and a rise in that of the secondary and tertiary sectors. This chapter reviews the changes which have taken place in the sub-sectors of industrial origin and their shares in the NDP during this period. Table 5.1 lists these sub-sectors, their index of growth and their share in the NDP during this period.

Table 5.1 shows that the annual compound rates of growth of the sub-sectors differ from their corresponding sectoral figures, some being lower than others. In the primary sector, agriculture and allied activities experienced a lower rate of growth than both forestry and fishing. In the secondary sector, electricity, gas and water supply showed a much higher rate and construction a much lower rate of growth than the sectoral rate, while registered manufacturing displayed a more or less similar rate. In the tertiary sector, public administration and defence, banking and insurance, transport other than by railways, and communication have a higher growth rate than the sectoral rate. All the others have a lower rate of growth in the following descending order: trade, hotels and restaurants, transport by railways, real estate, ownership of dwellings and business services, and other services. The sub-sectors whose rate of growth sharply exceeds that of the total NDP index of 271 are electricity (1596), public administration and defence (660), banking and insurance (807), transport other than by railways (578), registered manufacturing (488) and trade, hotels and restaurants (396), while the sub-sectors whose growth rates are sharply below that of the NDP are agriculture and allied activities (170) and forestry (193). The other sub-sectors have an index of growth more or less in line with that of the NDP as a whole.

However, these sub-sectors are not homogeneous in their composition—agriculture being confused with animal husbandry, electricity with gas and water supply, non-railway transport with storage, banking with insurance, and real estate with ownership of dwellings and business services. Fortu-

Table 5.1

Growth of Real NDP Industrial Groups

Sub-sector	*Share in NDP*		*Index of Growth*	*Compound Growth Rate*
	1950-51	*1979-80*	*1950-79*	*1950-79*
Agriculture & allied activities	54.11	33.83	169.63	2.10
Forestry	1.52	1.08	192.81	3.30
Fishing	0.49	0.53	288.89	4.00
Primary Sub-total	56.12	35.44	171.31	
Mining & quarrying	0.83	1.10	357.89	4.60
Regd. manufacturing	6.30	11.34	488.00	5.80
Unregd. manufacturing	5.36	6.86	347.44	4.10
Construction	4.49	4.83	291.71	4.90
Electricity, water & gas	0.26	1.55	1595.83	10.40
Secondary Sub-total	17.24	25.68	403.81	
Railways	1.66	2.12	347.02	4.80
Other transport & storage	1.61	3.43	577.55	6.40
Communication	0.37	0.85	617.65	6.50
Trade, hotels & restaurants	8.51	12.41	395.88	5.00
Banking & insurance	0.84	2.51	806.49	7.20
Real estate, ownership of dwellings & business services	3.09	3.64	319.15	4.20
Public administration & defence	3.64	8.85	659.64	7.00
Other services	6.92	5.07	199.84	2.30
Tertiary Sub-total	26.64	38.88	396.33	
TOTAL NDP	100.00	100.00	271.32	3.63

nately, desegregated data is available for the sub-sectors, which enables a more meaningful analysis of structural change in the sub-sectors of industrial origin on the basis of national accounts data.

First, the composite head of agriculture is divided into two main sub-heads—namely, agriculture and livestock—with sharply differing rates of growth and consequent changes in their percentage shares of the total. Over the period 1950-51 to 1979-80, agriculture proper had an annual compound growth in its NDP of 2.3 per cent, while that of livestock was only 1.6 per cent. This led to a drop in its share from 19.2 per cent in 1950-51 to 15.8 in 1979-80. Yet if we look at the data for the intermediate years, we find that, though the share of livestock shows a secular fall over the period, this is largely due to its lower growth rate in the fifties and a sharp fall from this rate during the sixties and the early seventies. However, it has recorded a sharp rise during the second half of the third decade, and has enabled livestock to record a marginal rise in its share from that in the first half of the seventies (see Table 5.2).

An examination of the growth in the NDP from agriculture proper shows that, while the gross value of its output at constant prices has risen from 100

Table 5.2

Average Percentage Share in Agriculture Sub-sectors

Period	*Agriculture*	*Livestock*
1950-51 to 54-55	81.68	18.31
1955-56 to 59-60	82.28	17.71
1960-61 to 64-65	83.43	16.56
1965-66 to 69-70	83.47	16.52
1970-71 to 74-75	84.18	15.82
1975-76 to 79-80	83.44	16.56

in 1950-51 to 207.16 in 1979-80, at an annual compound growth rate of 2.3 per cent, there is a wide difference in the growth rates of the principal categories of crops which constitute agricultural output. This is clearly seen in Table 5.3.

Table 5.3

Annual Compound Rates of Growth

Category	*1950-51 to 59-60*	*1960-61 to 69-70*	*1970-71 to 78-79*	*1950-51 to 78-79*
Cereals	3.7	2.8	2.3	2.9
Pulses	3.0	−0.7	−0.1	0.1
Oilseeds	3.6	1.6	−0.1	1.9
Sugar	4.9	2.4	2.2	3.0
Fibres	3.5	−0.3	2.7	2.3
Dyes & tanning materials	−11.8	4.7	5.2	1.4
Drugs & narcotics	1.9	2.6	1.6	2.2
Condiments & spices	2.1	0.9	2.8	1.8
Fruits & vegetables	3.6	6.1	2.8	4.2
Other crops	−0.7	0.4	−0.1	0.1
By–products	2.0	1.4	1.5	1.3
TOTAL	2.8	2.2	1.9	2.3

The effect of these differences in growth rates is seen in the change that has taken place in the percentage shares of these crop categories in the NDP from agriculture over and during the period. Table 5.4 gives the relevant data.

Cereals are obviously the prima donna of the crops and have also attracted the most attention. Sugar has also done well and is, in fact, the cultivator's preference to paddy even when he can have two crops in a year with assured irrigation. The surprising feature revealed by Tables 5.3 and 5.4 is the high rate of growth of fruits and vegetables and the share it occupies, which is next only to cereals in terms of its contribution to the NDP. It is also a welcome feature from the nutritional aspect. The same, however, cannot be said of pulses and oilseeds, whose rate of growth is low and whose percentage shares in the NDP have actually fallen over the period in spite of their nutritional importance. The fall in the share of by-products, which are mainly stalks and

Table 5.4

Average Per Cent Shares — Agriculture (1960-61 Prices)

Items	*1950-51 to 54-55*	*1955-56 to 59-60*	*1960-61 to 64-65*	*1965-66 to 69-70*	*1970-71 to 74-75*	*1975-76 to 79-80*
Cereals	42.47	43.76	45.45	45.39	48.25	50.03
Pulses	6.56	6.63	5.91	5.04	4.29	4.19
Oilseeds	8.15	8.83	8.75	8.29	8.30	7.52
Sugar	4.91	5.64	5.98	6.33	6.15	6.16
Fibres	4.97	5.40	5.56	4.87	5.32	5.26
Dyes & tanning	0.01	0.01	0.01	0.01	0.01	0.01
Drugs & narcotics	2.87	2.83	2.76	2.97	2.86	2.93
Condiments & spices	2.88	2.83	3.02	2.90	2.60	2.65
Fruits & vegetables	8.26	7.32	7.38	9.36	10.02	10.36
Other crops	10.04	8.50	7.56	7.63	6.46	5.70
By-products	8.82	8.64	8.09	8.21	7.11	6.84
Plus/Minus adjustments	+0.06	−0.39	−0.47	−1.00	−1.37	−1.65
TOTAL	100.00	100.00	100.00	100.00	100.00	100.00

straw, is another disquieting feature of the change that has taken place in Indian agriculture during the last thirty years. How far this is due to the increase in crop yields of cereals brought about by dwarf varieties is a matter that still needs investigation.

The other sub-head under the generic term agriculture is animal husbandry or livestock products. Livestock products also consists of a number of items, not all of which have had the same index of growth. Table 5.5 gives the annual compound growth rates of the different items.

Table 5.5

Annual Compound Growth Rates of Livestock Products

Category	*1950-51 60-61*	*1960-61 to 70-71*	*1970-71 to 79-80*	*1950-51 to 79-80*
Milk & products	1.1	1.4	3.7	2.0
Meat & products	0.8	1.1	2.3	1.3
Hides & skins	1.3	−0.16	1.0	0.5
Eggs & poultry	3.8	1.0	4.9	3.2
Wool & hair	0.8	0.9	2.1	1.0
Dung	1.0	−0.69	1.1	0.5
Increment in livestock	NA	NA	NA	NA
Other products	NA	NA	NA	NA
TOTAL	1.7	1.0	3.4	1.6

Eggs and poultry top the list in growth rate followed by milk and milk products. Meat and wool are next, while hides and skins and dung are last. The Table also shows that the third decade has seen a marked improvement not only in the overall growth rate of the total of livestock products, but also of that of each of its component items.

A better appreciation of the changes which have taken place in the pattern of livestock products output can be obtained by looking at the changes in their percentage shares of their NDP over the period. Table 5.6 gives the relevant figures at constant prices.

Table 5.6

Average Percentage Shares of Livestock Products

Items	*1950-51 to 54-55*	*1955-56 to 59-60*	*1960-61 to 64-65*	*1965-66 to 69-70*	*1970-71 to 74-75*	*1975-76 to 79-80*
Milk & products	63.95	61.99	63.39	64.77	65.67	67.25
Meat & products	9.37	8.99	8.99	9.08	8.81	8.30
Hides & skins	3.10	3.03	3.06	2.92	2.57	2.28
Eggs & poultry	4.80	5.30	5.96	5.70	6.66	7.14
Wool & hair	1.00	0.96	0.95	0.95	0.90	0.84
Dung	14.76	14.18	14.50	13.28	12.30	10.82
Increment in livestock	2.28	4.66	2.19	2.24	1.83	1.68
Other products	0.74	0.89	0.96	1.06	1.26	1.69
TOTAL	100.00	100.00	100.00	100.00	100.00	100.00

The dominant share is that of milk and milk products, which include butter and ghee, accounting for a little more than two-thirds of the total; and it has also increased its share in the total from 64.0 per cent in the beginning to 67.3 per cent towards the end of the period. The next major item is dung, but its share has decreased from 14.8 to 10.8 per cent. This is followed by meat and meat products with about 9 per cent of the total, but its share has also gone down from 9.4 to 8.3 per cent. The next in share—which constitutes the success story—is eggs and poultry, having increased its share from 4.8 to 7.1 per cent. Hides and skins have decreased their share from 3.1 to 2.3 per cent and wool and hair from 1 to 0.8 per cent. Livestock has had a fluctuating share and seems to average around a little over 2 per cent. Consistent growth over all the sub-periods is seen only in the case of eggs and poultry and, in the last four sub-periods, for milk and milk products. In the case of the other items, there is no consistent movement over the sub-periods, but the general trend is one of decline to the advantage of eggs, poultry, milk and milk products.

The other two sub-sectors in the primary sector are forestry and fishing. In the case of forestry, shares by products were only available up to 1970-71. From this, it appears that as against an index of growth of 180.3 for the gross ouptut of the total of forestry products, that of fuel wood was only 121.5 while that for industrial wood was 206.1, and for new plantations as much as 668.1. For minor forest products, it was 166.3. The figures underline the importance of social forestry and decentralised village production for meeting the rural requirement of fuel wood. While new plantations have shown a high rate of growth in their contribution to the NDP, their share in the total is marginal, being only 1.8 per cent in 1970-71, whereas industrial wood accounted for 58.1 per cent and minor forest products for 27.2 per cent, leaving fuel wood only 12.9 per cent. The major emphasis in forestry development has thus been commercial, and emphasises the imperative need for vigorous action in providing for alternative supplies of fuel wood for the rural population.

Fishing has shown a higher overall rate of growth than the other sub-sectors under the primary sector, with an index of growth of 312.7 in its contribution to the NDP in 1979-80. The index for marine fishing is only 250.2, as against 358.5 for inland fishing and 321.7 for subsistence fishing. Subsistence fishing only accounts for about 4 per cent of the total, while marine fishing accounts for about a third and inland fishing for a little less than two-thirds. Inland fishing thus plays a dominant role in the fishing industry contrary to popular impression, and has also been increasing its share over the period, unlike marine fishing whose share has been declining. Table 5.7 gives the relevant data at constant prices.

Table 5.7

Average Percentage Share of Items in Fishing Sector

Items	*1950-51 to 54-55*	*1955-56 to 59-60*	*1960-61 to 64-65*	*1965-66 to 70-71*	*1970-71 to 74-75*	*1975-76 to 79-80*
Inland fishing	58.17	62.48	64.63	64.94	62.64	61.57
Marine fishing	37.47	33.29	31.13	30.79	33.16	34.10
Subsistence fishing	4.36	4.23	4.24	4.27	4.20	4.33
TOTAL	100.00	100.00	100.00	100.00	100.00	100.00

Mining and quarrying are grouped under the sub-heads under the secondary sector. Minerals are categorised under major and minor in the CSO data. Major minerals account for more than 90 per cent of the NDP value of all mineral output and are classified under coal and lignite, metallic minerals and non-metallic minerals. Table 5.8 gives the index of growth and changing percentage shares of the total of the different items.

Minor minerals have had the highest index of growth followed by non-metallic minerals and then, at a long distance, by metallic minerals, and coal and lignite. While coal and lignite have decreased their share of the total from 70.8 per cent in 1950-51 to 53.8 per cent in 1978-79, iron ore has increased its share from 2.8 to 7.9 per cent, bauxite from 0.06 to 0.43 per cent, copper ore from 2.14 to 2.74 per cent, and limestone from 1.1 to 3.2 per cent. The share of manganese ore has fallen from 7.8 to 2.7 per cent, that of gold from 7.4 to 0.7 per cent, and mica from 3.1 to 0.2 per cent. As against this, non-metallic minerals, other than limestone and mica, and minor minerals have increased their share from 2.4 to 19.9 and from 0.8 to 7.0 per cent respectively. There has thus been a significant change in the product mix of minerals during the period under review, including a considerable measure of diversification in its products. The consistency of change over the period is seen from Table 5.9.

Table 5.8

Minerals — Growth and Changing Shares in Total

Items	*Index of Growth*	*Percentage Shares in Total*	
		1950-51	*1978-79*
Coal & lignite	331.7	70.79	53.82
Iron ore	1248.9	2.77	7.91
Manganese ore	149.0	7.83	2.67
Bauxite	3016.7	0.06	0.43
Copper ore	557.3	2.14	2.74
Gold	42.1	7.35	0.71
Other metallic minerals	402.0	1.57	1.45
Total metallic minerals	319.7	21.72	15.91
Limestone	1247.2	1.12	3.21
Mica	24.4	3.11	0.17
Other non-metallic minerals	3558.7	2.44	19.93
Total non-metallic minerals	1523.8	6.67	23.31
Total major minerals	409.3	99.18	93.04
Minor minerals	3697.5	0.82	6.96
TOTAL (all minerals)	436.3	100.00	100.00

Table 5.9

Average Percentage Share in the NDP from Mining and Quarrying — 1960-61 Prices

Item	*1950-51 to 54-55*	*1955-56 to 59-60*	*1960-61 to 64-65*	*1965-66 to 70-71*	*1970-71 to 74-75*	*1975-76 to 79-80*
Coal & lignite	67.56	67.32	63.84	58.14	55.87	55.38
Iron ore	3.40	5.21	8.15	8.38	9.56	8.74
Manganese ore	10.23	8.36	4.37	4.00	3.12	2.66
Bauxite	0.06	0.10	0.28	0.36	0.47	0.39
Copper ore	1.72	1.66	1.32	1.04	1.77	3.13
Gold	7.45	5.04	2.78	1.50	1.27	0.81
Other metallic minerals	1.62	1.96	0.85	0.64	1.17	1.59
Limestone	1.54	3.11	3.62	3.52	3.66	3.31
Mica	2.84	1.88	1.13	0.65	0.40	0.20
Other non-metallic minerals	2.37	2.59	4.69	11.96	15.45	18.09
Minor minerals	1.21	2.77	8.97	9.82	7.27	5.70
GROSS VALUE OF OUTPUT	100.00	100.00	100.00	100.00	100.00	100.00

Manufacture is another sub-category in this sector. We have already seen in Chapter 4 that registered manufacturing has grown faster than unregistered manufacturing. In fact, the index of growth of the former is 532 in 1979-80, while that of the latter is only 352.

Desegregated data on gross value added are available for 15 heads of industry and have been worked out at 1960-61 prices for the entire period.

The change that has taken place in the industrial product mix over the period and their different growth rates are given in Table 5.10.

Table 5.10

GDP from Manufacturing—1960-61 Prices

Head of Industry	*Index of Growth*	*Percentage Share*	
		1950-51	*1978-79*
Food products	310.4	14.45	8.85
Beverages & tobacco	359.4	2.64	1.87
Textiles & foot-wear	228.5	39.37	17.75
Wood & products except furniture	597.3	0.71	0.84
Paper, paper products, printing & publishing	441.9	4.16	3.63
Leather & products	153.3	0.60	0.18
Rubber products	997.0	2.25	4.42
Chemical products	997.6	6.16	12.12
Non-metallic minerals	605.1	2.86	3.42
Basic metal industries	629.8	6.26	7.78
Metal products except machinery	397.6	1.86	1.46
Machinery, except electrical	3032.5	1.43	8.58
Electrical machinery & appliances	2798.3	1.38	7.60
Transport equipment	322.1	7.98	5.07
Miscellaneous industries	425.5	2.88	2.42
Consumption of fixed capital	1357.6	5.20	13.92
TOTAL (Gross value added)	506.9	100.00	100.00

Against an overall growth index of 507, machinery, both electrical and non-electrical, experienced a growth index of nearly 3000, and chemical products and rubber products of about 1000 each. Their combined share in the NDP from registered manufacturing has increased from 11.2 per cent in 1950-51 to 32.7 per cent in 1978-79 or as much as three times. These are the fast growth industries which have radically altered the industrial pattern and product-mix during these thirty years. To these must be added the non-metallic minerals and the basic metal industries with a growth index of 605 and 630 respectively and an increase in their combined share from 9.1 to 11.2 per cent. These six industrial categories have increased their combined share in the NDP from registered manufacturing from 20.3 to 43.9 per cent or more than doubled their share during the period under review.

In contrast is the low growth of the textiles (including foot-wear) and food products industries with an index of 229 and 310 respectively and a fall in their combined share in the NDP from registered manufacturing from 53.8 per cent in 1950-51 to 26.6 per cent in 1978-79 or by a little more than half during this period. The fall in the share of paper, printing and publishing from 4.2 to 3.6 per cent and of leather manufacturing (other than foot-wear) from 0.6 to 0.18 during this period is also worth noting.

Altogether, the change has been from consumer goods to producer and intermediate goods, and should normally be regarded as a progressive feature associated with the developmental process. Only, in the Indian case, the volume of production is low and the change has come about so rapidly that the structure has become top-heavy and has led to our seeking export markets for our producer goods simultaneously importing some other types of producer and consumer goods. The pattern of our industrial development has been such that there has been no addition to the supply of manufactured consumption goods proportionate to the increase in the total of all manufactured goods.

Similar detailed data are not available for unregistered manufacturing. Moreover, the share of miscellaneous or other industries, which constitute a marginal item in the data relating to registered manufacturing, is a substantial item under unregistered manufacturing. Nevertheless, the data available shows that there have been differing rates of growth in its component items and significant changes in their shares, which are, to some extent, similar to those which have occurred in the registered manufacturing sector. Table 5.11 gives the relevant data at constant prices.

Table 5.11

Index of Growth and Percentage Shares of Individual Items in the Unregistered Manufacturing Sector

Head of Industry	*Index of Growth*	*Percentage Share*	
		1950-51	*1979-80*
Textiles & leather products	400.00	31.38	35.48
Wood & wood products	185.7	19.60	10.28
Metal manufacturing & engineering	385.9	12.74	13.90
Chemicals & products	584.7	2.50	4.13
Food, tobacco & drinks	177.1	20.81	10.42
Other industries	805.3	10.46	23.80
Consumption of fixed capital	587.3	2.51	4.15
Less computed bank charges	—	—	−2.16
TOTAL (Gross value added)	353.8	100.00	100.00

Here, too, we find the chemical industry growing faster and increasing its share as well as the metal manufacturing and the engineering industry. However, their progress is not of the same dimension as in the case of the registered manufacturing sector. Similarly, we also find a lower rate of growth on the part of the food and wood industries and a sharp decline in their share in the total.

There are, however, two striking differences between registered and unregistered manufacturing in respect of their changing product mix during the period under review. Whereas the textiles and leather group under registered manufacturing experienced a very sharp decline from 39.4 to 17.9 per cent, it has succeeded in improving its initial position under unregistered manufactures, its share in the total being 31.4 per cent in 1950-51 and 35.5 in 1979-80. Evidently, this is the result of the special encouragement it has received from the government at the expense of its counterpart under registered manufacturing.

The other difference is in respect of miscellaneous or other industries. Whereas under registered manufacturing this group has only a marginal place and has just managed to retain its position with 2.9 and 2.4 per cent respectively of the total in 1950-51 and 1979-80, it has an important position under unregistered manufacturing and has more than doubled its share of the total over the period from 10.5 to 23.8 per cent. While, in the absence of desegregated data under other industries, it is not possible to gauge the precise implications of the significant change that it has produced in the product mix under unregistered manufacturing, the figures do clearly indicate the presence of a dynamic element in its operation and a possible addition of new industries along with an expansion in some existing ones. This also could be traced to the increasing facilities and encouragement given by the government to the small and tiny sectors in manufacturing and the evident response it has evoked from the small entrepreneurial class. If the inference that has been drawn is correct, it constitutes a progressive feature of the country's industrial development from the point of view of dispersal of economic power and increased employment per unit of capital. This seems to have occurred particularly during the seventies or the third decade of the period under review, as can be seen from Table 5.12.

Table 5.12

Average Percentage Shares of Individual Items Under Unregistered Manufacturing at Constant Prices

Items	*1950-51 to 54-55*	*1955-56 to 59-60*	*1960-61 to 64-65*	*1965-66 to 69-70*	*1970-71 to 74-75*	*1975-76 to 79-80*
Food, tobacco & drinks	20.40	18.57	16.28	14.03	12.12	12.23
Textiles & leather products	33.58	35.90	35.07	35.31	31.55	32.17
Wood & wood products	18.69	19.15	19.80	20.66	12.63	11.78
Chemical products	2.39	2.32	2.47	2.76	3.90	4.17
Metal manufacturing & engineering	11.97	11.10	13.42	14.28	14.49	14.01
Other industries	10.47	10.46	10.46	10.46	22.38	23.08
Consumption of fixed capital	2.50	2.50	2.50	2.50	3.99	4.19
Less imputed bank charges	—	—	—	—	−1.06	−1.63
TOTAL	100.00	100.00	100.00	100.00	100.00	100.00

The other composite item in the secondary sector is electricity, gas and water supply. This was the fastest growing sub-sector, its index of growth reaching 1520 in 1979-80 as against 100 in 1950-51. This growth has been dominated by electricity with an index of 1845, while that for water supply is 475 and only 226 for gas. The share of electricity has increased from 77.6 to 94.2 per cent, with water supply falling from 16.01 to 4.8 per cent and gas from 6.4 to 1.0 per cent. The data only underscore the important place given to electricity in the country's development programmes after independence. It is interesting to note, however, that its annual compound growth rate has fallen to 7.4 per cent during the seventies after having remained at 12.7 per cent during both the fifties and sixties.

The tertiary sector is more composite in character than the other two sectors. It includes a large number of sub-heads; and some of them are a combination of two or more sub-heads which have been brought together by the CSO classification for no obvious reasons.

Two items given in the CSO Table pertain to railways, and other transport including storage. As desegregated data are available under the second item, it is possible to exclude storage and take transport as one item, with railways, and other transport as its sub-item. Table 5.13 gives the index growth and percentage changes in the shares of railways and other transport in the total NDP from transport at constant prices.

Table 5.13

Growth of Transport Sector (Value Added)

Item	*Index of Growth*	*Share in Total*	
		1950-51	*1979-80*
Railways	347.02	50.67	38.16
Other transport	577.55	49.33	61.84
TOTAL	460.74	100.00	100.00

Transport other than railways has been growing faster and has also increased its share in the total from 49.3 per cent in 1950-51 to 61.8 per cent in 1979-80. This increase has been consistent throughout the period, its compound annual growth rate being 5.7 per cent during 1950-51 to 1960-61, 5.8 per cent in the second decade and 7.5 per cent in the third decade up to 1979-80, whereas the corresponding figures for railways were 5.3, 4.3 and 4.5 per cent respectively. The slow growth of the railway sector is a matter of concern in the developmental process in view of the continental character of the country, its energy constraints, and the easier domestic availability of coal for moving the railways.

Within other transport, there are several sub-sectors; their rates of growth also show considerable variations. Table 5.14 gives the index of growth and percentage shares in the total of its different constituent items (the figures are at constant prices).

The highest growth is in the NDP from services incidental to transport, being 4341 as against 599 for the whole of the transport sector excluding railways; it has increased its share from 1.20 in 1950-51 to 8.71 in 1979-80. The next is air transport, the growth of which is more than four times that of either road transport or water transport and which has increased its share of the total at the expense of both these categories. Thus, the share of air

Table 5.14

Per Cent Distribution of Value Added from Transport

Type of Transport	*Index of Growth*	*Percentage Share in Total*	
		1950-51	*1979-80*
Road	538.27	78.71	70.73
Water	445.90	13.50	10.05
Air	2162.24	3.27	11.82
Services incidental to transport	4340.85	1.20	8.71
Storage	659.56	3.32	3.57
Imputed bank charges	NA	NA	−4.88
TOTAL (value added)	599.01	100.00	100.00

transport has increased from 3.3 to 11.8 per cent (or by more than 8.2 percentage points), while that of road transport has fallen from 78.7 to 70.7 (or by 8.0 percentage points) and that of water transport from 13.5 to 10.1 per cent (or by 3.4 percentage points). The socio-economic cost-benefit ratio of this increase in air transport has still to be worked out by the authorities concerned in comparison with those of road and water transport. The question is whether this partiality for air transport is not more of a bureaucratic, political, industrial convenience and commercial preference (all of whom meet the charges incurred on their expense account), than a matter of of costs and benefits involved from the point of view of the consumer or the tax payer?

The next item to be considered is trade and hotels and restaurants. As desegregated data are available for this head, Table 5.15 gives the growth and changes in percentage shares of these two items for the period under review at constant prices.

Table 5.15

Trade and Hotels — Growth and Shares

Items	*Index of Growth*	*Share in Total*	
		1950-51	*1979-80*
Trade	403.52	94.62	93.63
Hotels & restaurants	482.90	5.38	6.37
TOTAL	407.71	100.00	100.00

The growth rate of the NDP from hotels and restaurants is higher than that of trade, and it has, therefore, increased its share of the total from 5.4 to 6.4 per cent. But trade is the dominating item which accounts for 94 per cent of the total under this head.

Table 5.16 gives the index of growth and changes in the percentages shares of banking and insurance at constant prices.

Table 5.16

Distribution of Value Added — Banking

Items	*Index of Growth*	*Share in Total*	
		1950-51	*1979-80*
Banking	1025.58	62.20	78.24
Insurance	469.08	37.80	21.76
TOTAL	815.18	100.00	100.00

Banking has grown at more than double the rate of insurance, and has increased its share from 62.2 per cent to 78.2 per cent of the total. However, this increase has not been consistent during the three decades, the second decade showing a relatively smaller increase, while the fifties and the seventies show larger rates of increase (see Table 5.17).

Within the banking sector, however, there have been significant variations between the rates of growth of its different sub-sectors (see Table 5.18).

Table 5.17

Average Percentage Shares of Banking and Insurance

Items	*1950-51 to 54-55*	*1955-56 to 59-60*	*1960-61 to 64-65*	*1965-66 to 69-70*	*1970-71 to 74-75*	*1975-76 to 79-80*
Banking	59.87	63.36	63.44	66.05	67.35	70.09
Insurance	40.13	36.64	36.56	33.95	32.65	29.91
TOTAL	100.00	100.00	100.00	100.00	100.00	100.00

Table 5.18

Distribution of Financial Institutions — Value Added

Sub-sectors	*Index of Growth*	*Percentage Share in Total*	
		1950-51	*1979-80*
Banks	808.69	60.11	47.40
Banking deposits of RBI	866.46	13.51	11.41
Post office savings banks	180.23	1.76	0.31
Non-banking financial companies	1810.93	12.75	22.51
Co operative credit societies	1587.22	11.87	18.37
TOTAL	815.18	100.00	100.00

The striking features revealed by Table 5.18 is the rapid growth of the NDP from non-banking financial companies which is more than double the rate of growth of banking companies. This has enabled it to increase its share from 12.75 to 22.51 per cent. These non-banking financial intermediaries comprise hire-purchase finance companies, *nidhis* or mutual benefit financial companies, investment companies, loan companies, and various other companies who show deposit liabilities that cannot be used for making advances to other companies. Their growth shows the ability of the private sector to obtain funds from outside the regular banking system, the increasing role of non-banking financial companies in mobilisation and investment of funds and the consequent rise of the intermediation ratio in the Indian capital market. Next are the cooperative credit societies which have increased their share from 11.9 to 18.4 per cent. Banking proper has, therefore, declined in its share of the total from 60.11 per cent in 1950-51 to 47.40 per cent. Post office savings banks have grown in their contribution to the NDP only by 80.23 per cent, which is less than one-fourth of the growth in the entire banking sector. Their share in the total is marginal and even this has come down over the period from 1.76 to 0.31 per cent.

The startling growth of non-banking financial companies and the negligible growth and percentage share of post office savings banks raise important questions regarding the mobilisation of savings and the financing of investment which needs the attention of planners and the government. The growth of the share of cooperative credit socieities is, however, a welcome feature of the change in the contribution of the banking sector to the NDP.

In the insurance group, life insurance has had a higher index of growth of 575 as against 319 of non-life insurance, and its share was more than double that of the latter by the end of the period under review (see Table 5.19). Postal life insurance, like postal savings banks, has only a marginal position of about 0.2 per cent of the total and also a lower growth index of 329. The insignificant position occupied by postal life insurance and its lower rate of growth also requires the attention of planners and the government.

Table 5.19

Distribution of Insurance (Value Added)

Insurance Type	*Rate of Growth*	*Per Cent Share*	
		1950-51	*1979-80*
Life (other than postal)	575.03	58.73	71.94
Non-life	318.98	41.03	27.90
Postal	328.57	0.23	0.16
TOTAL	409.38	100.00	100.00

The next item is real estate, rentals of dwellings and business services. Table 5.20 gives the index of growth and changes in the percentage shares of these three items in the total.

Rentals of dwellings dominate this item, but its rate of growth has been less than that of the total. Its share has fallen from 94.7 per cent in 1950-51 to 88.4 per cent in 1979-80. Within the gross rentals of all dwellings, the index of

Table 5.20

Distribution of Value Added from Real Estate

Items	Index of Growth	Percentage Share in the Total	
		1950-51	1979-80
Real estate	277.71	0.69	0.77
Gross rental of dwellings	232.06	94.69	88.41
Gross rental of rural dwellings	189.14	61.83	47.05
Gross rental of urban dwellings	312.82	32.86	41.36
Business services	578.16	4.62	10.72
TOTAL	241.97	100.00	100.00

growth of urban dwellings has been much higher with 313 as against 189 for rural dwellings, and its share in rentals has increased from 32.9 per cent to 41.4 per cent. As the figures are at constant prices, it is a clear indication of the set-back that rural dwellings have suffered during this period as compared to urban dwellings. That this has been a consistent trend over the period is also seen from Table 5.21.

Table 5.21

Average Percentage Shares in Gross Rentals

Year	Rural	Urban	Total
1950-51 to 54-55	64.35	35.65	100.00
1955-56 to 59-60	61.91	38.09	100.00
1960-61 to 64-65	59.69	40.31	100.00
1965-66 to 69-70	58.13	41.87	100.00
1970-71 to 74-75	56.87	43.13	100.00
1975-76 to 79-80	54.20	45.80	100.00

Real estate occupies a marginal position in the total though its share has recorded a small rise from 0.69 to 0.77 during the period. Business services, however, have recorded an index of growth which is more than double that of the total, and increased its share from 4.6 to 10.7 per cent over the period.

The next composite item in the NDP by industrial origin is community and personal services, which is made up of two sub-items—public administration and defence, and other services. Table 5.22 gives the index of growth of their contributions to the NDP and the change in their percentage shares of the total over the period at constant prices.

Public administration and defence have been growing faster than other services with an index of 660 as against 200 of the latter. Their share in the total has also increased from 3.64 per cent in 1950-51 to 8.85 per cent in 1979-80. The figures emphasise the increasing role of the government sector in the generation of the country's NDP, which is in addition to its even more dominant role in economic activity through its departmental and non-departmental enterprises.

Table 5.22

Distribution of Value Added from Community Services

Item	Index of Growth	Percentage Share in Total NDP	
		1950-51	1979-80
Public administration & defence	659.64	3.64	8.85
Other services	199.84	6.92	5.07
TOTAL		10.56	13.92

Desegregated data on other services, which is made up of twelve kinds of services, are available from 1950-51 at constant prices. Table 5.23 gives their index of growth and changes in percentage shares to the total during the period.

Table 5.23

Distribution of Community Services

Items	Index of Growth	Changing Percentage Shares	
		1950-51	1979-80
I *Community Services*	543.7	27.41	71.36
Education, research & scientific	741.4	15.88	56.38
Medical & health	391.5	6.77	12.69
Religious & others	100.5	4.76	2.29
II *Legal Services*	149.0	4.05	2.89
III *Recreation & Entertainment Services*	106.3	3.51	1.79
IV *Personal Services*	210.4	17.77	17.89
Domestic	73.0	6.86	2.39
Laundry & allied	131.8	5.79	3.66
Barbers & beauty shops	143.8	4.11	2.83
Other personal services	1866.0	1.01	9.01
V *Sanitary Services*	159.4	4.21	3.21
VI *Other Service Activities*	13.4	42.82	2.74
VII *Gross Operating Surplus of Joint Stock Companies.*	96.7	0.26	0.12
TOTAL (Gross value added)	208.8	100.00	100.00

Table 5.23 shows that community services have grown at a higher rate than personal services, the former's index of growth being 544 as against 210 of the latter. Community and religious services, and recreation and entertainment services have shown hardly any increase during the period, their index of growth being only 101 and 106 respectively. Domestic services show an actual decline, its index of growth registering 73 as against 100 in 1950-51 and its share in the NDP from this sub-sector declining from 6.9 to 2.4 per cent over the period.

On the other hand, what are called 'other personal services' have shown an index of growth that is nearly nine times that of the total, and its share has increased from 1.0 to 9.0 per cent. It would be interesting to know the composition of these 'other personal services' and the class to which they cater.

The most surprising feature in this Table is the fall in the share of what are called 'other service activities' from 42.82 to 2.7 per cent over the period, which is evidently offset by the rise in what are called 'community services'. One possible explanation would be that education and medical services must have been a part of 'other service activities', and that, over this period, these have become community services. In any case, Table 5.23 does show a sharp drift towards community services, their share in the NDP from this sub-sector rising from 27.4 to 71.4 per cent. At the same time, it is also pertinent to note that the growth index of the total sub-sector of community and personal services, other than public administration and defence, is less than that of the NDP as a whole (271) during the period and much less than that of the tertiary sector (396). Sub-sectors which have had a higher growth index are mining, manufacturing, construction, electricity, transport and trade, communication, banking, insurance and public administration.

In conclusion, let us review some of the changes which have taken place in the composition of the NDP over the period under review. In the NDP at constant prices from agriculture, cereals have increased their average annual share in agricultural output from 42.5 per cent in the period 1950-51–1954-55 to 50.0 per cent during 1975-76–1979-80; fruits and vegetables from 8.3 to 10.4 per cent and sugar from 4.9 to 6.2 per cent. Pulses have declined from 6.6 to 4.2 per cent and oilseeds from 8.2 to 7.5 per cent. In the NDP from livestock products, the two items that have increased their share are milk and milk products (from 64.0 to 67.3 per cent) and eggs and poultry (from 4.8 to 7.1 per cent). Under forestry, it is industrial wood that has increased much faster than fuel wood, while under fishing, inland fishing has increased its share from 58.2 to 61.6 per cent, and that of marine fishing has fallen from 37.5 to 34.1 per cent.

Under minerals, coal and lignite have lost their dominant position, their share declining from 70.8 to 53.8 per cent. Similarly metallic minerals, including iron ore, have declined from 21.7 to 15.9 per cent, though iron ore by itself has increased its share from 2.8 to 7.9 per cent. Non-metallic minerals have increased their share from a low of 6.7 per cent to 23.3 per cent. Under the NDP from registered manufacturing, textiles and foot-wear have declined in their share from 39.4 per cent to 17.8 per cent, and food products from 14.5 to 8.9 per cent. Against this, machinery and chemical products including rubber have increased their share nearly three-fold from 11.2 per cent in 1950-51 to 32.7 per cent in 1979-80.

Altogether, the change has been from consumer goods to producer and intermediate goods which is a normal feature of developmental progress. In the Indian case, however, it has not had the same progressive effect because of an inadequate domestic market, a low rate of growth of domestic purchasing power in real terms and a low output of consumer goods. A similar tendency has been found also in the case of the NDP from unregistered manufacturing, except that textiles and leather products have improved their 1950-51 percentage position. In the case of the NDP from transport services, railways have recorded a sharp decline in its share to the advantage of other means of transport, especially road and air transport and services incidental to their growth and maintenance. While the CSO classification under national accounts has clubbed trade and hotels together, it is trade which accounts for more than 90 per cent of the NDP from this head. Similarly, under the CSO combined head of banking and insurance, it is banking which now accounts for 70 per cent of its combined NDP, and it has gained at the expense of insurance during the period under review. One striking feature of the NDP growth from banking, however, is the fast growth of non-banking financial companies which have increased their share from 12.8 to 22.5 per cent during the thirty years under review. An equally conspicuous feature of the growth of the banking and insurance sector is the negligible growth and percentage share of postal savings and postal insurance in spite of the advantage they have of a much wider territorial coverage, especially in rural and semi-urban areas.

The gross rentals of dwellings shows a rate of growth which is considerably lower than that of the tertiary sector as a whole; and within it the gross rental of rural dwellings a lower rate of growth than that of urban dwellings. Under the NAS head of community and personal services, it is public administration and defence which has increased its share in the NDP from 3.6 to 8.9 per cent, while that of other services has declined from 6.9 to 5.1 per cent over the three decades. In the other services, education and medical services have increased their share significantly, while surprisingly, for a religious country like India, the share of religious services in the NDP from the sector on community and personal services (other than public administration and defence) is not only low, but has also declined from 4.8 to 2.3 per cent during the period. Domestic services also show a sharp decline from 6.9 to 2.4 per cent, but what are called 'other personal services' have shown a conspicuous rise from 1.0 to 9.0 per cent. The product mix is certainly moving in what may be called a modern direction, but whether it is equally an evidence of growth in real welfare is questionable.

Addendum to Chapter 5

PRODUCT MIX OF THE FACTORY SECTOR

It is relevant to refer to the changes which have taken place in the product mix of the factory sector in the Indian economy, even though they are not drawn from NAS data. Figures are available from 1960-61 to 1976-77. The sector has been divided into twenty broad industry groups. According to the *Annual Survey of Industries Report* (ASI) of 1977-78, results accounted for 87 per cent of the value added, 83 per cent of the total employment and 93 per cent of the fixed capital in the registered manufacturing sector. The data was compiled by the Industrial Statistics Division of the CSO and published in 1981 as Bulletin No. 8 in their ISD series.

Table 5.24 gives the figures of gross value added at 1960-61 prices and percentage distribution by twenty industry groups of the total value added by the factory sector.

While the gross value added in the factory sector as a whole has grown by

Table 5.24

Gross Value Added in the Factory Sector 1960-61 to 1976-77 at 1960-61 Prices

Industry	*Amount*		*Index of Growth*		*Percentage Shares*	
	1960-61	*1976-77*	*1960-61*	*1976-77*	*1960-61*	*1976-77*
Chemicals	81.32	345.66	100.00	425	9.35	14.18
Cement	13.30	37.56	100.00	282	1.53	1.54
Iron & steel	68.49	193.75	100.00	283	7.88	7.95
Non-ferrous basic metals	12.31	17.83	100.00	145	1.42	0.73
Electric light & power	28.57	313.13	100.00	1096	3.29	12.84
Machinery except electrical	37.31	216.72	100.00	581	4.29	8.89
Electrical machinery & appliances	33.62	209.83	100.00	624	3.87	8.61
Ship-building & repairs	7.91	14.31	100.00	181	0.91	0.59
Railroad equipment	36.81	37.60	100.00	102	4.23	1.54
Motor vehicles	28.12	108.55	100.00	386	3.23	4.45
Repairs to motor vehicles	11.12	38.91	100.00	350	1.28	1.60
Metal products	27.47	68.11	100.00	248	3.16	2.79
Rubber products	24.64	46.23	100.00	188	2.83	1.90
Petroleum refining	15.31	46.09	100.00	295	1.76	1.85
Structural	8.49	17.02	100.00	201	0.98	0.70
Spinning & weaving	279.55	482.89	100.00	173	32.15	19.80
Paper pulp & paper products	18.04	73.55	100.00	408	2.07	3.02
Miscellaneous food products	73.86	82.45	100.00	112	8.49	3.38
Tobacco manufacturing	24.25	31.29	100.00	129	2.79	1.28
Sugar	39.06	57.78	100.00	148	4.49	2.37
ALL INDUSTRIES	869.55	2439.26	100.00	280	100.00	100.00

180 per cent at constant prices during the seventeen years covered by the period 1960-61 to 1976-77, the industries which have grown fastest are electric, light and power (996 per cent), machinery other than electrical (481 per cent), electrical machinery (524 per cent), chemicals (325 per cent), paper pulp and paper products (308 per cent), motor vehicles (286 per cent) and motor vehicle repairs (250 per cent).

The industries which have more or less kept pace with the overall growth rate of the factory sector are petroleum refining (195 per cent), cement (182 per cent) and iron and steel (183 per cent). The industries which have grown at a rate significantly below that of the factory sector as a whole are rubber products (88 per cent), spinning and weaving (73 per cent), sugar (48 per cent), tobacco (29 per cent), ship-building and repairs (81 per cent), non-ferrous basic metals (45 per cent), miscellaneous food products (12 per cent) and railroad equipment (2 per cent).

These varying rates of growth have brought about a significant change in the industrial mix of the factory sector over the period. Thus, electricity has increased its share from 3.29 to 12.84 per cent, chemicals from 9.35 to 14.18 per cent, machinery (both electrical and non-electrical) from 8.16 to 17.50 per cent, between them accounting for 44.52 per cent in 1976-77 as against only 20.8 per cent in 1960-61. They have thus more than doubled their share and account for nearly half of the total value added by the factory sector in 1976-77. Curiously, while electricity and machinery have recorded a sharp rise in their share, cement, and iron and steel have only retained their initial share of about 1.5 and 7.9 per cent respectively, and petroleum refining at about 1.8 per cent.

The factory sector industry which has recorded the sharpest fall in its share is spinning and weaving (from 32.15 to 19.80 per cent). Non-ferrous basic metals and metal products have also experienced a reduction in their share from 1.42 to 0.73 and from 3.16 to 2.79 per cent respectively; and rubber products from 2.83 to 1.90 per cent. Miscellaneous food products have declined from 8.49 to 3.38 per cent or by more than half, while the share of sugar has fallen from 4.49 to 2.37 per cent. A very disquieting fall is that of railroad equipment (from 4.23 to 1.54 per cent). Though the factory sector as a whole accounted for 10.71 per cent of the GDP in 1976-77 at 1960-61 prices and has increased its share of the same from 6.25 per cent in 1960-61, consumer goods industries and some of the infrastructural and basic industries have either declined in their share or only kept their initial levels. On the whole the factory sector does not seem to have developed in a balanced manner in its product mix; and this unbalanced development accounts for some of the problems which have faced the Indian economy during this period.

Consumption: Growth and Structure 6

In the last three chapters, the growth and structure of the economy were analysed from the income and output angle. In this chapter changes in the economy will be analysed from the aspect of expenditure. Expenditure is usually divided into four major heads — personal (private) consumption, government purchases of goods and services, domestic investment and net foreign investment. The first of these items gives an idea about the structure of consumption and the changes that have taken place in regard to the living standards of the people that constitute the economy, as well as the magnitude of the reduction/increase in consumption inequalities.

Due to data limitations that have already been discussed in Chapter 2, it is necessary to use 1970-71 instead of 1960-61 as the base year for the constant price series covering the period. Given this departure from the norm adopted in earlier chapters, it is not desirable to use absolute figures of consumption expenditure for analysing growth and shares in consumption. Instead, our analysis will be based on index numbers of consumption expenditure and its components. Table 6.1 gives the index numbers of the growth of aggregate private final consumption expenditure and its major component categories at constant prices (base 1970-71) for quinquennial periods.

Table 6.1

Index of Consumption Growth

Consumption	*1950-51*	*1979-80*	*1950-51 to 54-55*	*1955-56 to 59-60*	*1960-61 to 64-65*	*1965-66 to 69-70*	*1970-71 to 74-75*	*1975-76 to 79-80*
Food	100	208	100	114	135	150	172	194
			(67.61)	(66.29)	(65.35)	(62.72)	(61.44)	(59.16)
Non-food	100	287	100	121	149	185	226	280
			(32.39)	(33.71)	(34.65)	(37.28)	(38.56)	(40.84)
TOTAL	100	249	100	116	139	161	190	222

Note: Figures in brackets are per cent shares in total expenditure.

It is evident from Table 6.1 that while the total expenditure on consumption has grown by 149 per cent between 1950-51 and 1979-80, expenditure on food has grown by only 108 per cent. If we take quinquennial averages during this period, expenditure on food has increased by only 94 per cent from 1950-54 to 1975-79, against an increase of 122 per cent in total consumption. In fact, the percentage of food expenditure to total consumption expenditure has falled from 67.56 per cent in 1950-51 to 56.44 per cent in 1979-80 or from 67.61 per cent in the first quinquennium to 59.16 per cent in the last quinquennium. Further, whereas during the first three quinquennial periods the decline in the share of food was only 2.26 percentage points, it was as much as 6.19 percentage points in the following three quinquennial periods. This indicates its much more rapid fall during the last fifteen years of the period under review. The expenditure on non-food items has correspondingly increased from 32.44 per cent in 1950-51 to 43.54 per cent in 1979-80 or from 32.39 per cent in the first quinquennium to 40.84 per cent in the last quinquennium. This change in the consumption pattern is in line with the historical experience of developed countries. This is, of course, at the macro level and takes no account of the distortions caused by unequal distribution.

The change in the pattern of food consumption, however, is not so satisfactory. Table 6.2 gives the average shares of the component food items in quinquennial periods during 1950-51 to 1979-80.

Table 6.2

Growth of Expenditure—Food Items

Items	*Index of Growth*		*Average Shares*					
	1950-51	*1979-80*	*1950-51 to 54-55*	*1955-56 to 59-60*	*1960-61 to 64-65*	*1965-66 to 70-71*	*1970-71 to 74-75*	*1975-76 to 79-80*
Cereals & substitutes	100	219	44.74	45.27	44.96	45.41	44.83	45.61
Milk & products	100	178	16.09	14.86	13.54	12.76	13.20	14.14
Edible oils	100	167	7.77	8.20	8.13	7.80	8.03	6.62
Meat, fish, eggs	100	173	5.12	5.28	5.14	4.86	4.35	4.36
Sugar	100	222	6.62	7.47	7.90	7.66	7.33	6.88
Salt	100	416	0.25	0.26	0.33	0.37	0.38	0.40
Other foods	100	228	19.41	18.66	20.00	21.16	21.88	21.99
TOTAL	100	208	100.00	100.00	100.00	100.00	100.00	100.00

Table 6.2 shows that cereals have increased their share in food consumption, while milk and milk products, edible oils, and meat, fish and eggs have recorded a decline. The share of sugar shows a marginal rise while that of salt shows a more significant rise. Miscellaneous foods, which includes pulses, fruits and vegetables, also shows a small increase in its share. On the whole, what emerges is the increasing domination of cereals and sugar and the falling share of quality foods, indicating a decline in the nutritional quality of overall food consumption.

As far as non-food items are concerned, the rate of increase in their consumption by individual items does not show any uniformity. This is clearly shown in Table 6.3, which presents the percentage shares of each non-food item in the total expenditure on all consumption for the initial and final years of the period, as well as by quinquennial averages during the period.

It is seen from Table 6.3 that the items which have shown the most significant increase are clothing (from 4.22 to 9.87 per cent), furniture, furnishings and household equipment (from 1.20 to 3.25 per cent), personal transport (from 0.25 to 1.33 per cent), other transport including hired services (from 3.35 to 5.25 per cent), medical care and health (from 1.14 to 2.86 per cent), and education (from 1.33 to 2.48 per cent). There are, however, some items which have declined significantly, indicating that the increased share of the above-mentioned non-food items has been not only at the expense of the share of food items but also of some non-food items. These are: pan and alcoholic beverages declining from 2.30 to 1.83 per cent, tobacco from 3.68 to 2.82 per cent, fuel and power from 5.09 to 3.58 per cent, and domestic services from 1.00 to 0.43 per cent.

These data on private final consumption expenditure imply that over the period 1950-51 to 1979-80, national consumption has progressively increased, with non-food expenditure increasing its share of total consumption expenditure. The decline in the share of food expenditure has been accompanied not so much by a decline in the share of cereals as by that on milk, milk products, edible oils, meat, eggs and fish. To this extent, the change that has taken place in the national diet cannot be considered to be progressive. In the case of non-food expenditure, however, the change in the consumption pattern is distinctly progressive with items like pan, alcoholic beverages, tobacco and domestic services declining in their share and items like clothing, foot-wear, transport, medical care and education increasing their share of the total expenditure on consumption.

We have concentrated so far on national aggregates of consumption expenditure and not on per capita expenditure, which includes population growth during the period. It is the per capita changes in consumption expenditure that reflect the real change in consumption levels and patterns from the point of view of economic welfare. Table 6.4 gives the index numbers of the growth of per capita final consumption expenditure during the period 1950-51 to 1979-80, both in the total and in its main component categories.

It is seen from Table 6.4 that while the per capita expenditure at constant prices of total final consumption over the thirty years has increased by 34 per cent, that on some categories of consumption has increased by several times this figure. Thus, the per capita expenditure on medical care and health has increased by 239 per cent, on clothing and foot-wear by 210 per cent, transport and communication by 145 per cent, furniture, furnishings and domestic equipment by 125 per cent, and on education, recreation, entertainment, and cultural services by 148 per cent.

On the other hand, the per capita expenditure on food has increased by only 12 per cent, on gross rent, taxes, fuel and power by 17 per cent, on

Table 6.3

Per Cent Shares of Non-food Expenditure

Item Category	1950-51	1979-80	1950-51 to 54-55	1955-56 to 59-60	1960-61 to 64-65	1965-66 to 69-70	1970-71 to 74-75	1975-76 to 79-80
I *Alcoholic beverages, pan & intoxicants*	2.30	1.83	2.28	2.35	2.27	2.01	1.78	1.80
II *Tobacco*	3.68	2.82	3.64	3.76	3.52	3.65	2.88	2.52
III *Clothing & foot-wear*	4.62	10.68	5.48	6.18	6.43	7.43	8.02	9.68
Clothing	4.22	9.87	5.04	5.67	5.93	6.95	7.56	9.10
Foot-wear	0.40	0.81	0.44	0.51	0.50	0.48	0.46	0.58
IV *Gross rent, taxes & power*	8.39	7.29	7.93	7.45	7.43	7.29	7.22	7.03
Rent	3.28	3.60	3.20	3.22	3.53	3.40	3.63	3.51
Taxes	0.02	0.11	0.02	0.03	0.05	0.07	0.09	0.10
Fuel & power	5.09	3.58	4.71	4.20	3.85	3.82	3.50	3.42
V *Domestic services*	1.00	0.43	0.97	0.97	0.86	0.70	0.56	0.45
VI *Furnishings*	1.20	3.25	1.13	1.28	1.52	1.91	2.69	3.14
VII *Medical care*	1.14	2.86	1.15	1.27	1.65	2.23	2.44	2.76
VIII *Personal transport*	0.25	1.33	0.26	0.40	0.52	0.73	1.01	1.20
IX *Other transport*	3.35	5.25	3.23	3.46	3.67	4.21	4.34	4.93
X *Education*	1.33	2.48	1.39	1.68	2.15	2.86	3.06	2.45
XI *Recreation & entertainment*	0.56	1.00	0.51	0.45	0.39	0.48	0.77	0.92
XII *Miscellaneous goods & services*	4.63	4.34	4.42	4.46	4.26	3.76	3.79	3.96
TOTAL NON-FOOD	32.44	43.54	32.39	33.71	34.67	37.28	38.56	40.84

Table 6.4

Indices of Growth in Per Capita Consumption Expenditure at 1970-71 Prices

	1950-51 to 54-55	*1955-56 to 59-60*	*1960-61 to 64-65*	*1965-66 to 69-70*	*1970-71 to 74-75*	*1975-79 to 79-80*	*1950-51 to 79-80 (50-51 = 100)*
I *Food*	100	105	109	109	111	112	112
Cereals & substitutes	100	107	110	112	112	114	118
Milk & products	100	97	92	87	91	99	96
Edible oils	100	111	115	110	115	96	90
Meat, eggs & fish	100	109	110	104	94	96	93
Sugar	100	119	131	126	123	117	120
Salt	100	111	141	164	170	181	226
Other food	100	101	113	116	126	127	123
II *Non-alcoholic beverages*	100	101	137	112	148	151	153
III *Others excluding non-alcoholic beverages*	100	101	111	116	124	125	121
IV *Pan, intoxicants & alcoholic beverages*	100	111	113	104	96	101	106
V *Tobacco*	100	111	110	118	97	89	103
VI *Clothing & foot-wear*	100	121	133	159	179	226	310
Clothing	100	121	133	162	184	231	314
Foot-wear	100	126	128	127	127	168	270
VII *Gross rent, taxes & power*	100	101	106	108	111	114	117
Rent	100	108	125	125	139	141	147
Taxes	100	167	256	389	522	633	775
Fuel & power	100	96	92	95	91	93	95
VIII *Furniture, etc.*	100	115	129	146	189	219	225
Domestic services	100	107	101	85	70	60	58
Furniture	100	122	152	198	292	356	365
IX *Medical care & health*	100	119	164	228	261	308	339
X *Transport & communication*	100	119	136	166	187	225	245
Personal transport	100	164	226	331	476	589	712
Other transport	100	115	129	153	164	195	210
XI *Education, recreation, etc.*	100	121	151	206	247	227	248
Education	100	130	175	241	270	226	251
Others	100	94	87	111	184	230	240
XII *Miscellaneous goods & services*	100	109	109	100	105	115	125
TOTAL PRIVATE FINAL CONSUMPTION	100	108	113	117	122	128	134

miscellaneous goods and services by 25 per cent, on pan, alcoholic beverages and intoxicants by 6 per cent and on tobacco by 3 per cent. There has thus been a significant change in the pattern of per capita consumption expenditure at constant prices which seems to be a progressive development. This observation is qualified if one takes into account the varying growth rates of the individual items constituting the food basket over the quinquennial periods.

Table 6.5

Average Shares in Non-food Items

	1950-51 to 54-55	*1955-56 to 59-60*	*1960-61 to 64-65*	*1965-66 to 69-70*	*1970-71 to 74-75*	*1975-76 to 79-80*
Pan, alcoholic intoxicants	2.28	2.35	2.27	2.01	1.78	1.80
Tobacco	3.64	3.76	3.52	3.65	2.88	2.52
Clothing	5.04	5.67	5.93	6.95	7.56	9.10
Foot-wear	0.44	0.51	0.50	0.48	0.46	0.58
Rent	3.20	3.22	3.53	3.40	3.63	3.51
Taxes	0.02	0.03	0.05	0.07	0.09	0.10
Fuel & power	4.71	4.20	3.85	3.82	3.50	3.42
Furniture & domestic equipment	1.13	1.28	1.52	1.91	2.69	3.14
Domestic services	0.97	0.97	0.86	0.70	0.56	0.45
Medical care & health	1.15	1.27	1.65	2.23	2.44	2.76
Personal transport	0.26	0.40	0.52	0.73	1.01	1.20
Other transport	3.23	3.46	3.67	4.21	4.34	4.93
Education	1.39	1.68	2.15	2.86	3.06	2.45
Recreation, etc.	0.51	0.45	0.39	0.48	0.77	0.92
Miscellaneous goods & services	4.42	4.46	4.26	3.76	3.79	3.96
TOTAL NON-FOOD	32.39	33.71	34.67	37.28	38.56	40.84

There has also been a significant change in the pattern of per capita consumption of individual non-food items. Table 6.5 gives the average share of individual non-food items in per capita expenditure on total consumption by quinquennial periods.

Per capita expenditure on the consumption of non-food items has increased from 32.39 per cent in the first quinquennial period to 40.84 per cent in the last quinquennial period; but the increase in its component items has been of varying degrees with some items actually registering a decline. The items which have increased most are clothing (from 5.04 to 9.10 per cent), medical care and health (from 1.15 to 2.76 per cent), education (from 1.39 to 2.45 per cent), furniture and domestic equipment (from 1.13 to 3.14 per cent), personal transport (from 0.26 to 1.20 per cent), transport other than personal, including hired services (from 3.23 to 4.93 per cent) and recreation and cultural services (from 0.51 to 0.92 per cent). A significant fall in shares in the last quinquennial period over the first were recorded by pan, alcohol and intoxicants (from 2.28 to 1.80 per cent), tobacco (from 3.64 to 2.52 per cent), fuel and power (from 4.71 to 3.42 per cent), domestic services (from 0.97 to 0.45 per cent); and miscellaneous goods and services (from 4.42 to 3.96 per cent).

The rise in the share of non-food items from 32.39 to 40.84 per cent in the total per capita expenditure on consumption is a progressive change in the consumption pattern. Similarly, the rise in their shares of consumption expenditure of clothing, foot-wear, personal and hired transport equipment, household furniture and equipment, and education, and the fall in the shares of alcoholic beverages, tobacco and domestic services is a progressive trend. The fall in the share of expenditure on fuel and power is difficult to explain and cannot be considered a progressive feature, nor can the fall in the share of miscellaneous non-food goods and services be treated as a progressive change.

Considering per capita consumption over the twenty years including both food and non-food items, it would not be incorrect to suggest that the change has been progressive and oriented towards improvement in the quality of living. But in terms of the level of living, the change has not been of a major magnitude, which reflects the twin consequences of an inadequate rate of economic growth and a high rate of population increase.

It would be interesting to find out what happened over this period to the distribution of private final consumption between rural and urban areas in the country, between expenditure groups of ascending size in the population, and by inter-state population groups. The NAS gives only national totals of private final consumption expenditure. However, NSS data on surveys of consumption expenditure by sample households are available separately for urban and rural areas, and by different states in the Indian Union as well as by monthly per capita expenditure classes. These data are available from 1956-57 to 1973-74 when household consumption surveys were conducted in the annual NSS rounds, after which it was decided to conduct them only once every five years. The latest NSS round which covered consumption expenditure by households was 1978-79; but the results of this survey have not yet become available.

Earlier, when referring to the availability of this NSS data, we had pointed out that they are of doubtful validity in estimating national totals because they do not tally with figures in the NAS data. However, they are quite accurate for estimating the distribution of consumption expenditure by rural/urban, inter-state, and monthly per capita expenditure classes. This study proposes to apply ratios or patterns of distribution obtained from the NSS data to the NAS data. As NSS data are available from 1956-57 up to 1973-74, estimates for the remaining years of the period under review are obtained by an extrapolation of the linear trends shown by the period covering 1956-57 to 1973-74.

Figures of the index of growth of private final consumption expenditure by rural and urban areas, separately and collectively, are given in Table 6.6 for every fifth year during the period 1950-51 and 1979-80. They have been calculated on the basis of the expenditure totals at 1970-71 prices given in the NAS data and the rural/urban ratios of household consumption expenditure obtained from the NSS data.

Table 6.6 indicates a higher growth over the period of rural consumption expenditure (158.24 per cent) than that of urban expenditure (127.96 per cent). This is contrary to the popularly accepted thesis of growing deterioration in the rural sector, which has also been propounded by Michael Lipton.[1] In fact, when account is taken of the higher rate of growth of the urban population as compared to the rural, and its consequent effect on per capita

Table 6.6

Growth in Total Rural and Urban Expenditure

Year	*Index of Growth*			*Percentage Distribution*	
	Total	*Rural*	*Urban*	*Rural*	*Urban*
1950-51	100.00	100.00	100.00	68.71	31.29
1954-55	118.31	125.54	102.44	72.91	27.09
1959-60	135.13	145.66	112.00	74.07	25.93
1964-65	167.06	178.64	141.64	73.47	26.53
1969-70	190.93	201.75	168.28	72.42	27.58
1974-75	211.75	226.56	179.21	73.52	26.48
1979-80	248.76	258.24	227.96	71.32	28.68

consumption expenditure, the comparative position in terms of change over the period as a whole appears to be even more favourable for the rural population. But while the rural sector's share of the national total of private consumption expenditure rose from 68.71 per cent in 1950-51 to 74.07 per cent in 1959-60, it fell marginally to 72.42 per cent in 1969-70 and then more sharply to 71.32 per cent in 1979-80, though it was still significantly higher than its earlier position in 1950-51. The rural sector seems to have fared better in consumption during the fifties compared to its position in the seventies. This is in keeping with what has been pointed out in Chapter 3 about the improvement in the terms of trade between agriculture and non-agriculture in the earlier years of the period under review and its deterioration during the later years, especially the late 1970s. This is further confirmed by the quinquennial averages of rural and urban shares in the national total of consumption expenditure during 1950-51 to 1979-80, given in Table 6.7.

Table 6.7

Percentage Share of Rural and Urban Sectors

Period	*Rural*	*Urban*
1950-51 to 54-55	70.76	29.24
1955-56 to 59-60	72.63	27.37
1960-61 to 64-65	73.90	26.10
1965-66 to 69-70	72.76	27.24
1970-71 to 74-75	73.15	26.85
1975-76 to 79-80	72.07	27.93

The per capita consumption figures are actually better indicators of the difference in economic welfare between the rural and urban population. Accordingly, Table 6.8 gives the figures of rural and urban per capita consumption expenditure at constant prices, as well as rural per capita consumption expenditure as a percentage of urban per capita expenditure at five-year intervals during the periods 1950-51 to 1979-80.

Table 6.8

Growth of Rural and Urban Per Capita Consumption Expenditures

Year	Index of Growth			Rural as Per Cent of Urban
	Total	Rural	Urban	
1950-51	100.00	100.00	100.00	45.91
1954-55	109.40	116.41	93.49	57.19
1959-60	113.36	122.96	91.23	61.87
1964-65	125.69	136.80	98.31	63.87
1969-70	128.53	139.57	99.34	64.50
1974-75	127.38	142.37	95.91	72.96
1979-80	134.24	147.03	98.44	74.79

Table 6.8 only confirms the conclusions that emerge from Table 6.6 and 6.7. In terms of per capita expenditure on consumption, the rural sector has recorded a significant growth over the period, while the urban per capita expenditure has actually been declining from 1950-51 and has just about managed to regain its initial position in the final year. The result is the rise in rural per capita consumption as a percentage of urban per capita consumption. This does not, however, make the rural per capita expenditure on consumption higher than the urban; it has only meant a narrowing down of the difference between the urban and the rural per capita consumption expenditure. Thus, while the rural per capita consumption expenditure was only 45.91 per cent of the urban in 1950-51, it went up to 74.29 per cent in 1979-80. A partial explanation for this comparative improvement in rural per capita consumption expenditure is, apart from the slower growth in rural population, the increase that has taken place in the rate of national savings during the period, the major share of which must have been in urban areas.

This comparative improvement in rural per capita consumption expenditure is also borne out by the average per capita consumption expenditure figures by quinquennial periods as can be seen from Table 6.9.

It would be interesting to find out if this comparative improvement in rural per capita consumption expenditure is concentrated on some or all items of

Table 6.9

Average Per Capita Consumption Expenditure at 1970-71 Prices by Quinquennial Periods

	1950-51 to 54-55	1955-56 to 59-60	1960-61 to 64-65	1965-66 to 69-70	1970-71 to 74-75	1975-76 to 79-80
TOTAL	100.00	105.16	113.91	118.41	124.36	109.80
Urban	100.00	96.96	96.20	98.79	97.39	100.49
Rural	100.00	108.54	120.45	124.89	133.45	141.01
Rural as per cent of urban	50.89	56.97	63.76	64.33	69.74	71.41

consumption. Item-wise details of per capita consumption expenditure can be compiled only from 1960-61 and that too at current prices (see Table 6.10).

Table 6.10

Per Capita Consumption Expenditure at Current Prices—1960-1978 (Rs)

Items	*1960-61*		*1979-80*		*Percentage Increase in 1979-80 over 1960-61*	
	Rural	*Urban*	*Rural*	*Urban*	*Rural*	*Urban*
Cereals & substitutes	78.69	66.01	252.07	195.71	220.33	196.48
Milk & products	19.05	32.79	77.07	119.78	304.56	265.29
Edible oils	9.42	16.54	35.19	61.59	273.56	272.37
Meat, fish & eggs	6.74	12.43	28.44	45.52	321.95	266.21
Sugar	22.66	22.16	63.68	70.42	181.02	217.77
Salt	0.61	0.37	3.59	3.91	488.52	956.75
Other foods	30.07	46.74	130.98	146.28	335.58	212.96
Total food	156.24	197.04	591.03	643.21	278.28	226.43
Pan, tobacco & intoxicants	17.00	23.11	43.69	45.92	157.00	98.70
Fuel & light	10.15	14.37	44.14	58.45	334.87	306.75
Clothing	17.69	19.32	125.07	100.57	607.00	420.54
Foot-wear	2.84	3.63	10.16	8.83	257.74	143.25
Durables	5.41	8.23	54.93	70.10	915.34	751.76
Rents	0.63	78.49	3.55	132.14	463.49	68.35
Taxes	0.12	0.34	0.35	2.15	191.66	532.35
Other non-food items	42.07	18.51	179.63	192.83	326.98	941.76
Total non-food	95.93	166.00	461.52	610.62	381.10	267.84
TOTAL—FOOD & NON-FOOD	252.17	363.04	1052.55	1253.83	317.40	245.36

Rural per capita expenditure has risen faster than the urban at current prices for both food and non-food items. However, there is a continuing inequality in the absolute levels of expenditure. But that the rural per capita consumption is catching up with the urban can be seen from Table 6.11 which gives the percentage of rural per capita expenditure item-wise as compared to the urban for 1960-61 and 1979-80.

Except for salt, taxes, and some miscellaneous non-food items, the rural per capita consumption has risen as a percentage of the urban in the case of other items. This increase has been particularly marked in the case of sugar, other foods, foot-wear, pan, intoxicants, and tobacco, and rents. There is a marginal rise in meat, fish and eggs, and milk and milk products. The marginal rise in the expenditure on cereals and cereal substitutes is also worth noting. Above all, there is a noticeable improvement in the per capita rural expenditure on the totals of all items and, separately, of both food and non-food items, the latter being higher.

Table 6.11

Percentage of Rural Per Capita Expenditure to Urban for 1960-61 and 1979-80 at Current Prices

Items	*1960-61*	*1979-80*
Cereals & substitutes	119.21	128.79
Milk & milk products	58.10	64.34
Edible oils	56.95	57.13
Meat, fish and eggs	54.22	62.47
Sugar	52.62	90.42
Salt	164.86	91.81
Other foods	64.33	89.54
Total foods	79.29	91.88
Pan, intoxicants & tobacco	73.56	95.97
Fuel & light	70.63	75.51
Clothing	91.56	124.36
Foot-wear	78.24	115.06
Durable goods	65.74	78.35
Rents	0.80	2.68
Taxes	35.29	16.27
Other non-food items	227.28	98.24
Total non-food	57.79	75.58
TOTAL—FOOD AND NON-FOOD	69.46	83.94

This certainly seems to indicate a comparative improvement in the per capita rural level of living as compared to the urban over this period of thirty years. However, it still leaves it below the urban in absolute terms, being only 74.29 per cent of urban per capita consumption in 1979-80. A partial explanation for this comparative deterioration in the urban per capita consumption may be, as indicated earlier, an increase in the rate of urban per capita saving. It may to some extent be due to the export of poverty from the rural to the urban areas caused by the massive drift of the rural unemployed to the urban areas in search of employment and some means of livelihood. It may also be because of the massive investment in irrigation, rural electrification and meeting rural basic needs which have been part of the developmental programmes undertaken by the government in its five year plans. Another partial explanation may be that the NSS estimates of food production are higher than the CSO figures. The truth probably lies in a combination of all these explanations. Whatever is the explanation, the data does reveal an improvement in rural per capita consumption from its pre-plan levels, which is at a higher rate than in the case of urban per capita consumption.

NSS data on monthly per capita consumption by expenditure classes are available from 1956-57 to 1973-74 with some missing years. During this period, there has been a change in the number and range of expenditure classes. Instead of taking all the years for which data are available, we have taken for our analysis only four years; namely, 1960-61, 1965-66, 1970-71 and 1973-74. For each of these years, the NSS data by per capita monthly expenditure classes has been recalculated on the basis of population deciles, after which the percentage share of each decile group in the total consumption of all the groups taken together has been calculated. Using these data, one can estimate the distribution of consumption by decile groups of the population, the pattern of inequality it reveals and changes therein during the period for which data are available. This was done separately for the rural and urban populations and then combined to give the needed data for the total population. The percentage distribution of consumption by deciles thus reached is applied to the totals of private final consumption expenditure given in the NAS accounts. Table 6.12 gives the all-India figures arrived at as a result of this exercise.

Table 6.12

Final Urban and Rural Consumption Expenditure at Current Prices in Rs Crores (Based on NSS Data)

Decile Group (Per Cent)	*Percentage of Total Consumption Expenditure*			
	1960-61	*1965-66*	*1970-71*	*1973-74*
0 to 10	3.27	3.59	3.56	3.80
10 to 20	4.57	4.97	4.94	5.21
20 to 30	5.55	5.94	5.88	6.12
30 to 40	6.50	6.82	6.78	6.96
40 to 50	7.47	7.75	7.63	7.91
50 to 60	8.58	8.54	8.39	8.92
60 to 70	9.92	10.01	10.07	10.39
70 to 80	11.77	11.68	11.81	11.99
80 to 90	15.12	14.48	14.78	14.68
90 to 100	27.25	25.92	26.16	24.02
TOTAL	100.00	100.00	100.00	100.00

It is seen from Table 6.12 that, during the period, the percentage of consumption expenditure of the first eight deciles has gone up while that of the ninth and tenth deciles has gone down — the former by 0.44 percentage points and the latter, more significantly, by 3.23 percentage points. This fall of 3.67 percentage points of the top two deciles in total consumption is offset by a corresponding rise in that of the first eight deciles, which is distributed among them, as given in Table 6.13.

The percentage rise in the decile share of total consumption gets progressively less as one moves up from the first to the eighth decile (with the exception of the seventh), while the percentage fall in the ninth decile is only 2.91 as compared to 11.85 in the tenth decile.

The change in the distributional pattern of consumption is illustrated even more clearly if one looks at the share in consumption expenditure of the first five deciles, or the bottom half of the population, which has risen from 27.36 per cent in 1960-61 to 30.0 per cent in 1973-74 or by 2.64 percentage points, which is equal to a rise of 9.65 per cent. Correspondingly, the share of the top

Table 6.13

Per Cent Rate of Increase in Consumption Share

Deciles	*Rise in Percentage Points*	*Percentage of Rise*
First decile	0.53	16.21
Second decile	0.64	14.00
Third decile	0.57	10.27
Fourth decile	0.46	7.08
Fifth decile	0.44	5.89
Sixth decile	0.34	3.96
Seventh decile	0.47	4.74
Eighth decile	0.22	1.87
TOTAL	3.67	8.66

half of the population has gone down from 72.64 per cent to 70.0 per cent or by 3.63 per cent. Within the two halves of the population, the last three deciles have fared better than the top two deciles. The top two deciles in the lower half of the population show a marginal rise, while those in the top half of the population show a larger fall, with the fall in the top decile accounting for 88 per cent of the rise that has taken place in the bottom 8 deciles and 81.7 per cent of the rise in the bottom 5 deciles or the lower half of the population.

Obviously the change that has taken place in the decile distribution of total expenditure has been in the direction of a reduction in inequality. However, the consumption pattern continues to exhibit a high level of absolute inequality with the bottom 30 per cent of the population having a share of 15 per cent of the total consumption in 1973-74 and the top 30 per cent a share of 51 per cent, the intermediate 40 per cent having a share of 34 per cent.

Using the data given in Tables 6.12 and 6.13 and the analysis accompanying it, one can form an idea about the change, if any, that has occurred in both the magnitude and the intensity of poverty between 1960-61 and 1973-74. Taking the Planning Commission's figure of the monthly per capita expenditure of Rs 20 as indicating the poverty line in 1960-61 and raising it for 1973-74 to allow for the rise in the national cost of living during the period, the poverty line for 1973-74 may be placed around Rs 53.60. Table 6.14 gives the per capita monthly expenditure on consumption at current prices by decile groups on the basis of the NSS data for those two years.

The poverty line was delineated by the Planning Commission on the basis of a report submitted by an expert working group which dealt specifically with the year 1960-61. In both 1960-61 and 1973-74 the first five deciles have a per capita monthly consumption expenditure below the poverty line. In 1960-61, the sixth decile also fell below the poverty line, as its per capita monthly consumption expenditure was below Rs 20. In 1973-74, however, its average per capita consumption expenditure (Rs 54.57) was slightly above the poverty line. Obviously, therefore, there has been a decline in the magnitude of poverty from about 60 per cent of the population in 1960-61 to about 58 per cent in 1973-74. The fall has been marginal in spite of several years of planned

Table 6.14

Per Capita Per Cent Distributions of 1960-61 and 1973-74

Decile Groups (Per Cent)	*Monthly Per Capita Expenditure (in Rs)*		*Percentage Difference between 1973-74 and 1960-61*
	1960-61	*1973-74*	
0 to 10	7.42	23.24	213.2
10 to 20	10.38	31.87	207.0
20 to 30	12.60	37.43	197.1
30 to 40	14.76	42.57	188.4
40 to 50	16.96	48.38	185.3
50 to 60	19.48	54.57	180.1
60 to 70	22.52	63.56	182.2
70 to 80	26.73	73.34	174.4
80 to 90	34.34	89.80	161.5
90 to 100	61.87	146.92	137.5
Poverty line	20.00	53.60	168.0

economic growth and substantial public investment and cannot be a cause for satisfaction.

Table 6.14 also shows a decline in the intensity of poverty. The rise in the per capita expenditure of the bottom-most decile between 1973-74 and 1960-61 is higher than that of the other deciles below the poverty line. Even in the case of the other five deciles the rise is higher than that of the deciles above the poverty line. We have also seen that the percentage share of each of the first three deciles (i.e., 0 – 30) in the total consumption of all deciles has gone up more than the other deciles, though not enough to bring them above the poverty line.

The conclusion that follows from this analysis is that while there has been no marked decline in the proportion of the population below the poverty line between 1960-61 and 1973-74, there has definitely been no increase. At the same time, the per capita consumption of the bottom three deciles has shown an improvement as compared to that of the next three deciles below the poverty line, thus indicating a decline in the intensity of poverty during this period.

Some indication of the difference in the standard of living of different expenditure classes can be found by looking at the percentage distribution of individual items in each expenditure class in 1973-74, which is the latest year for which NSS data are available on the subject. Instead of reducing the data into decile groups, we have taken the data on item-wise consumption by expenditure classes and the proportion of the total population in each expenditure class. The resulting figures have been rearranged into five classes, each covering approximately 20 per cent of the population. The advantage of this method is that it leaves the original data by expenditure classes undisturbed for about 80 per cent of the population, aggregation of several expenditure classes (7 out of 11 expenditure classes in ascending order) being resorted to

Table 6.15

Per Capita Item-wise Distribution of Personal Consumption

Percentage of Population	Expenditure Classes Covered (Rs)	Percentage of Expenditure Item-wise in Total Consumption Expenditure									
		Cereals	Milk Products	Edible Oils	Meat, Fish, Eggs	Sugar	Salt	Other Foods	Total Food	Pan, Tobacco, etc.	Fuel & Power
21.13	0-34	61.50	2.73	3.67	2.27	2.38	0.30	10.04	82.89	2.94	7.29
18.07	34-43	36.05	4.77	5.53	2.40	5.45	0.25	17.78	72.23	4.23	3.73
20.36	43-55	33.07	6.59	5.59	2.52	5.80	0.19	16.47	70.23	4.24	3.49
20.58	55-75	29.08	8.43	5.72	2.76	6.38	0.16	14.29	66.82	3.83	3.27
19.86	75 & above	19.04	10.32	5.15	2.80	5.86	0.12	11.48	54.75	3.99	2.67
ALL EXPENDITURE CLASSES		27.70	7.85	5.36	2.63	5.76	0.18	14.52	64.00	4.05	3.22

Percentage of Population	Expenditure Classes Covered (Rs)	Percentage of Expenditure Item-wise in Total Consumption Expenditure							
		Clothing	Foot-wear	Rent	Taxes	Durable Goods	Other Non-foods	Total Non-foods	Total Consumption Expenditure
21.13	0-34	1.83	0.10	0.17	0	0.04	4.74	17.11	100.00
18.07	34-43	3.06	0.12	0.88	0	0.10	15.65	27.77	100.00
20.36	43-55	4.52	0.23	1.61	0	0.19	15.49	29.77	100.00
20.58	55-75	7.24	0.38	2.22	0.06	0.37	15.81	33.18	100.00
19.86	75 & above	12.34	0.86	5.61	0.14	9.02	10.60	45.25	100.00
ALL EXPENDITURE CLASSES		7.76	0.48	3.10	0.07	3.62	13.70	36.00	100.00

for about 20 per cent of the population. The results of this exercise are given in Table 6.15.

Table 6.15 shows clearly the difference in the level of living of the five groups of population (approximately 20 per cent each) which belong to ascending expenditure classes. The contrast, of course, is sharpest between the top 20 per cent and the bottom 21 per cent of the population in both food and non-food expenditure, the food expenditure of the former being much lower (54.75 per cent as against 82.89) and non-food expenditure correspondingly higher (45.25 per cent as against 17.11).

The greatest difference is seen in the percentage of total consumption expenditure on cereals (19.04 as against 61.50), durable goods (9.02 as against 0.04), clothing (12.34 as against 1.83), rent (5.61 as against 0.17), milk and milk products (10.32 as against 2.73) and foot-wear (0.86 as against 0.10). There was not much difference, however, between the percentage expenditure on edible oils, sugar, and pan, intoxicants and tobacco, while there was actually a fall with regard to fuel and power. The contrast was also quite sharp between the fourth 20 per cent of the population (which is above the poverty line), and the fifth (or the top) 20 per cent of the population. The figures are conspicuously indicative of the extent of nutritional inequality and of inequality in the expenditure on clothing, foot-wear and durable goods.

Reference

1. Michael Lipton, *Why the Poor Stay Poor,* London, Temple Smith & Co., 1978.

Regional Distribution of NDP 7

In this chapter, we will examine the regional distribution of the NDP in terms of industrial origin. Regions are identified here with the principal states which comprise the Indian Union because of the limitations of available data. It must be remembered that, unlike previous chapters, the data used here are based on RBI publications, as the NAS data do not contain any details of the SDPs by industrial origin. Also, since it is difficult to compare SDPs measured at constant prices, our analysis will be based on measurements valued at current prices only.

Table 7.1 lists the SDP shares in the NDP at current prices in 1960-61 and 1976-77. We can infer from the data that the geographical distribution of the NDP has become less skewed over time. While the first six states in 1960-61 had an aggregate share of 59 per cent of the NDP, it declined to 52.46 per cent in 1976-77. In this group, only Maharashtra increased its share from 11.98 to 12.54 per cent. The last six states had an aggregate share of 13.98 per cent in 1960-61 which increased to 15.23 per cent in 1976-77; three of them increased their individual shares, while two suffered a reduction and one retained its initial share. The middle group of four states reduced their aggregate share from 20.96 to 20.13 per cent, though one increased its individual share from 5.53 to 5.97 per cent. Generally, there is some measure of reduction in inequality in inter-state shares in the NDP at current prices during this period. Except for Maharashtra, the bigger states have all shown a fall in their individual shares, while the smaller states have fared better, especially Punjab, Haryana, Gujarat and Kerala. The minor states not covered in the Table, including Delhi and other Union Territories, have increased their share from 6.06 per cent to 12.18 per cent.

The rankings in Table 7.1 do not indicate any significant changes in the relative positions of different states. Of the first six states, while there has been no change in the positions of two states, two have exchanged ranks by one place, and two by two places. These six states together retain in 1976-77 the top six places they held in 1960-61. Similarly, in the middle group of four

Table 7.1

SDP Share in NDP at Current Prices (Percentages)

State	SDP Share (Percentage)		Ranking	
	1960-61	1976-77	1960-61	1976-77
Uttar Pradesh	13.82	11.77	1	2
Maharashtra	11.98	12.54	2	1
West Bengal	10.04	8.85	3	3
Tamil Nadu	8.34	6.26	4	6
Bihar	7.45	6.48	5	5
Andhra Pradesh	7.37	6.56	6	4
Madhya Pradesh	6.24	5.41	7	8
Gujarat	5.53	5.97	8	7
Karnataka	5.00	4.84	9	9
Rajasthan	4.19	3.91	10	11
Kerala	3.24	3.36	11	12
Punjab	2.87	4.04	12	10
Orissa	2.80	2.42	13	14
Assam	2.52	2.17	14	15
Haryana	1.84	2.53	15	13
Jammu & Kashmir	0.71	0.71	16	16
TOTAL	93.94	87.82		
ALL INDIA	100.00	100.00	–	–

states, there has been no change in one, and two have exchanged ranks by one place, but one has moved down to the last group of six. Of the six states in the bottom group, two have moved up by two places with one of them getting into the middle group; three have moved down by one place; and one has not changed its position.

On the whole, our analysis of the changes in relative ranking shows that five have moved up, seven have moved down and four have not changed their positions. Of the five which have moved up, two, belonging to the bottom group, have moved by two places. Of the seven which have fallen, the one that has moved down by two places belongs to the top group. There seems to be a general trend towards a slight reduction in inter-state SDP inequalities in NDP shares, which is not attributable to the differences in the size of their population or the magnitude of their natural resources. To this extent, perhaps, some credit can be taken by the government for inducing this change through their economic policies, programmes and planning.

This comforting conclusion is, however, not borne out if we look at the changes in per capita SDPs over the period. We are giving the figures for per capita SDPs and per capita NDP, as these are at current prices and may give a misleading idea of the increase that has taken place between 1960-61 and 1976-77. Table 7.2 gives the percentages of the per capita SDPs in relation to per capita NDP in both the years. It also relates the individual SDP to the highest per capita SDP during these two years.

The growth in inequality among the per capita SDPs at current prices between 1960-61 and 1976-77 is obvious (see Table 7.2). Thus, the range of per capita SDPs as a percentage of the per capita NDP, which was 70.0 to 133.2 in 1960-61, has widened from 60.1 to 165.2 in 1976-77. The lowest per capita SDP has gone down while the highest per capita SDP has gone up in proportion to the per capita NDP.

Table 7.2

Per Capita SDPs and Per Capita NDP and their Relationship at Current Prices

State	*Percentage of Per Capita SDP to Per Capita NDP*		*Percentage of Per Capita SDP to Highest Per Capita SDP*	
	1960-61	*1976-77*	*1960-61*	*1976-77*
Andhra Pradesh	89.6	82.1	67.2	49.7
Assam	102.6	77.6	77.0	47.0
Bihar	70.0	63.8	52.6	38.6
Gujarat	117.9	122.2	88.5	74.0
Haryana	106.5	134.2	80.0	81.2
Jammu & Kashmir	87.6	81.2	65.8	49.5
Karnataka	93.2	91.1	69.9	55.1
Kerala	84.4	86.4	63.3	52.3
Madhya Pradesh	84.7	69.2	63.6	41.9
Maharashtra	133.2	137.2	*100.0*	83.1
Orissa	70.7	60.1	53.1	36.4
Punjab	113.0	165.2	84.8	*100.0*
Rajasthan	92.5	80.9	69.4	49.0
Tamil Nadu	108.8	86.4	81.7	52.3
Uttar Pradesh	82.1	74.3	61.6	45.0
West Bengal	127.0	109.6	95.4	66.3
ALL INDIA PER CAPITA NDP/SDP	100.00	100.00	75.1	60.5

There have also been changes in the comparative position of SDPs *vis-a-vis* the per capita NDP. Eleven of the sixteen states listed in Table 7.2 have recorded a decline in the proportion of their per capita domestic product to the per capita NDP of the country as a whole, while the remaining five have recorded an increase. Of these, the most conspicuous improvement is in Haryana (from 106.5 to 134.2 per cent of the per capita NDP) and Punjab (from 113.0 to 165.2 per cent). The other three states—namely, Gujarat, Maharashtra and Kerala—have registered a marginal increase. Of the states whose per capita SDP in relation to the per capita NDP has gone down, the states with a decrease of more than 10 percentage points are Assam (from 102.6 to 77.6), Madhya Pradesh (from 84.7 to 69.2), Orissa (from 70.7 to 60.1), Rajasthan (from 92.5 to 80.9), Tamil Nadu (108.8 to 86.4), and West Bengal (127.0 to 109.6). The others show a fall of less than 8 percentage points. Uttar Pradesh tops this list with 7.8 percentage points (from 82.1 to 74.3). In 1976-77, one finds five states which have a per capita SDP higher than the per capita NDP. These are Punjab (165.2), Maharashtra (137.2),

Haryana (134.2), Gujarat (122.2) and West Bengal (109.6). Four states have a per capita SDP of less than 75 per cent of the per capita NDP for that year. They are, U.P. with 74.3 per cent, Madhya Pradesh with 69.2 per cent, Bihar with 63.8 per cent and Orissa with 60.1 per cent. The remaining seven states have an NDP per capita percentage of between 75 and 100 per cent, the highest among them being Karnataka with 91.1 per cent.

Inequality between per capita SDPs has also grown as a percentage of the highest per capita SDP between the years 1960-61 and 1976-77. Thus the range in 1960-61 was from 52.6 to 95.4 per cent of the highest per capita SDP in that year, while the corresponding range in 1976-77 was from 36.4 to 83.1 per cent.

There has also been a change in the relative position of the per capita SDPs. Punjab has replaced Maharashtra in the highest per capita SDP position, pushing the latter to the second place, while Haryana has reached the third position with 81.2 per cent, overtaking West Bengal, Gujarat and Tamil Nadu, all of which were ranked higher than Haryana in 1960-61. All the other states have also registered a decrease in the proportion of their per capita SDPs to the highest per capita SDP. The largest decreases have taken place in Assam (from 77 to 47 per cent), Tamil Nadu (from 81.7 to 52.3 per cent) and West Bengal (from 95.4 to 66.3 per cent).

There has been considerable change in the relative position of SDPs. Table 7.3 gives their relative ranking in 1960-61 and 1976-77.

Table 7.3

Inter-state Position in Respect of Per Capita SDPs Ranking

State	*Percentage of Per Capita SDP to Per Capita NDP*		
	1960-61	*1976-77*	*Rise or Fall from 1960-61*
Andhra Pradesh	10	9	+1
Assam	7	12	−5
Bihar	16	15	+1
Gujarat	3	4	−1
Haryana	6	3	+3
Jammu & Kashmir	11	10	+1
Karnataka	8	6	+2
Kerala	13	7.5	+5.5
Madhya Pradesh	12	14	−2
Maharashtra	1	2	−1
Orissa	15	16	−1
Punjab	4	1	+3
Rajasthan	9	11	−2
Tamil Nadu	5	7.5	−2.5
Uttar Pradesh	14	13	+1
West Bengal	2	5	−3

Of the six states which were at the top in 1960-61 in the percentage of per capita SDP to the per capita NDP, (or to the highest per capita SDP) four states—Maharashtra, West Bengal, Gujarat and Tamil Nadu—have fallen from their original rank while the smaller states of Punjab and Haryana have gone up in rank. Of the six states which were at the bottom in 1960-61, four have improved their rank and two have gone down. In the middle group, two states have gone up and two have come down in rank. The shifts in ranking correspond with the percentage of per capita SDP to the NDP and to the highest SDP, except for Bihar which has improved its position at the expense of Orissa. Taking all the states together, five of the top eight have fallen in rank in 1976-77, while five of the bottom eight have improved their position. The overall change in ranking seems to be in a progressive direction though the difference between the top and the bottom states has widened.

Let us now analyse the shares of the different states in the NDP under the three basic sectors—primary, secondary and tertiary. The figures in Table 7.4 are based on the SDP and NDP at current prices, and are the average for the first and last four year sub-periods of 1960-61 to 1976-77. Sub-periods have been selected to avoid annual fluctuations which are more likely to occur in the individual sectors of industrial origin.

Table 7.4

Average Percentage Share of Primary, Secondary and Tertiary Sectors in NDP

State	*Primary*		*Secondary*		*Tertiary*	
	1960-61 to 1963-64	*1973-74 to 1976-77*	*1960-61 to 1963-64*	*1973-74 to 1976-77*	*1960-61 to 1963-64*	*1973-74 to 1976-77*
Andhra Pradesh	8.89	8.50	4.91	5.24	7.12	6.61
Assam	2.80	NA	1.70	NA	1.45	NA
Bihar	7.74	8.33	5.91	7.01	7.98	4.05
Gujarat	NA	4.75	NA	7.20	NA	6.12
Haryana	NA	3.08	NA	1.90	NA	1.75
Jammu & Kashmir	0.91	0.91	0.33	0.53	0.56	0.55
Karnataka	6.01	6.45	3.73	4.76	4.34	4.24
Kerala	3.45	3.78	2.43	2.71	3.35	3.33
Madhya Pradesh	7.41	7.35	5.16	5.70	4.80	4.15
Maharashtra	9.12	8.72	16.53	17.96	13.41	13.55
Orissa	3.83	3.94	2.40	1.91	2.48	1.69
Punjab	3.46	5.03	2.78	2.74	2.97	3.97
Rajasthan	4.49	5.36	3.12	3.03	3.60	2.92
Tamil Nadu	7.60	4.93	7.54	8.50	8.54	6.87
Uttar Pradesh	15.67	14.78	8.06	8.38	13.59	9.86
West Bengal	7.92	8.05	13.37	10.81	11.31	8.32
ALL INDIA	100.00	100.00	100.00	100.00	100.00	100.00

With the exception of Andhra Pradesh, Uttar Pradesh, Tamil Nadu and Maharashtra (and in Madhya Pradesh which experienced a marginal decline), all the other states have increased their share of the NDP from the primary sector during the first and last sub-periods while Jammu and Kashmir had no change in its share. In the secondary sector, all the states, except for Orissa, Rajasthan, Punjab and West Bengal, increased their share of the NDP from that sector; the most significant fall being in the share of West Bengal which declined from 13.37 to 10.81 per cent. As for the tertiary sector, the majority of the states—Andhra Pradesh, Bihar, Madhya Pradesh, Orissa, Rajasthan, Tamil Nadu, Uttar Pradesh and West Bengal—had all reduced their share of the NDP, while Karnataka and Kerala experienced only a marginal decline. The only states which increased their share, and that too only marginally, were Maharashtra and Punjab. The two states, Gujarat and Haryana for which data were not available for the first sub-period, had a total share of 7.83 per cent in the primary sector, 9.10 per cent in the secondary sector, and 7.87 per cent in the tertiary sector in the last sub-period.

Regarding changes in the states' shares in the individual sub-sectors of industrial origin within these three major sectors, data are not available for Gujarat, Assam and Haryana. Table 7.5 gives the relevant data for the other states covering the first and last sub-periods for the sub-sectors within the primary sector.

It will be seen from Table 7.5 that while five states, including Uttar Pradesh, have suffered a reduction in their share in agriculture from 49.02 to 44.33 per cent, seven others have increased their share from 37.07 to 41.06 per cent. As indicated in Table 7.5, comparable figures are not available for both the first and last sub-periods for three states — Assam, Haryana and Gujarat — under the primary sector which also includes agriculture. This not only applies to agriculture but to other sectors of industrial origin as well. The most notable loss has been that of Tamil Nadu (from 7.68 to 4.98 per cent), while the most significant gain has been that of Punjab (from 3.59 to 5.21 per cent). In regard to forestry and logging, six states have reduced their share from 27.51 to 20.71 per cent, the most notable falls being that of Orissa (from 6.30 to 2.31 per cent) and Rajasthan (from 2.55 to 0.91 per cent). Seven states have increased their share from 44.37 to 64.50 per cent, the most remarkable being Bihar (from 4.73 to 9.76 per cent), Karnataka (from 3.88 to 8.60 per cent) and Jammu and Kashmir (from 3.64 to 6.67 per cent). Fishing shows the largest spectrum of change. While seven states have reduced their share from 80.17 to 55.67 per cent, four other have doubled their share from 13.41 to 26.75 per cent. Significant among the losers are West Bengal (from 26.53 to 21.49 per cent), Bihar from (16.33 to 7.15 per cent) and Tamil Nadu (from 13.99 to 6.21 per cent), while conspicuous among the gainers are Kerala (from 4.96 to 11.89 per cent) and Maharashtra (from 6.41 to 11.37 per cent).

Regarding the secondary sector, Table 7.6 shows that while four states have reduced their share of mining and quarrying from 61.94 to 54.83 per cent, six states have increased their share from 28.83 to 37.77 per cent. Notable among the reductions are those of West Bengal (from 19.90 to 15.87 per cent) and of Jammu and Kashmir (from 3.98 to 2.78 per cent). Significant among the increases are those of Madhya Pradesh (from 11.46 to 14.70 per

Table 7.5

Changes in Primary Sector Shares (Percentages)

State	*1960-61 to 1963-64*	*1973-74 to 1976-77*	*State*	*1960-61 to 1963-64*	*1973-74 to 1976-77*
I *Agriculture*					
Uttar Pradesh	15.97	15.02	West Bengal	7.86	7.95
Maharashtra	9.13	8.64	Bihar	7.72	8.31
Andhra Pradesh	9.07	8.53	Rajasthan	4.60	5.54
Tamil Nadu	7.68	4.98	Karnataka	6.08	6.44
Madhya Pradesh	7.17	7.16	Orissa	3.75	3.99
TOTAL	49.02	44.33	Punjab	3.59	5.21
			Kerala	3.47	3.62
			TOTAL	37.07	41.06
II *Forestry & Logging*					
Maharashtra	10.18	9.92	Madhya Pradesh	18.55	20.46
Orissa	6.30	2.31	Uttar Pradesh	11.03	13.83
Andhra Pradesh	4.24	3.83	Bihar	4.73	9.76
Rajasthan	2.55	0.91	Karnataka	3.88	8.60
West Bengal	2.18	1.81	Jammu & Kashmir	3.64	6.67
Tamil Nadu	2.06	1.93	Kerala	2.18	4.36
TOTAL	27.51	20.71	Punjab	0.36	0.82
			TOTAL	44.37	64.50
III *Fishing*					
West Bengal	26.53	21.49	Maharashtra	6.41	11.37
Bihar	16.33	7.15	Kerala	4.96	11.89
Tamil Nadu	13.99	6.21	Uttar Pradesh	1.75	2.71
Andhra Pradesh	13.41	12.42	Rajasthan	0.29	0.78
Karnataka	5.25	4.12	TOTAL	13.41	26.75
Orissa	3.79	3.55			
Madhya Pradesh	0.87	0.73			
TOTAL	80.17	55.67			

cent), Orissa (from 4.94 to 6.40 per cent) and Punjab (from 3.03 to 6.48 per cent). As regards manufacturing, seven states reduced their share from 38.67 to 33.08 per cent, while six states increased their share from 39.27 to 43.20 per cent. The share of West Bengal fell from 14.62 to 10.87 per cent, while among the increases were Maharashtra (from 19.31 to 20.37 per cent), Karnataka (from 2.34 to 4.00 per cent), Andhra Pradesh (from 4.19 to 4.94 per cent), and Kerala (from 2.70 to 3.00 per cent).

In construction, the share of four states fell from 24.38 to 19.07 per cent, while nine states had an increase from 42.27 to 64.64 per cent. Notable among the decreases were Karnataka (from 8.54 to 7.10 per cent), Andhra Pradesh (from 7.04 to 5.85 per cent), and Orissa (from 4.09 to 1.67 per cent). Among the increases were Maharashtra (from 10.87 to 13.76 per cent), West Bengal (from 7.73 to 9.84 per cent), Uttar Pradesh (from 10.76 to 13.10 per cent), Tamil Nadu (from 3.14 to 7.24 per cent), Madhya Pradesh (from 2.66 to 6.51 per cent), Jammu and Kashmir (from 0.51 to 1.47 per cent), and Bihar (from 1.42 to 7.06 per cent). As for electricity, six states reduced their share from 47.20 to 34.51 per cent, while six states increased their share from 35.68 to 46.18 per cent. Notable among the decreases were West Bengal (from 14.75 to 9.06 per cent), Tamil Nadu (from 14.16 to 10.58 per cent), and Punjab (from 6.49 to 4.35 per cent). Among the increases were Maharashtra (from 16.81 to 19.44 per cent), Bihar (from 3.54 to 5.78 per cent), Rajasthan (from 1.18 to 4.22 per cent), and Madhya Pradesh (from 4.42 to 5.87 per cent).

Table 7.6

Changes in Secondary Sector Shares

State	*1960-61 to 1963-64*	*1973-74 to 1976-77*	*State*	*1960-61 to 1963-64*	*1973-74 to 1976-77*
I *Mining & Quarrying*					
Bihar	35.19	34.17	Madhya Pradesh	11.46	14.70
West Bengal	19.90	15.87	Orissa	4.94	6.40
Jammu & Kashmir	3.98	2.78	Andhra Pradesh	4.78	5.08
Uttar Pradesh	2.87	2.01	Maharashtra	2.55	2.65
TOTAL	61.94	54.83	Punjab	3.03	6.48
			Tamil Nadu	2.07	2.46
			TOTAL	28.83	37.77
II *Manufacturing*					
West Bengal	14.62	10.87	Maharashtra	19.31	20.37
Uttar Pradesh	7.57	7.32	Tamil Nadu	9.06	9.21
Madhya Pradesh	5.53	4.76	Andhra Pradesh	4.19	4.94
Bihar	5.31	5.06	Karnataka	2.34	4.00
Jammu & Kashmir	0.29	0.28	Kerala	2.70	3.00
Punjab	2.65	2.56	Orissa	1.67	1.68
Rajasthan	2.70	2.23	TOTAL	39.27	43.20
TOTAL	38.67	33.08			
III *Construction*					
Karnataka	8.54	7.10	Maharashtra	10.87	13.76
Andhra Pradesh	7.04	5.85	West Bengal	7.73	9.84
Orissa	4.09	1.67	Uttar Pradesh	10.76	13.10
Rajasthan	4.71	4.45	Tamil Nadu	3.14	7.24
TOTAL	24.38	19.07	Madhya Pradesh	2.66	6.51
			Jammu & Kashmir	0.51	1.47
			Bihar	1.42	7.06
			Kerala	1.86	2.06
			Punjab	3.32	3.60
			TOTAL	42.27	64.64
IV *Electricity*					
West Bengal	14.75	9.06	Maharashtra	16.81	19.44
Tamil Nadu	14.16	10.58	Andhra Pradesh	6.49	6.97
Uttar Pradesh	8.26	8.20	Madhya Pradesh	4.42	5.87
Punjab	6.49	4.35	Kerala	3.24	3.90
Orissa	2.95	2.16	Bihar	3.54	5.78
Jammu & Kashmir	0.59	0.16	Rajasthan	1.18	4.22
TOTAL	47.20	34.51	TOTAL	35.68	46.18

In the two sub-sectors of the tertiary sector for which data can be used, it is seen (Table 7.7) that eight states decreased their share of NDP from transport and communications from 64.4 per cent to 40.2 per cent, while five states increased their share from 34.91 to 39.57 per cent. Notable among the states whose share fell were Uttar Pradesh (from 16.27 to 9.19 per cent), West Bengal (from 12.63 to 8.65 per cent), Karnataka (from 10.67 per cent to 4.33 per cent), and Bihar from 10.37 to 6.37 per cent. Under banking and insurance four states decreased their share from 35.65 to 30.58 per cent, while the other nine states increased their share from 43.72 to 47.89 per cent. The share of West Bengal fell from 14.29 to 10.80 per cent, while among the increases the notable ones were of Karnataka (from 3.54 to 5.84 per cent), Punjab (from 2.56 to 3.17) per cent), Rajasthan (from 2.44 to 2.80 per cent), and Kerala (from 2.69 to 2.93 per cent).

Table 7.7

Changes in Tertiary Sector Shares

State	*1960-61 to 1963-64*	*1973-74 to 1976-77*	*State*	*1960-61 to 1963-64*	*1973-74 to 1976-77*
I *Transport & Communication*					
Uttar Pradesh	16.27	9.19	Andhra Pradesh	7.35	7.46
West Bengal	12.63	8.65	Kerala	2.84	4.16
Karnataka	10.67	4.33	Maharashtra	16.64	17.75
Bihar	10.37	6.37	Orissa	1.60	1.78
Madhya Pradesh	7.21	5.10	Tamil Nadu	6.48	8.42
Jammu & Kashmir	0.62	0.59	TOTAL	34.91	39.57
Punjab	2.88	2.81			
Rajasthan	3.75	3.16			
TOTAL	64.40	40.20			
II Banking & Insurance					
West Bengal	14.29	10.80	Maharashtra	24.66	24.96
Tamil Nadu	8.91	8.22	Karnataka	3.54	5.84
Uttar Pradesh	7.57	7.30	Kerala	2.69	2.93
Andhra Pradesh	4.88	4.26	Punjab	2.56	3.17
TOTAL	35.65	30.58	Rajasthan	2.44	2.80
			Bihar	2.93	2.94
			Jammu & Kashmir	0.24	0.32
			Madhya Pradesh	3.66	3.76
			Orissa	1.00	1.17
			TOTAL	43.72	47.89

If one reviews the gains and losses made by the states in all the industry-wise sub-sectors, one observes that most of them had a more or less equal number of losses and gains except for four states. They are West Bengal with 11 losses and 2 gains, Uttar Pradesh with 9 losses and 4 gains, while Kerala had 11 gains and 2 losses and Maharashtra 10 gains and 3 losses.

However, too much should not be read into these figures, as there is an unidentified measure of error, omission and non-comparability among SDP figures. This is especially so when sector and sub-sector-wise analysis is done, as in this chapter. In spite of this, the foregoing analysis may give a general idea of the changing position of the SDPs in regard to their comparative position in the incomes generated by industrial origin.

It is even more difficult to divide the national consumption figure into its component state shares. However, as seen in Chapter 6, it is possible to apply the NSS ratios of inter-state per capita consumption expenditure for all expenditure classes to the consolidated figures of private final consumption expenditure given in the national accounts. This is what has been done here. As the most recent NSS data on household expenditure only relates to 1973-74, and as the initial year used in this chapter for our analysis is 1960-61, we have confined our rèview of the consumption-mix by states to this period. Table 7.8 provides the shares of fifteen states for which NSS data are available. Punjab and Haryana are lumped together, as separate figures are not given for them for both the years. The states are arranged in descending order of their shares in 1960-61. The figures used are at current prices.

Table 7.8 shows that there is comparative stability in the inter-state shares of national consumption expenditure, as far as ranking is concerned, with only three states shifting by two places—Rajasthan and Madhya Pradesh in an upward direction, and West Bengal in a downward direction. Six states have shifted their ranking by one place—Maharashtra and Andhra Pradesh upward, and Tamil Nadu, Punjab and Haryana, Karnataka and Gujarat downward. The remaining states have retained their original places.

Table 7.8

Inter-state Variations in Consumption Shares

State	Shares (Per Cent)		Ranking	
	1960-61	1973-74	1960-61	1973-74
Uttar Pradesh	15.24	15.00	1	1
Bihar	11.85	10.37	2	2
West Bengal	9.04	7.39	3	5
Maharashtra	9.03	9.89	4	3
Andhra Pradesh	7.50	7.47	5	4
Tamil Nadu	6.93	6.89	6	7
Punjab & Haryana	6.43	5.67	7	8
Madhya Pradesh	6.24	7.11	8	6
Karnataka	5.48	5.28	9	10
Gujarat	5.16	5.00	10	11
Rajasthan	4.84	5.39	11	9
Kerala	3.18	3.90	12	12
Assam	2.95	3.35	13	13
Orissa	2.61	3.15	14	14
Jammu & Kashmir	0.90	1.15	15	15
Others	2.62	2.99	–	–

When viewing the shares by individual states between the two years, one finds that there has been some change in the case of every state listed in Table 7.8. Some states have had a sharp decline in their share—such as, West Bengal (from 9.04 to 7.39 per cent), Bihar (from 11.85 to 10.37 per cent) and Punjab-Haryana (from 6.43 to 5.67 per cent). Others have had a significant rise—like Maharashtra (from 9.03 to 9.89 per cent), Madhya Pradesh (from 6.24 to 7.11 per cent), Rajasthan (from 4.84 to 5.39 per cent), Kerala (from 3.18 to 3.90 per cent) and Orissa (from 2.61 to 3.15 per cent). The other states have experienced either upward or downward shifts by fewer percentage points. The change in percentage shares by different states in national consumption is far more widespread than that in percentage shares of SDPs in the national NDP, indicating the possibility of differences in the development of inter-state saving behaviour during the period.

These figures relate to the state shares in national consumption expenditure and cannot indicate the inter-state position in regard to consumption welfare. For this, one has to look at the per capita position. Table 7.9 gives the figures of estimated per capita expenditure on consumption by different states at current prices for 1960-61 and 1973-74 as well as their percentage growth between the two years and the changes in their ranking. The states are arranged in descending order of magnitude in 1960-61.

The per capita state-wise expenditure figures on consumption provided in Table 7.9 show sharp differences in the initial year and greater changes in the

Table 7.9

Inter-state Per Capita Expenditure on Consumption (At Current Prices)

State	Per Capita Expenditure on Consumption		Growth Per Cent	Per Capita Expenditure on Consumption (Rank)	
	1960-61	1973-74		1960-61	1973-74
Punjab & Haryana	378.9	972.2	257	1	1
West Bengal	309.7	672.8	217	2	14
Bihar	305.3	740.2	242	3	6
Jammu & Kashmir	302.6	697.4	231	4	9
Gujarat	299.2	748.4	250	5	4
Assam	297.4	699.9	235	6	8
Rajasthan	287.5	827.1	288	7	2
Karnataka	278.0	722.6	260	8	7
Maharashtra	273.3	789.1	289	9	3
Andhra Pradesh	262.5	692.8	264	10	10
Uttar Pradesh	247.3	680.9	275	11	13
Tamil Nadu	246.2	684.6	278	12	12
Madhya Pradesh	230.6	684.6	297	13	12
Kerala	225.2	745.5	331	14	5
Orissa	178.0	583.9	328	15	15
ALL INDIA	272.5	734.0	269	–	–

final year. Per capita consumption expenditure in 1960-61 ranged from Rs 178 for Orissa to Rs 379 for Punjab-Haryana, while as a proportion of national per capita expenditure it ranged from 65.3 to 139.0 per cent. In 1973-74, the inter-state range in per capita consumption expenditure was from Rs 584 for Orissa to Rs 972 for Punjab-Haryana. Though the top and bottom positions of Punjab-Haryana and Orissa did not change, the range of difference between them fell from 2.1 in 1960-61 to 1.7 in 1973-74. As a percentage of national per capita expenditure, Orissa's figure increased from 65.3 to 79.5, while that of Punjab and Haryana declined from 139.0 to 132.5. This is in sharp contrast to the position regarding SDPs and NDP, where the range widened between the two years. It also lends further support to the tentative thesis stated earlier of a change in inter-state consumption behaviour during the period.

It is also possible to analyse inter-state per capita shares in the national per capita consumption expenditure in rural and urban areas separately. Earlier, NSS ratios had been used for desegregating the NDP by rural and urban areas. They are now used to disaggregate the national private consumption expenditure by rural and urban areas, and by different states. Table 7.10 gives the shares of different states in national private consumption expenditure in rural areas in 1960-61 and 1973-74. The states are arranged in descending order of their shares, based on current prices.

Table 7.10

State-wise Distribution of National Consumption in Rural Areas (At Current Prices)

State	*State Share (Percentage)*		*Growth in Absolute Amounts of State Shares*	*Ranking in Shares*	
	1960-61	*1973-74*		*1960-61*	*1973-74*
Uttar Pradesh	16.73	16.95	353	1	1
Bihar	14.05	12.39	307	2	2
West Bengal	7.79	6.89	308	3	6
Andhra Pradesh	7.50	7.69	357	4	4
Maharashtra	7.03	7.84	388	5	3
Punjab & Haryana	6.59	5.99	316	6	7
Madhya Pradesh	6.48	7.62	409	7	5
Tamil Nadu	5.94	5.86	343	8	9
Rajasthan	5.06	5.92	407	9	8
Karnataka	5.02	5.03	309	10	10
Gujarat	4.65	4.58	343	11	11
Assam	3.41	3.96	404	12	13
Kerala	3.37	4.25	439	13	12
Orissa	3.09	3.69	416	14	14
Jammu & Kashmir	0.99	1.11	390	15	15
Others	2.30	0.23	–	–	–

Before analysing Table 7.10, it is necessary to draw attention to the fall from 2.30 to 0.23 in the share of other territories not listed in the Table. This probably includes some errors and omissions in the percentage shares of the states listed in the Table. Subject to this qualification, Table 7.10 appears to show some stability in inter-state consumption rankings.

Thus, seven of the fifteen states listed show no change in their ranking, while five have only changed by one place, two by two places and one by three places. However, there has been some change in the individual shares of all the states between 1960-61 and 1973-74. Three states have shown a sharp fall in their share—Bihar from 14.05 to 12.39 per cent, West Bengal from 7.79 to 6.89 per cent, and Punjab and Haryana from 6.59 to 5.99 per cent. Tamil Nadu and Gujarat have shown a marginal fall from 5.94 to 5.86 per cent and from 4.65 to 4.58 per cent respectively. The other states have shown a rise in their share. Significant increases were recorded by Maharashtra (from 7.03 to 7.84 per cent), Madhya Pradesh (from 6.48 to 7.62 per cent), Rajasthan (from 5.06 to 5.92 per cent), Assam (from 3.41 to 3.96 per cent), Kerala (from 3.37 to 4.25 per cent) and Orissa (from 3.09 to 3.69 per cent).

The position regarding state shares in national private consumption expenditure in urban areas is provided in Table 7.11. The states are arranged in descending order of their shares in the initial year, based on current prices.

The increase in the share of other areas from 3.8 to 8.4 per cent is high. This is, perhaps, not so unrealistic because of the faster growth both in

Table 7.11

Share of States in National Consumption Expenditure in Urban Areas (at Current Prices)

State	State Shares (Percentages)		Growth in Absolute Amount of State Shares	Ranking in Shares	
	1960-61	1973-74		1960-61	1973-74
Maharashtra	15.63	15.42	400	1	1
West Bengal	13.14	10.74	266	2	2
Uttar Pradesh	10.31	9.75	356	3	3
Tamil Nadu	10.19	9.66	381	4	4
Andhra Pradesh	7.50	6.87	359	5	5
Karnataka	6.81	5.93	339	6	7
Gujarat	6.85	6.15	358	7	6
Punjab & Haryana	5.89	4.82	316	8	10
Madhya Pradesh	5.43	5.76	407	9	8
Bihar	4.61	4.92	376	10	9
Rajasthan	4.10	3.97	371	11	11
Kerala	2.58	2.96	444	12	12
Assam	1.46	1.19	430	13	14
Orissa	1.03	1.71	583	14	13
Jammu & Kashmir	0.63	0.64	796	15	15
Others	3.85	4.68	–	–	–

numbers and per capita income of Delhi, which is included in Table 7.11. Nevertheless, there could be some error and omissions in the shares of the states listed in the Table, though not of a magnitude significant enough to vitiate the findings revealed by it. Subject to this qualification, the following comments can be made. In terms of inter-state rankings in shares, there seems to be even greater stability in urban consumption, seven of the fifteen states listed showing no change. Of the seven which did, only one showed a change by two places, while the remaining six showed a change by only one place. Surprisingly, the largest change in ranking was in the case of Punjab-Haryana, which fell from eighth place in 1960-61 to the tenth place in 1973-74. But all the states showed some change in their individual shares between 1960-61 and 1973-74. Seven states have shown a sharp fall in their percentage shares—West Bengal from 13.14 to 10.74, Uttar Pradesh from 10.31 to 9.75, Andhra Pradesh from 7.49 to 6.87, Karnataka from 6.81 to 5.93, Gujarat from 6.85 to 6.15, and Tamil Nadu from 10.19 to 9.66 per cent. Punjab-Haryana's share fell from 5.89 to 4.82 per cent, while Bihar showed a marginal fall from 4.99 to 4.92 per cent. All the other states showed a rise in their shares, the most significant being Orissa (from 1.03 to 1.71 per cent) and Jammu and Kashmir which more than doubled its share from 0.63 to 1.25 per cent.

These figures, however, relate to the share of the total urban and rural consumption of the states in the national totals or urban and rural consumption, and would include the increase in consumption due to a rise in numbers besides an increase in income and change in consumption behaviour. Table 7.12 gives the per capita rural and urban consumption expenditure of the different states at current prices in 1960-61 and 1973-74, their ranking and percentage of growth during the period.

Taking the rural sector first, the per capita expenditure figures on consumption in rural areas shows sharp inter-state variations in the initial year and sharper changes in the final year, as indicated in Table 7.12. Per capita consumption expenditure in the rural areas in the states in 1960-61 varied from Rs 170.3 in Orissa to Rs 368.1 in Punjab-Haryana, while as a proportion of national rural per capita consumption expenditure, it ranged from 67.7 to 146.4 per cent. In 1973-74 the inter-state range in rural per capita consumption expenditure was from Rs 555.1 for Orissa to Rs 963.7 for Punjab-Haryana. Though the top and bottom positions of Punjab and Haryana and Orissa did not change, the range of difference between them fell from 2.16 in 1960-61 to 1.74 in 1973-74. As a proportion of national rural per capita consumption expenditure, Orissa improved its position from 67.7 per cent in 1960-61 to 80.6 per cent in 1973-74, while that of Punjab-Haryana declined in its comparative superiority from 146.4 per cent in 1960-61 to 139.5 per cent in 1973-74. The figures seem to show some lessening of inter-state inequality in rural per capita consumption between these two years. There has been, however, no uniformity in the increase in rural per capita consumption expenditure in different states, and there have been some conspicuous changes in ranking.

Table 7.12

Inter-state Variations in Per Capita Consumption Expenditure

State	Rural Per Capita Expenditure (in Rs)		Rural Growth (Per Cent)	Ranking		Urban Per Capita Expenditure (in Rs)		Urban Growth (Per Cent)	Ranking	
	1960-61	1973-74		1960-61	1973-74	1960-61	1973-74		1960-61	1973-74
Andhra Pradesh	228.7	658.7	288	10	11	347.7	825.3	237	9	11
Assam	281.9	675.7	240	4	9	454.4	903.0	186	1	3
Bihar	299.3	728.0	243	3	3	371.2	840.5	226	6	8
Gujarat	275.0	708.9	258	5	5	368.8	806.4	219	7	13
Jammu & Kashmir	302.0	691.7	229	2	6	305.3	711.6	233	13	15
Kerala	212.8	718.9	338	13	4	295.0	875.2	297	14	4
Maharashtra	224.4	679.3	303	11	8	397.6	1018.4	256	4	1
Karnataka	248.3	679.8	274	8	7	344.8	820.6	238	10	12
Madhya Pradesh	211.6	655.2	310	14	12	381.4	846.8	222	5	7
Orissa	170.3	555.1	326	15	15	291.7	858.6	294	15	6
Punjab & Haryana	368.1	963.7	262	1	1	421.6	1002.9	238	3	2
Rajasthan	271.8	819.4	302	6	2	368.2	860.5	234	8	5
Uttar Pradesh	235.9	667.0	283	9	10	321.0	758.1	239	12	14
Tamil Nadu	217.9	620.7	285	12	13	323.9	826.2	255	11	10
West Bengal	267.5	617.7	231	7	14	440.3	834.3	189	2	9
ALL INDIA	251.5	689.1	274	—	—	368.3	895.2	243	—	—

As regards the urban sector, the per capita expenditure figures on consumption also show sharp inter-state variations in the initial year and more pronounced changes in the final year (see Table 7.12). Per capita consumption expenditure in the urban areas in the states varied from Rs 291.7 in Orissa to Rs 454.4 in Assam in 1960-61, while as a proportion of national urban per capita expenditure it ranged from 79.2 to 131.5 per cent. It will be seen that this range is lower than the corresponding rural figures given earlier, indicating a smaller measure of inter-state inequality in urban per capita consumption expenditure. In 1973-74, the inter-state range in urban per capita consumption expenditure varied from Rs 711.6 for Jammu and Kashmir to Rs 1018.4 for Maharashtra. Both the top and bottom states changed in 1973-74, but the range of difference between the top and bottom fell from 1.66 in 1960-61 to 1.43 in 1973-74, indicating a decline in inter-state inequality in urban per capita consumption expenditure. There have been sharp variations in the individual growth rates of the various states in consumption and ranking.

It is interesting to see the differences in the per capita rural and urban consumption in the different states in 1960-61 and the change that has taken place in 1973-74. Table 7.13 gives the percentage of per capita rural to per capita urban consumption expenditure at current prices in different states in 1960-61 and 1973-74.

Table 7.13

Rural-Urban Differentials in Per Capita Consumption Expenditure (At Current Prices)

State	*1960-61*	*1973-74*
Andhra Pradesh	65.8	79.8
Assam	58.2	74.8
Bihar	80.6	86.6
Gujarat	74.5	87.9
Jammu & Kashmir	98.9	97.2
Kerala	72.1	82.1
Maharashtra	56.4	66.7
Karnataka	72.0	82.8
Madhya Pradesh	55.5	77.4
Orissa	58.4	64.7
Punjab & Haryana	87.3	96.1
Rajasthan	73.8	95.2
Uttar Pradesh	73.5	88.0
Tamil Nadu	67.3	75.1
West Bengal	60.8	74.0
ALL INDIA	68.3	77.0

It is evident from Table 7.13 that there is considerable variation in the proportion of rural to urban per capita consumption expenditure in both the initial and final years of the period covered. In 1960-61, it ranged between 55.5 per cent in Madhya Pradesh to 98.9 per cent in Jammu and Kashmir, and 64.7 per cent in Orissa to 97.2 per cent in Jammu and Kashmir in 1973-74, thus narrowing the gap in 1973-74. It is remarkable that the comparative improvement in rural per capita consumption expenditure witnessed at the all-India level in 1973-74 over 1960-61 is widespread over all the states, every state listed in the Table increasing its percentage of rural to urban per capita consumption with the solitary exception of Jammu and Kashmir. This comparative improvement in rural per capita consumption expenditure in practically all the states lends further support to the thesis advanced in an earlier chapter of the comparative overall betterment in rural areas that has accompanied Indian economic development after 1960-61.

It may be added, however, that differences in rural/urban per capita expenditure on consumption continued even in 1973-74, which is the last year for which NSS data are available on rural and urban expenditure on consumption. Thus in 1973-74, there were two states where the rural/urban ratio of per capita consumption expenditure was less than 70 per cent—Orissa (64.7) and Maharashtra (66.7). There were five states where the ratio was between 70 and 80 per cent—Andhra Pradesh (79.8), Assam (74.8), Madhya Pradesh (77.4), Tamil Nadu (75.1) and West Bengal (74.0). The states that had a ratio between 80 and 90 per cent were also five—namely, Bihar (86.6), Gujarat (87.9), Kerala (82.1), Karnataka (82.8) and Uttar Pradesh (88.0). Three states had a ratio of over 90 per cent—Jammu and Kashmir (97.2), Punjab-Haryana (96.1) and Rajasthan (95.2). The prevalence of a rural/urban ratio of per capita consumption expenditure exceeding 80 per cent in as many as eight out of the fifteen states listed in Table 7.13 in 1973-74 is certainly a significant feature of the consumption pattern. It is also a matter for satisfaction that the number of states with a rural/urban per capita consumption expenditure exceeding 80 per cent has increased from three in 1960-61 to eight in 1973-74.

Another aspect of the inter-state position is in respect to the number of factory workers, their average monthly earnings and the position of workers in manufacturing industries earning less than Rs 400 a month. The data available is limited to the period 1961 to 1974.

Table 7.14 deals with the estimated average daily employment in all factories in India and their distribution by different states in 1961 and 1974. The first group of five states, each of which has a share of more than 8 per cent of the all-India total of factory workers, accounted for 25.95 lakh factory workers and a share of 66.23 per cent in the all-India total. While the number of workers increased to 34.82 lakhs in 1974, their share in the all-India total dropped to 61.33 per cent.

The second group of five states, each of which had a share of between 4 and 6 per cent of the all-India figure of factory workers, had 9.39 lakhs of workers and accounted for a share of 23.97 per cent of the all-India total in 1961. The number of workers increased to 15.28 lakhs in 1974, while their share in the all-India total increased to 26.91 per cent.

Table 7.14

Average Daily Employment in Factories

State	No. (000s) 1961	No. (000s) 1974	Percentage 1961	Percentage 1974	Increase in 1974 over 1961 (%)	Ranking 1961	Ranking 1974
Maharashtra	827	1093	21.11	19.25	32.2	1	1
West Bengal	739	884	18.86	15.57	19.6	2	2
Gujarat	361	523	9.21	9.21	44.9	3	3
Uttar Pradesh	338	466	8.63	8.21	37.9	4	5
Tamil Nadu	330	516	8.42	9.09	56.4	5	4
Total 5 States	2595	3482	66.23	61.33	34.2		
Andhra Pradesh	228	368	5.82	6.48	61.4	6	6
Bihar	192	319	4.90	5.62	66.2	7	8
Karnataka	178	335	4.54	5.90	88.2	8	7
Kerala	172	261	4.39	4.60	51.7	9	9
Madhya Pradesh	169	245	4.31	4.31	45.0	10	10
Total 5 States	939	1528	23.97	26.91	62.7		
Assam	80	78	2.04	1.37	−2.5	11	14
Punjab	78	132	1.99	2.32	69.2	12	11
Rajasthan	57	100	1.45	1.76	75.4	13	13
Haryana	54	109	1.38	1.92	101.9	14	12
Orissa	38	75	0.97	1.32	97.4	15	15
Total 5 States	307	494	7.83	8.70	60.9		
Total 4 States (Excluding Assam)	227	416	5.79	7.33	83.3	–	–
Others	77	175	1.97	3.08	127.3	–	–
ALL INDIA	3918	5679	100.00	100.00	–	–	–

The third group of five states, each of which had a share of less than 2 per cent of the all-India total, had 3.07 lakhs of factory workers in 1960 and accounted for a share of 7.83 per cent of the national total. This number increased to 4.94 lakhs in 1974 and their share of the all-India total to 8.70 per cent. Their rates of growth in the number of factory workers for the period 1961-1974 were 34.2 per cent for the first group, 62.7 per cent for the second group, and 60.9 per cent for the third group. If Assam, which was conspicuous for its industrial stagnation during the period having a negative growth rate in the number of its factory workers, is omitted from the third group, its rate of growth becomes 83.3 per cent, and its share in the national total 7.33 per cent in 1974 as against 5.79 per cent in 1961. Of the increase of 17.61 lakhs of factory workers, the first group had a share of only 50.4 per cent as against their initial share of 66.2 per cent in 1961; the second group's share was 33.4 per cent against an initial share of 24.0 per cent, and the third group got 10.6 per cent against their initial share of 7.8 per cent. All the states which had a share of more than 8 per cent of factory workers registered a reduction in their individual shares, with the exception of Tamil Nadu; and all the other states registered an increase in their individual shares with the exception of Assam. Among them, three had a growth rate in the number of factory workers much above the all-India rate of 45 per cent—Haryana with 102 per cent, Orissa with 99 per cent, and Karnataka with 88 per cent. On the other hand, the dominant industrial states of Maharashtra and West Bengal had a growth rate of only 32 and 19 per cent respectively. It is clear from this analysis that the direction of change in the distribution of factory workers in 1974 over 1960 has been towards a reduction in inter-state inequality.

As regards the growth of monthly earnings in the manufacturing industries at current prices, the inter-state position is shown in Table 7.15. Against the all-India index of growth of 206.9 in 1974 (with 1961 = 100) eight states had an index of growth above this average. They were Rajasthan (391.5), Kerala (267.9), West Bengal (265.7), Punjab and Haryana (258.1), Orissa (252.5), Uttar Pradesh (247.6), and Andhra Pradesh (229.6). The remaining seven states had an index of growth in the monthly earnings of their workers in manufacturing industries which was less than the all-India figure. They were Madhya Pradesh (198.5), Maharashtra (195.0), Tamil Nadu (199.5), Assam (162.7), Karnataka (160.0), Gujarat (154.6) and Bihar (131.4).

Table 7.15

Index Numbers of Money Earnings of Workers in Manufacturing Industries

States	*1961*	*1970*	*1974*
Andhra Pradesh	100	178.1	229.6
Assam	100	151.8	162.7
Bihar	100	147.4	131.4
Gujarat	100	175.1	154.6
Himachal Pradesh	100	229.5	268.9
Karnataka	100	181.0	160.0
Kerala	100	199.0	267.9
Madhya Pradesh	100	158.2	198.5
Maharashtra	100	174.8	195.0
Orissa	100	219.7	252.5
Punjab & Haryana	100	199.8	258.1
Rajasthan	100	328.1	391.5
Tamil Nadu	100	176.7	199.5
Uttar Pradesh	100	183.1	247.6
West Bengal	100	196.6	265.7
ALL INDIA	100	180.1	206.9

It is difficult to identify the different factors responsible for the difference in the growth rate of earnings without making a special study of the subject. It is interesting to note, however, that of the five states listed in the first group in Table 7.14, three had an index of growth in earnings below the all-India figure. The corresponding figure for the second group of five states was three, and for the third group of five states only one. Evidently, the third group — which has the least share in the national total of factory workers and whose members had an individual share of less than 2 per cent — had fared better than the other two groups, with a larger collective and individual share both in respect of growth in the number of factory workers as well as in the index of monthly earnings of workers in manufacturing industries.

When one looks at the increase in the number of workers with annual earnings below Rs 400 (for which separate data is available) different trends emerge. Table 7.16 gives the number of such workers in manufacturing industries in different states in 1961 and 1974 and their percentage to the total number of factory workers. The states are arranged in the same order as in Table 7.14.

It is seen that the top group of five states, which increased their total number of workers from 25.95 lakhs to 34.82 lakhs, actually suffered a decline in the number of workers earning below Rs 400 per annum (from 18.51

Table 7.16

Number of Workers with Annual Earnings Below Rs 400 and their Percentage to the Total Number of Factory Workers

State	*No. of Workers with Earnings Below Rs 400 Per Year (figure in 000s)*		*Percentage to Total Number of Workers*	
	1961	*1974*	*1961*	*1974*
Maharashtra	601	501	72.7	45.8
West Bengal	569	413	77.0	46.7
Gujarat	279	207	77.3	39.6
Uttar Pradesh	178	214	52.7	45.9
Tamil Nadu	224	291	67.9	56.4
Total 5 States	1851	1626	71.3	46.7
Andhra Pradesh	54	139	23.7	37.8
Bihar	130	136	67.7	42.6
Karnataka	81	121	45.5	36.1
Kerala	49	30	28.5	11.5
Madhya Pradesh	32	76	18.9	31.0
Total 5 States	346	502	36.9	32.9
Assam	12	16	15.0	37.8
Punjab	46	68	59.0	51.5
Rajasthan	15	54	26.3	54.0
Haryana	39	72	72.2	66.1
Orissa	18	19	47.4	25.3
Total 5 States	130	229	42.3	46.4
Total 4 States (Excluding Assam)	118	213	52.0	37.8
Others	62	97	80.50	3.95
ALL INDIA	2389	2454	61.0	100.00

lakhs to 16.26 lakhs), their percentage to the total dropping from 71.3 to 46.7. In the second group of five states, while the total number of workers increased from 9.39 lakhs to 15.28 lakhs, or by a larger percentage, their workers who earned less than Rs 400 per year also increased from 3.46 lakhs to 5.02 lakhs but their percentage to the total dropped from 36.9 to 32.9 per cent. The bottom group of four states, which recorded an increase in the total number of workers from 2.27 lakhs to 4.16 lakhs, also recorded a sharp increase in the number of workers with earnings below Rs 400 per year (from 1.18 lakhs to 2.13 lakhs), their percentage to the total increasing from 5.44 to 8.68. In spite of this, the percentage of workers with earnings below Rs 400 per annum is approximately the same as in the top group of five states with their much larger percentage of the total number of factory workers employed in 1974.

Factor Shares in the National Product 8

It is customary for analysts of national income data to identify the shares of the factors of production in the national product and the changes, if any, in these shares over a given period for which a time series data is available. The traditionally accepted factors of production are four — land, labour, capital and enterprise; their shares are described as rent, wages and salaries or employee compensation, interest and profits. The *UN Yearbook of National Accounts*, 1979, which is the latest available edition, does not go into the details of these four categories of factor incomes, but groups them under two heads, namely, employee compensation and operational surplus. Operational surplus is a catch-all which remains after deducting employee compensation from the NDP; or, if GDP is used, after deducting from it, besides employee compensation, indirect taxes minus subsidies and consumption of fixed capital. Table 8.1 gives a consolidated picture of the data contained in these tables on the share of employee compensation in the NDP and GDP of India.

The UN tables give a misleading picture of the share of employee compensation in the national product, making it much higher than that of any other

Table 8.1

Share of Employee Compensation (Percentage)

Year	*Share in NDP*	*Share in GDP*
1970	84.7	73.0
1971	63.6	72.0
1972	83.7	72.0
1973	85.8	74.0
1974	85.5	73.0
1975	84.5	71.0
1976	82.7	69.0
1977	83.1	70.0

country listed in its yearbook. This is because it has included the mixed income of the self-employed in the Indian national product while tabulating the share of employee compensation. In actual fact, the mixed income of the self-employed includes payment for all the four factors of production; but as it is not possible to segregate them, and as they all accrue to the self-employed, they have been lumped together under the category 'mixed income of the self-employed'. It is impossible to segregate the whole of the Indian national product, net or gross, into its constituent factor shares. To do so would only give a misleading picture of the Indian economy. It is, however, possible to identify the shares of the different factors of production in the national product if the share of the mixed income of the self-employed is excluded. After making some adjustments like the one proposed earlier, we found that factor incomes can be estimated for nearly two-thirds of the Indian NDP.

Table 8.2 gives the amount and percentage shares of different factor incomes (excluding the mixed income of the self-employed) in the NDP.

Table 8.2

Factor Incomes in NDP (Excluding the Mixed Income of the Self-employed) at Current Prices (Rs Crores)

Factor Income	*1960-61*	*1979-80*	*1960-64*	*1965-69*	*1970-74*	*1975-79*
Wages & salaries	4497	34988	27054	46981	82792	147141
	(62.34)	(67.80)	(62.83)	(67.55)	(68.02)	(67.08)
Rent	692	3726	4126	5718	10176	16029
	(9.59)	(7.22)	(9.58)	(8.22)	(8.36)	(7.31)
Interest	425	6598	2938	6105	12479	26964
	(5.89)	(12.78)	(6.82)	(8.77)	(10.25)	(12.29)
Profits & dividends	1600	6296	8940	10741	16263	29205
	(22.18)	(12.20)	(20.77)	(15.46)	(13.37)	(13.32)
TOTAL	7214	51608	43058	69545	121710	219339
	(100.00)	(100.00)	(100.00)	(100.00)	(100.00)	(100.00)

Note: Figures in brackets are a percentage of each group to the total in the year or period concerned.

It is seen from Table 8.2 that the share of employees' compensation or wages and salaries has increased from Rs 4,497 crores in 1960-61 to Rs 34,988 crores in 1979-80 at current prices, or from 62.34 per cent to 67.80 per cent, the index of growth being 778. Profits and dividends have increased from Rs 1,600 crores to Rs 6,296 crores, with an index of growth of only 394 and its percentage share falling from 22.18 to 12.20. Interest, however, has increased from Rs 425 crores to Rs 6,598 crores or from 5.89 to 12.78 per cent with an index of growth of 1552. The share of rent has increased from Rs 692 to Rs 3,726 crores, with an index of growth of 538 and a fall in its percentage share from 9.59 to 7.22 per cent. If we take the operational surplus as defined by the UN as distinguished from employee compensation, the increase is from Rs 2,717 crores to Rs 16,620 crores; the index of growth is 612 and the fall in percentage share in the NDP is from 36.7 to 32.2. It is interesting to note that the trend of change in the share of employee compensation in the NDP is upward. This is in contrast to the UN figures where the movement is downward, obviously because it has included the mixed income of the self-employed in the profits of unincorporated enterprises under employee compensation.

Table 8.3

Share of Sectors of Industrial Origin in the Totals of Factor Incomes at Current Prices
(Percentages)

Sector	*Employee Compensation*		*Rent*		*Interest*	
	1960-61	*1979-80*	*1960-61*	*1979-80*	*1960-61*	*1979-80*
Primary	37.36	21.15	28.32	16.26	52.95	26.81
Secondary	29.06	32.00	5.63	10.97	26.59	49.75
Tertiary	33.58	46.85	66.05	72.77	20.46	23.44
TOTAL	100.00	100.00	100.00	100.00	100.00	100.00

Sector	*Profits & Dividends*		*Total Factor Incomes*	
	1960-61	*1979-80*	*1960-61*	*1979-80*
Primary	37.50	22.22	37.44	21.65
Secondary	44.70	62.05	30.14	36.80
Tertiary	17.80	15.73	32.42	41.55
TOTAL	100.00	100.00	100.00	100.00

We will now study the shares of the three basic sectors of industrial origin in the individual factor incomes as well as the total of all factor incomes over the period 1960-80 (Table 8.3). It must be noted that the primary sector referred to here excludes a large share of its NDP which is attributable to the mixed income of the self-employed, accounting for 67.3 per cent of that sector in 1979-80. Similarly, the secondary sector dealt with here excludes 19.1 per cent of the mixed income of the self-employed from that sector. In the case of the tertiary sector, the mixed income of the self-employed accounted for 50.8 per cent of the NDP for transport, communication and trade, whereas the corresponding figure for finance and real estate was only 2.4 per cent and for community and personal services only 9.4 per cent. This must be borne in mind when interpreting the tables relating to factor shares and their distribution between different sectors of industrial origin.

Table 8.3 shows that, taking factor incomes as a whole, the primary sector's share fell from 37.44 to 21.65 per cent, while that of the secondary sector increased from 30.14 to 36.80 per cent and the tertiary sector from 32.42 to 41.55 per cent. However, the change in individual factor incomes in the different sectors did not correspond to that of their total factor incomes in the case of the secondary and tertiary sectors while it was more or less similar in the case of the primary sector. In the primary sector, while the fall in its total factor income was 57.8 per cent, the fall in employee compensation was 56.6 per cent, in rent 57.4 per cent, in interest 50.6 per cent and in profits 59.3 per cent. All these figures indicate an increase in self-employment or mixed income that must have accompanied the growth of the primary sector during this period and its green revolution. In the secondary sector, while the rise in its total factor income was 22.1 per cent, the increase in its employee compensation was only 10.1 per cent, while the increase in its rent, interest and profit incomes were 94.8, 87.1 and 38.8 per cent respectively, indicating a probable increase in self-employment in this sector as well as a fall in the wage component of its total factor income. In the tertiary sector, the position was in sharp contrast to that in the secondary sector. While the increase in its total factor income was 28.2 per cent, that in its employee compensation was higher with 39.5 per cent, while it was lower in the case of rent and interest with 10.2 and 14.6 per cent respectively and was actually negative in the case of interest with a fall of 11.5 per cent.

There is also considerable difference between the distribution of factor incomes in the total of all sectors of industrial origin and in that of each sector of industrial origin. Table 8.4 gives the relevant data. The caution must be repeated that these sectors of industrial origin exclude the mixed income of the self-employed.

Public administration and other community and personal services are significant insofar as their factor income is almost completely identical with employee compensation. It is only in regard to the other sectors of industrial origin that one can meaningfully analyse factor share distribution. The sectors which have an employee compensation of more than 50 per cent of their factor income are agriculture, fishing, mining and quarrying, manufacturing, construction, railways, communication and banking and insurance. The sectors in which interest gets a share of more than 10 per cent are only agriculture, electricity, gas and water supply and railways. The sectors in which rent has a share of more than 10 per cent are transport other than railways and trade, hotels and restaurants. The sector where rent claims more than 90 per cent of its factor income is real estate (including business houses and ownership of residential houses).

As regards profits and dividends, a share of more than 20 per cent of the sectoral factor incomes is found in fishing, mining and quarrying, manufacturing, construction, transport other than railways, communication, trade and catering, and banking and insurance. Forestry and logging have the highest percentage of profits and dividends with more than 70 per cent of its total factor income. Some sectors which started with a profit percentage of more than 20 per cent of factor incomes in the first sub-period have lost this position during the fourth sub-period. Thus, profits in mining and quarrying have come down from 28.23 to 9.31 of their factor incomes, construction from 22.74 to 7.17 per cent, railways from 19.97 to 7.48 per cent, transport other than railways from 29.28 to a negative figure of 17.21 per cent, and trade and catering from 33.40 to 5.77 per cent. In fact, all the sectors have

Table 8.4

Factor Shares in Sectoral Incomes

Sector of Industrial Origin	1960-61 to 1964-65				1975-76 to 1979-80			
	Employee Compensation	Rent	Interest	Profits	Employee Compensation	Rent	Interest	Profits
Agriculture	67.71	8.83	11.04	12.42	65.99	6.42	16.08	11.51
Forestry & logging	21.73	—	0.09	78.18	30.16	—	—	69.84
Fishing	54.99	—	6.33	38.68	64.54	—	10.49	24.97
Mining & quarrying	64.72	3.89	3.16	28.23	71.60	4.23	14.86	9.31
Manufacturing	55.83	1.67	4.98	37.52	55.31	2.33	17.09	25.27
Construction	71.84	1.46	3.96	22.74	83.22	1.25	8.36	7.17
Electricity, water & gas	38.12	1.07	46.90	13.91	47.49	1.86	43.16	7.49
Railways	60.18	—	19.85	19.97	69.81	—	22.71	7.48
Other transport	49.74	13.35	7.63	29.28	89.95	8.60	18.66	−17.21
Communication	70.34	—	6.37	23.29	62.09	—	5.67	32.24
Trade, hotels & restaurants	45.86	14.35	6.39	33.40	64.20	10.88	19.15	5.77
Banking & insurance	53.35	2.11	—	44.54	49.11	2.98	—	47.91
Real estate	4.04	94.81	0.31	0.84	11.25	87.95	0.37	0.43
Public administration	100.00	—	—	—	100.00	—	—	—
Other services	94.83	3.21	1.13	0.83	98.47	0.60	0.74	0.19
TOTAL	62.83	9.58	6.82	20.77	67.08	7.31	12.29	13.32

experienced a reduction in the percentage of their profits to their total factor incomes except for communication and banking while, with regard to interest, all the sectors have registered a higher percentage with the exception of electricity, gas and water, and communication. Employee compensation has been rising as a percentage of factor incomes in all the sectors with the exception of agriculture, communication and banking. As far as change between the first and fourth sub-periods are concerned, they are in line with the changes referred to earlier in the macro-picture of factor shares in the total of factor incomes of all the sectors of industrial origin.

We will now analyse the changing shares of the public and private sectors separately in each category of factor incomes (Table 8.5). The private sector has been divided into the organised and unorganised segments. The unorganised segment includes unincorporated and individual enterprises. The figures are given in percentages at current prices, both for quinquennial periods and for the initial and final years of the period 1960-61 to 1979-80.

Table 8.5

Shares of Public and Private Sectors in Each Category of Factor Income (Percentages)

Factor Incomes	*1960-61*	*1979-80*	*1960-64*	*1965-69*	*1970-74*	*1975-79*
I *Employee Compensation*						
Public	25.97	38.78	27.81	30.51	33.17	37.58
Private organised	24.57	20.94	25.16	23.82	21.09	20.43
Private unorganised	49.46	40.28	47.03	45.67	45.74	41.99
TOTAL (PRIVATE)	74.03	61.22	72.19	69.49	66.83	62.42
II *Rent*						
Public	0.59	6.82	0.70	2.19	3.25	5.68
Private organised	6.07	6.39	6.28	8.03	5.71	6.11
Private unorganised	93.34	86.79	93.02	89.78	91.04	88.21
TOTAL (PRIVATE)	99.41	93.18	99.30	97.81	96.75	94.32
III *Interest*						
Public	28.24	35.98	30.67	34.97	28.67	33.59
Private organised	18.12	25.33	16.61	20.79	23.17	25.32
Private unorganised	53.64	38.69	52.72	44.24	48.16	41.09
TOTAL (PRIVATE)	71.76	64.02	69.33	65.03	71.33	66.41
IV *Profits & Dividends*						
Public	4.60	14.57	5.41	5.47	7.64	16.41
Private organised	27.00	27.09	27.84	28.98	26.08	25.41
Private unorganised	68.40	58.34	66.75	65.55	66.28	58.18
TOTAL (PRIVATE)	95.40	85.43	94.59	94.55	92.36	83.59

The public sector has increased its share in the national total of factor incomes from 19.71 per cent in 1960-61 to 34.94 per cent in 1979-80 at current prices. Its share of employee compensation has gone up from 25.97 to 38.78 per cent, rent from 0.59 to 6.82 per cent, interest from 28.24 to 35.98 per cent and profits from 4.60 to 14.57 per cent. The growing role of the public sector is, in fact, one of the major developments in the Indian economy during this period.

It is also seen from Table 8.5 that the public sector has increased its share of total employee compensation from 27.81 per cent in the first sub-period to 37.58 per cent in the last sub-period. This has been at the expense of both segments of the private sector — the organised has dropped from 25.16 to 20.43 per cent and the unorganised segment from 47.03 to 41.99 per cent. Another fact that emerges is that the largest share of employee compensation remains with the unorganised segment of the private sector.

As regards rent, the dominant share is held by the private unorganised sector. This has fallen marginally from 93.02 to 88.21 per cent, the remaining 4.8 percentage points becoming the gain of the public sector. Under interest, which has doubled its share in the total of factor incomes from 5.9 to 12.8 per cent, the private organised sector has increased its share from 16.61 to 25.32 per cent, and the public sector from 30.67 to 33.59 per cent, the loser being the private unorganised sector (from 52.72 to 41.09 per cent). This illustrates the decreasing role of loan finance in the private unorganised sector. In the sector of profits, the public sector has increased its share from 5.41 to 16.41 per cent, while the private sector has decreased its share from 94.59 to 83.59 per cent.

Two points emerge from this analysis. One is the significant role over the whole period of the private unorganised sector in its share of each of the factor incomes — with 88.2 per cent of rent, 58.2 per cent of profits, 41.1 per cent of interest and 42.0 per cent of employee compensation. The other is the consistent increase in the share of the public sector in all the four categories of factor incomes — from 27.8 to 37.6 per cent in employee compensation, 0.7 to 5.7 per cent in rent, 30.7 to 33.6 per cent in interest and 5.4 to 16.4 per cent in profits, which has already been pointed out in Table 8.4. It must be noted, however, that the conspicuously higher rate of growth of profits in the public sector and its increased share in the national total of profits is not entirely the result of increased efficiency in the public sector. It is also due to its low base in 1960-61, the higher investment in the public sector as compared to the private sector, and the nationalisation of private incorporated enterprises in insurance, banking and mines during the period.

We will now look at the changing factor share composition separately for the public and private sectors. Table 8.6 gives the relevant figures for 1960-61 and 1979-80 at current prices.

It is seen from Table 8.6 that while employee compensation in the public sector has gone down from 82.14 per cent in 1960-61 to 75.24 per cent in 1979-80 (or by 9.17 per cent), it has risen in the case of the private sector from 47.45 to 53.71 (or by 13.19 per cent). In the private sector, it has gone up from 55.61 to 57.91 per cent in the organised segment (or by 4.14 per cent), while in the unorganised segment it has gone up from 44.22 to 51.76 per cent (or by 17.05 per cent). In spite of these differential changes, the share of employee compensation in the public sector still remains above that in the private sector; and within the private sector the share of the organised seg-

Table 8.6

Shares of Factor Incomes in Public and Private Sectors

Factor Income	1960-61				1979-80			
	Public	Private			Public	Private		
		Organised	Unorganised	Total (Private)		Organised	Unorganised	Total (Private)
Employee compensation	82.14	55.61	44.22	47.45	75.24	57.91	51.76	53.71
Rent	0.28	2.11	12.85	9.81	1.41	1.88	11.87	8.70
Interest	8.44	3.88	4.53	4.35	13.17	13.21	9.37	10.59
Profits	9.14	38.40	38.40	38.40	10.18	27.00	27.00	27.00
TOTAL	100.00	100.00	100.00	100.00	100.00	100.00	100.00	100.00

ment has fallen below that of the unorganised segment. What nearly twenty years of development has done is to reduce the difference in the share of employee compensation in the public sector to almost that of the private sector, and within the private sector to effect a larger percentage increase in the unorganised sector as compared to that in the organised sector.

The share of rent in the public sector has increased from 0.28 to 1.41 per cent, while it shows a marginal decline in the private sector from 9.81 to 8.70 per cent. Within the private sector, the share of rent is much higher in the case of its unorganised segment as compared to its organised segment, mainly because of the larger role of dwelling rentals in the case of the former.

It is in regard to the share of interest that one finds the largest changes between 1960-61 and 1979-80. It has increased from 8.44 per cent to 13.17 per cent in the case of the public sector or by 56 per cent, while in the private sector it has increased from 4.35 to 10.59 per cent or by 143 per cent. Within the private sector, the organised segment saw an increase in the share of interest from 3.88 to 13.21 per cent (or by 240 per cent), while the corresponding figures for the unorganised segment were 4.53 to 9.37 per cent or 107 per cent.

This sharp rise in the share of interest in the case of the private sector, especially the organised segment, is a clear indication of the increasing role of loan capital in financing the development of non-self-employed economic activity. The decline in the share of profits further confirms this finding. This is also supported by the evidence available from the data on the sources and uses of funds in the corporate sector and the rapid growth of bank advances to the industrial sector. Thus, loan capital is playing a more important role than risk capital in the non-self-employed sector of the economy.

Even in the self-employed sector, which is mainly agricultural, loan capital has become more significant which is evident from the large increase in the advances made to cultivators by the banking system. The growth of the private corporate sector has also witnessed a similar phenomenon, which is seen from the increasing share of loan capital in its development. Credit has thus played a crucial role in India's economic development. Further proof of this is the phenomenal growth of the banking and insurance sector in the Indian economy during recent years. While this may have slackened the pace of innovation and risk-based growth in the Indian economy, it also underlines the need for strengthening the ethic of payment of interest and repayment of loans by entrepreneurs in both the incorporated and unincorporated sectors so as to maintain an even pace in the current rate of economic growth, apart from raising it. This observation is induced by the populist pressure for non-payment or reduction in the payment of interest and capital loans, which seems to have gained in intensity after the nationalisation of banks and the subsequent growth of opportunistic political behaviour.

It is more difficult to delineate the respective roles of risk capital and loan capital in the case of public enterprises. Though factor incomes under public enterprises show interest and profits separately, the share of equity capital in financing public enterprises cannot be treated on par with that in the private sector. The equity investments in the public sector do not come from the general public but from the government which acts as the equity investor or risk bearer. It does this by raising finances from its current revenue and capital receipts. The government also supplies the loan capital required by these enterprises. To this extent, the distinction between loan capital and risk capital and interest and profits gets blurred in the case of public enterprises.

Table 8.6 also shows clearly that employee compensation has a larger role in the public sector than in the incorporated private sector, and a more significant role in the incorporated private sector than in the unincorporated one. A part of the explanation is that public administration and defence are included in the public sector and they have employee compensation of 100 per cent. It could also mean a larger staffing per unit of value added or a higher employee compensation per worker in the public sector than in the incorporated private sector and similarly in the incorporated as compared with the unincorporated private sector. It is not possible to allocate weights to these three possibilities on the basis of the national accounts data, but it does seem plausible that between them they may account for the difference in the employment compensation patterns in these three sectors.

Table 8.6 also illustrates clearly that the profits generated in the public sector are lower per unit of value added as compared to that in the private sector. The explanation for this is public knowledge, namely, that public enterprises, both departmental and non-departmental, have a record of lower profitability than the private sector. This may be due either to lower operational efficiency or an uneconomic pricing policy or both. In addition, it must be remembered that the public sector NDP includes public administration and defence which, by definition, are not conducted on the criterion of profitability. The identity between the share of profits in the two sections of the private sector is obviously the result of the formula we adopted earlier for estimating the profits accruing to its non-incorporated section.

While the share of profits in the public sector increased from 9.14 to 10.18 per cent (or by 11 per cent), in the private sector it fell from 38.40 to 27.00 per cent or by 42 per cent. This decline in the share of profits and the accompanying large increase in that of interest may be an explanation for the slow growth of corporate savings in the economy between 1960-61 and 1979-80.

A detailed discussion of employee compensation follows. This is not only the most important of the factor incomes in magnitude but also in terms of the number of people affected. We will use all available data — the national acounts, RBI bulletins and Indian labour yearbooks.

The national accounts data on employee compensation by the CSO sectors of industrial origin are considered first.

Table 8.7 shows that in the last quinquennial period (1975-76 to 1979-80) agriculture leads with 20.45 per cent of the total employee compensation, followed by manufacturing with 17.94 per cent. Public administration and defence are next with 12.93 per cent, followed by community and personal services, other than public administration and defence, with 10.65 per cent;

Table 8.7

Sectoral Shares in Employee Compensation by Quinquennial Periods at Current Prices

Sector of Industrial Origin	*Percentages*					
	1960-61 to 64-65	*1965-66 to 69-70*	*1970-71 to 74-75*	*1975-76 to 79-80*	*1960-61*	*1979-80*
Agriculture	34.48	31.75	24.05	20.45	35.69	19.49
Forestry & logging	0.87	0.92	0.84	0.86	0.80	0.97
Fishing	0.84	0.86	0.76	0.74	0.87	0.69
Mining & quarrying	1.97	1.86	1.47	2.23	1.96	2.44
Manufacturing	18.57	18.56	18.44	17.94	18.03	17.87
Construction	7.99	9.90	10.09	10.61	8.47	9.85
Electricity, water & gas	0.66	0.85	1.10	1.67	0.60	1.84
Railways	3.45	3.17	2.54	2.30	3.56	2.11
Other transport & storage	2.51	3.05	4.37	5.35	2.27	5.75
Communication	1.06	1.18	1.14	1.17	1.07	1.21
Trade, hotels & restaurants	2.71	2.60	9.04	8.61	2.71	8.48
Banking & insurance	2.15	2.61	3.34	3.78	1.93	4.12
Real estate	0.34	0.26	0.57	0.71	0.38	0.77
Public administration	12.80	13.24	12.71	12.93	11.96	13.06
Others	9.60	9.20	9.54	10.65	9.70	11.35
TOTAL	100.00	100.00	100.00	100.00	100.00	100.00

construction with 10.61 per cent; trade, hotels and restaurants with 8.61 per cent; transport other than railways with 5.35 per cent; banking and insurance with 3.78 per cent; railways with 2.30 per cent; mining and quarrying with 2.23 per cent; electricity, water and gas with 1.67 per cent; and communication with 1.17 per cent. The remaining three sectors each have a share of less than 1 per cent and taken together account for less than 2.50 per cent of the total.

Between the quinquennial periods of 1960-61 to 1964-65 and 1975-76 to 1979-80, it is agriculture which has recorded a steep decline in its share of total employee compensation (from 34.48 per cent to 20.45 per cent). The sectors which have shown an increase in their share are trade, hotels and restaurants (from 2.71 per cent to 8.61 per cent), construction (from 7.99 to 10.61 per cent), transport other than railways (from 2.51 to 5.35 per cent), banking and insurance (from 2.15 to 3.78 per cent), and electricity, gas and water supply (from 0.66 to 1.67 per cent). Changes in other sectors, including manufacturing, public administration and community and personal services, are marginal. Hence there has been a significant change in the sectoral shares of employee compensation between the two sub-periods. On the whole, it is the non-major sectors of industrial origin that have contributed the most to the increase which has taken place in the share of employee compensation in the total of all factor incomes.

The *Indian Labour Yearbook* gives figures of per capita average daily earnings of all employees in major groups of industries and services from 1963-64 to 1975-76. This classification of industries was changed in 1971-72. However, it is possible to obtain a continuous time series of the per capita earnings of all employees in the manufacturing sector for the period 1963-64 to 1975-76. Table 8.8 gives the daily average per capita earnings of employees in all manufacturing industries and services for which data is available for the period 1963-64 to 1975-76.

Table 8.8

Indices of Growth in Real Earnings of Industrial Workers

Year	*Per Capita Daily Earnings*	*Index of Growth*	*All India CPI*	*Index of Real Growth of Earnings*	*Index of Real Growth of Per Capita NDP*	*Col. 4/ Col. 5*
1963-64	5.61	100.0	100	100.0	100.00	1.0000
1964-65	6.32	112.7	115	98.0	105.34	0.9303
1965-66	6.84	121.9	124	98.3	97.94	1.0037
1966-67	7.43	132.4	140	94.6	96.59	0.9794
1967-68	8.67	154.6	156	99.1	102.33	0.9684
1968-69	9.44	168.3	158	106.5	102.90	1.0350
1969-70	9.86	175.8	161	109.2	107.05	1.0201
1970-71	10.72	101.1	169	113.1	110.18	1.0265
1971-72	11.36	202.3	175	115.6	109.59	1.0548
1972-73	—	—	—	—	—	—
1973-74	13.97	249.0	227	109.7	108.66	1.0096
1974-75	17.33	308.9	288	107.3	107.86	0.9948
1975-76	19.39	345.6	285	121.3	115.16	1.0533

Source: Per capita daily earnings – *Indian Labour Yearbook*, New Delhi, Government of India; All India Consumer Price Index – *Economic Survey*, New Delhi, Government of India; Per capita NDP at 1960-61 prices – October 1976, NAS CSO publications (New Delhi, Government of India) from 1970-71 onwards to base is corrected to 1960-61 prices.

The data in this Table show that from 1968-69 the index of real per capita daily earnings of all employees has been rising. It suddenly jumped to 121.3 in 1975-76 from 100 in 1963-64. It was also higher than the growth of real per capita NDP in 1975-76, showing a difference of nearly 6 percentage points (the highest difference during the period under review).

Generally, we can say that employee per capita compensation in manufacturing industries and services has fared slightly better than the growth of the NDP as a whole. This does not mean, however, that they have not suffered any differential effects from inflation during the period, as their earnings do not reflect their increased per capita productivity, which has grown faster than that of all workers contributing to the NDP, as we have seen in Chapter 3.

When we look at the data by individual manufacturing industries and services constituting the average given in Table 8.8, we find considerable differences among them, both in the level of their per capita earnings and in their rate of growth. This is true both for the period 1963-64 to 1971-72 on the old classification, and 1971-72 to 1975-76 for which the classification is different as indicated earlier. Tables 8.9 and 8.10 deal with data for 1963-64 to 1971-72 and 1971-72 to 1975-76 respectively.

Table 8.9 gives the figures of the per capita average daily earnings of the employees by twenty-four sectors of manufacturing industries at current prices and their percentage growth in real terms (as corrected by the all-India consumer price index with base 1960-61 = 100) for the initial and terminal years of the period 1963-64 to 1971-72. They are arranged in ascending order of the per capita earnings at current prices in the initial year.

Table 8.10 contains similar data but includes twenty-seven categories covering the period 1971-72 to 1975-76.

It is seen from Table 8.9 that the per capita earnings per employee in 1963-64 ranged from a low of Rs 3.25 for industries manufacturing wood products to a high of Rs 10.63 for industries manufacturing petroleum and coal products, the range being 3.28. Eleven industries and services were below the overall average (Rs 5.61), while thirteen were above it. The lowest two were the industries manufacturing wood and wood products (Rs 3.25) and food manufacturing industries except beverages (Rs 3.53), while the highest two were the industries manufacturing rubber and products (8.57) and those manufacturing petroleum and coal products (Rs 10.63). In 1971-72, the average per capita daily earnings increased at current prices to Rs 11.36, with twelve industries and services below the average, but the range increased to 3.64. The lowest and highest two positions were held by the same industries which had held them in 1963-64, with the industries manufacturing paper and products joining those below the overall average.

This apparent stability of the employee compensation structure was, however, not seen in terms of the ranking of the different industries and services in their per capita employee earnings during the initial and final years of the period, which is evident from the last column of Table 8.9. This Table also shows that while the overall average per capita earnings had increased by 102.5 per cent during the period at current prices, the real increase was only 15.7 per cent when we convert them into constant prices on the 1963-64 base. When we look at the real increase in per capita earnings of the different industries, we find that eighteen out of the twenty-four have an increase which is below the average, but of these, nine have average per capita daily earnings at current prices per employee above the average in 1963-64, while only nine were among those whose average earnings per employee were below the average in that year. In fact, one industry, whose per capita worker earnings was below the average in 1963-64, had gone above the average in 1971-72. Evidently, there has been some movement within the group towards a reduction in inter-industry differentials during the period.

When we look at Table 8.10 which deals with the period 1971-72 to 1975-76, it is seen that per capita earnings ranged from Rs 5.10 in the manufacture of food products (II) to Rs 16.20 in the manufacture of rubber, plastics, petroleum and coal products, giving a range of 3.18 in 1971-72. The average

Table 8.9

Industry-wise Growth of Real Per Capita Earnings (1963-72)

Industry	1963-64	1971-72	Index of Growth at Current Prices	Index of Real Growth of Per Capita Earnings at 1963-64 Prices	Real Per Capita Earnings (1971-72)	Ranking in Per Capita Earnings (Current)	
						1971-72	1963-64
Wood manufacturing & products	3.25	6.04	185.9	106.2	3.45	1	1
Food manufacturing industries except beverages	3.53	6.64	188.1	107.5	3.79	2	2
Leather & fur products (except foot-wear & apparel)	4.28	7.59	177.3	101.3	4.34	4	3
Non-metallic mineral products	4.31	7.85	182.1	104.1	4.49	5	4
Beverage industries	4.49	9.17	204.2	116.7	5.24	9	5
Personal services	4.60	8.96	194.8	111.3	5.12	7	6
Water & sanitary services	4.65	9.11	195.9	111.9	5.21	8	7
Tobacco	5.14	6.85	133.3	76.2	3.91	3	8
Manufacturing of textiles	5.20	9.79	188.3	106.7	5.59	10	9
Foot-wear & apparel made of textiles	5.28	8.23	155.9	89.1	4.70	6	10

Contd . . .

Table 8.9 Continued

Industry	1963-64	1971-72	Index of Growth at Current Prices	Index of Real Growth of Per Capita Earnings at 1963-64 Prices	Real Per Capita Earnings (1971-72)	Ranking in Per Capita Earnings (Current)	
						1971-72	1963-64
Miscellaneous manufacturing industries	5.46	11.75	215.2	123.0	6.71	13	11
Paper & products	5.67	10.59	186.8	106.7	6.05	11	12
Furniture & furnishing	6.42	13.34	207.8	118.7	7.62	17	13
Printing & publications	6.42	12.93	201.4	115.1	7.39	16	13
Metal products (except machinery & transport equipment)	6.44	11.90	184.8	105.6	6.80	15	14
Recreation services	6.48	10.74	165.7	94.7	6.14	12	15
Machinery except electrical	6.64	13.52	203.6	116.3	7.73	18	16
Basic metal industries	6.91	14.70	212.7	121.5	8.40	21	17
Electrical machinery & appliances	6.92	14.64	211.6	120.9	8.37	20	18
Electricity, gas & water	7.21	11.83	164.1	93.8	6.76	14	19
Transport equipment	7.31	14.49	198.2	113.3	8.28	19	20
Chemicals & products	7.39	14.92	201.9	115.4	8.53	22	21
Rubber & products	8.57	15.46	180.4	103.1	8.83	23	22
Petroleum & coal products	10.63	21.96	206.6	115.4	12.55	24	23
ALL INDUSTRIES	5.61	11.36	202.5	115.7	6.49		

was Rs 11.36; fourteen industries and services were below the average while thirteen were above it. The two lowest were manufacture of food products (II) (Rs 5.10), and wood products, furniture and fixtures (Rs 6.94), while the two highest were rubber, plastics, petroleum and coal products (Rs 16.20) and transport equipment (Rs 15.31). In 1975-76, the average per capita daily earnings had increased to Rs 19.39 at current prices with eighteen industries and services below the average as against fourteen in 1971-72 and nine above it as against thirteen in 1971-72. The range had increased from 3.18 to 3.32. The analysis indicates that there is a tendency towards equalisation in the comparative growth of the twenty-seven industries and services listed in the tables.

Table 8.10 also shows that while the overall average of per capita earnings increased by 70.7 per cent at current prices, the real growth has only been 4.7 per cent, reflecting the impact of severe inflation during this period.

Tables 8.9 and 8.10 show changes in the ranking of the different industries and services in terms of per capita earnings. Thus, of the eleven industries and services below the average in 1963-64, seven improved their rank in 1971-72, while two fell in rank and the remaining two maintained their original position. Of the fourteen categories below the average in 1971-72, six improved their original position, five fell and three retained their original rank. This also confirms the earlier finding of a tendency towards reduction in the inequality in per capita employee earnings between industries throughout the period 1963-64 to 1975-76.

This tentative finding can be checked by the data which is available from *Bulletin No. ISD/8* of 1981-82 released by the Planning Commission on the number of employees, their break up into workers and supervisory, managerial and technical staff, and the per capita earnings for workers and for total employees. These data are available for twenty industries in the factory sector, over the period 1960 to 1977 at current prices. It is possible to compile from these figures the comparative per capita earnings of workers and managerial, technical and supervisory staff (supervisory staff in short) and the changes therein between 1960 and 1977. Table 8.11 gives the per capita earnings of workers and supervisory staff at current prices and their numbers in 1960 and 1977.

It is seen from Table 8.11 that between 1960 and 1977 the total number of employees in the factory sector (covering twenty industries) increased from 2.96 million to 5.86 million or by 97.8 per cent. Of this number, workers other than supervisory, managerial and technical staff numbered 2.63 million in 1960 or 88.8 per cent, while the supervisory staff numbered 0.33 million or 11.2 per cent. By 1977, however, the percentage of workers to total employees fell to 78.4 per cent, while that of the supervisory staff increased to 21.6 per cent. As the supervisory staff have higher per capita earnings than workers, this increase meant that, taking employees in the factory sector as a whole, more of them were now occupying a better per capita earning position. To this extent, there was a diminution in inequality of per capita earnings within the category of employees in the factory sector.

Table 8.10

Industry-wise Growth of Real Per Capita Earnings (1971-72 to 1975-76)

	1971-72	1975-76	Index of Growth at Current Prices	Index of Real Growth of Per Capita Earnings at 1971-72 Prices	Real Per Capita Earnings	Ranking in Per Capita Earnings (Current) 1971-72	Ranking in Per Capita Earnings (Current) 1975-76
Manufacture of food products (II)	5.10	8.22	161.2	98.9	5.04	1	1
Wood & products, furniture & fixtures	6.94	11.33	163.3	100.2	6.95	2	3
Non-metallic mineral products	7.83	14.59	186.3	114.3	8.95	3	9
Manufacture of food products (I)	7.93	13.33	168.1	103.1	8.18	4	6
Storage & warehousing	7.97	13.20	165.6	101.6	8.10	5	5
Leather & fur products	8.09	18.87	233.3	145.6	11.58	6	18
Beverages, tobacco products	8.12	11.20	137.9	84.6	6.87	7	2
Textile products including apparels	8.44	13.63	161.5	99.1	8.36	8	7
Waterworks & supply	8.52	13.02	152.8	93.7	7.99	9	4
Personal services	8.96	13.88	154.9	95.0	8.52	10	8
Jute, hemp & mesta	9.14	16.71	182.8	112.2	10.25	11	11
Cotton textiles	9.96	18.04	181.1	111.1	11.07	12	15
Wool, silk & synthetic fibre	10.16	16.83	165.7	101.7	10.33	13	12
Recreational services	10.74	17.60	163.9	100.6	10.80	14	13
Other manufacturing industries	11.47	21.55	187.9	115.3	13.22	15	20
Gas & steam	11.58	26.20	226.3	138.8	16.07	16	25

Contd . . .

Table 8.10 Continued

	1971-72	1975-76	Index of Growth at Current Prices	Index of Real Growth of Per Capita Earnings at 1971-72 Prices	Real Per Capita Earnings	Ranking in Per Capita Earnings (Current) 1971-72	Ranking in Per Capita Earnings (Current) 1975-76
Electricity	11.84	17.78	150.2	92.2	10.91	17	14
Repair services	11.86	18.67	157.4	96.6	11.45	18	17
Paper & products, printing & publications	11.90	18.34	154.1	94.5	11.25	19	16
Sanitary services	12.24	16.12	131.7	80.8	9.89	20	10
Metal products & parts (except machinery & transport equipment)	12.26	20.34	165.9	101.8	12.48	21	19
Machine tools except electrical machinery	13.55	23.03	170.0	104.3	14.13	22	21
Electrical machinery appliances & parts	14.61	26.23	179.5	110.1	16.09	23	26
Basic metal & alloy industries	14.72	24.96	169.6	104.1	15.31	24	22
Chemicals & products	14.93	25.59	171.4	105.2	15.70	25	24
Transport equipment	15.31	25.23	164.8	101.1	14.48	26	23
Rubber, plastics, petroleum & coal products	16.20	27.30	168.5	103.4	16.75	27	27
ALL INDUSTRIES	11.36	19.39	170.7	104.7	11.90		

There has been an improvement in the position of those who remained in the category of workers whose per capita earnings were less than those of the increased supervisory staff during this period. While the per capita earnings of workers constituted 32.3 per cent of that of the supervisory staff in 1960, it increased to 41.5 per cent in 1977. Thus the 4.59 million workers in the factory sector had comparatively better per capita earnings in 1970 as compared with the earnings of the 2.63 million workers in 1960. Their earning position in relation to the supervisory staff improved as well. At the same time, the number of supervisory staff, whose per capita earnings were higher than that of the workers, increased from 0.33 million in 1960 to 1.27 million in 1977 or by nearly four times. These figures confirm the thesis of a movement towards reduction in inequality in inter-personal per capita earnings in the factory sector.

This thesis, however, does not hold good for the improvement effected in the per capita earnings of non-supervisory workers in all the twenty different industries of the factory sector. While the improvement in respect of per capita earnings of all such workers in the factory sector gave them 41.5 per cent as a percentage of that of the supervisory staff in 1977, workers in six industries had a per capita earning below it. These were chemicals and products, ship-building and repairs, structural clay, spinning and weaving, pulp and paper, and miscellaneous food products. Together, these six industries employed 2.1 million workers, or 45 per cent of the number of workers in 1977. On the other hand, there were six industries whose per capita earnings of workers equalled or exceeded 50 per cent of that of their supervisory staff as against the overall percentage of 41.5. They employed 1.25 million (or 27.2 per cent) of the number of workers in 1977. The industries concerned were iron and steel, electric power and lighting, railroad equipment, repair of motor vehicles, petroleum refineries and tobacco manufacturing. Inter-industry disparity in the percentage of workers' per capita earnings to that of the supervisory staff has diminished, the number below the overall average in 1977 being only six as against nine in 1960 out of the total of twenty, and the percentage of workers being only 45 against 57 in 1960.

As regards the fall in the ratio of workers to supervisory staff and the consequent improvement in the per capita earnings of employees as a whole, the position varied between different industries. While every industry showed a fall in the ratio of workers to supervisory staff from the overall average of 7.92 in 1960 to 3.63 in 1977, fourteen industries showed a ratio below this figure in 1977; the number of workers in these industries was 2.16 million or 53.1 per cent of the total number of workers. The industries whose worker-supervisor ratio was more than the overall average of 3.63 numbered six and accounted for 46.9 per cent of the total workers. The industries falling in this category were repair of motor vehicles, structural clay, spinning and weaving, pulp and paper, miscellaneous food products and tobacco manufacturing. On the whole, the movement in the inter-personal wages of workers and emoluments of supervisory staff and in their numbers, as well as in their inter-industry disparities between them has moved in a socially prog-

Table 8.11

Number and Earnings of Workers and Supervisory Staff at Current Prices

Industry	No. of Workers		No. of Supervisory Staff		Per Capita Wages of Workers	
	1960	1977	1960	1977	1960	1977
Chemicals & products	116984	283382	24533	130934	1436	5787
Cement	22393	35623	5745	10712	1416	6572
Iron & steel	154427	334751	27491	119741	1792	7181
Non-ferrous basic	18431	33677	3970	12972	1584	6687
Electric light & power	36348	450185	14402	177181	1697	5434
Machinery except electric	131497	265354	20672	118569	1332	5751
Manufacturing of electric machinery, etc.	71186	187236	15483	86433	1442	6705
Ship-building & repair	26532	28665	4576	10641	1873	6646
Railroad equipment	145407	95833	17388	29799	1494	7042
Motor vehicles	40447	94763	8365	37999	1598	7170
Repair of motor vehicles	46846	99246	6827	22507	1238	5769
Metal products except machinery equipment	81982	148655	12141	46056	1192	4560
Rubber products	34538	61186	5171	20786	1604	5047
Petroleum refinery	3978	5967	916	3626	3922	16324
Structural clay	55857	78896	5068	12356	776	2387
Spinning, weaving, etc.	1074273	1217565	79347	165047	1423	5378
Pulp, paper & products	43850	89893	7285	21469	1300	4794
Miscellaneous food products	247182	370006	33714	67449	589	1417
Tobacco manufacturing	169048	299932	13049	34103	571	1667
Sugar	108800	411735	25719	136616	940	1668
ALL INDUSTRIES	2630006	4592550	331862	1264996	1284	4749

Table 8.11 (Continued)

Industry	*Per Capita Wages of Supervisory Staff*		*% of Supervisory Staff to Total Employees*		*Ratio of No. of Workers to Supervisory Staff*		*Percentage of Per Capita Earnings of Workers to Supervisory, Staff*	
	1960	*1977*	*1960*	*1977*	*1960*	*1977*	*1960*	*1977*
Chemicals & products	4430	14723	17.34	31.60	4.77	2.16	32.42	39.31
Cement	4139	13826	20.42	23.12	3.90	3.33	34.21	47.53
Iron & steel	5041	13011	15.11	26.35	5.62	2.80	35.55	55.19
Non-ferrous basic	5319	14972	17.72	27.81	4.64	2.60	29.78	44.66
Electric light & power	3780	10890	28.38	28.24	2.52	2.54	44.89	49.90
Machinery except electric	3261	12208	13.58	30.88	6.36	2.24	40.85	47.11
Manufacturing of electric machinery, etc.	3967	15111	17.86	31.58	4.60	2.17	36.35	44.37
Ship-building & repair	5068	20694	14.71	27.07	5.80	2.69	36.96	32.12
Railroad equipment	4031	10499	10.68	23.72	8.36	3.22	37.06	67.07
Motor vehicles	5829	15304	17.14	28.62	4.84	2.49	27.41	46.85
Repair of motor vehicles	2472	9897	12.72	18.49	6.86	4.41	50.08	58.29
Metal products except machinery equipment	3417	10077	12.90	23.65	6.75	3.23	34.88	45.25
Rubber products	6926	12098	13.02	25.36	6.68	2.94	23.16	41.72
Petroleum refinery	21393	29782	18.72	37.80	4.34	1.65	18.33	54.81
Structural clay	2615	6848	8.32	13.54	11.02	6.39	29.67	34.86
Spinning, weaving, etc.	4723	14953	6.88	11.94	13.54	7.38	30.13	35.97
Pulp, paper & products	4325	14167	14.25	19.28	6.02	4.19	30.06	33.84
Miscellaneous food products	2397	5295	12.00	15.42	7.33	5.49	24.57	26.76
Tobacco manufacturing	2385	3273	7.17	10.21	12.95	8.79	23.94	50.93
Sugar	2185	3450	19.12	24.91	4.23	3.01	43.02	48.35
ALL INDUSTRIES	3974	11438	11.20	21.60	7.92	3.63	32.31	41.52

ressive manner towards a reduction in inequality. Whether this also indicates an improvement in working efficiency is a question that cannot be answered without detailed investigation of the relevant data for each industry.

To conclude, while it is not possible to obtain a break up of the entire NDP by factor shares because of the significant category of mixed income of the self-employed, it is possible to do so for about 60 per cent of the NDP, as indicated in Chapter 4. It is found that employee compensation, which includes both wages and salaries, increased its share of factor income identifiable NDP from 62.3 per cent in 1960-61 to 67.8 per cent in 1979-80, and interest from 5.9 to 12.8 per cent. Rent declined from 9.6 to 7.2 per cent and profits from 22.2 to 12.2 per cent. The increase in interest and decline in profits was found to hold not only for the total of identifiable factor incomes in the NDP but also separately for those in the public sector, the incorporated or organised private sector, and the unincorporated or unorganised private sector.

A partial explanation for the fall in profits may be due to low or negative profitability in the public sector. The major reason, however, is the increasing role of loan finance in all economic activity identifiable by factor incomes. This is somewhat disturbing, not only because of the bias it introduces against risk-taking and innovation in development but also because of the adverse pressure from populist agitations and opportunist politics on the ethics of payment of interest and repayment of capital loans.

The study of the changes in factor shares of the NDP identifiable by factor incomes also shows that in the case of agriculture (which excludes the larger contribution to the NDP of mixed income of the self-employed in the agricultural sector) the fall in the employee compensation, rent and interest has been steeper than that in its contribution to the NDP as a whole, while profits have fallen only marginally. This indicates a greater measure of self-managed cultivation as a result of the green revolution. It was also found that the public sector has increased its share of the total of employee compensation during the period from 25.97 to 38.78 per cent, while the private organised sector's share fell from 24.57 to 20.94 per cent and that of the private unorganised sector from 49.46 to 40.28 per cent.

As neutralisation of the rise in the cost of living is bound to be inadequate or negligible in the case of the unorganised private sector, their employees will face more acutely the brunt of inflation; and they constituted the largest section among the employee class in the economy, even in 1979-80. What is significant, however, is that, within the individual sectors, the share of employee compensation is higher in the public sector, less in the organised private sector and least in the unorganised private sector. Within individual sectors by industrial origin of the NDP identifiable by factor incomes, the largest shares were held in 1979-80 by manufacturing (17.87 per cent), agriculture and allied activities (19.49 per cent), public administration (13.06 per cent), other community and personal services (11.35 per cent), trade, hotels and restaurants (8.48 per cent) and transport other than railways and storage (5.75 per cent).

Employee compensation in manufacturing industries and services for the years 1963-64 to 1975-76 on the basis of data available in the *Indian Labour Yearbook* showed a reduction in the inequality in per employee earnings across the industries dealt with during the period. This finding was also confirmed by the data available in the Planning Commission's *Bulletin No. ISD/8* (of 1981-82) on the number of employees and their per capita earnings for twenty industries in the factory sector. The data cover the period 1960 to 1977 and are at current prices. They provide a break up of the employees by workers and supervisory staff. An analysis of the data shows that the percentage of supervisory staff with higher per capita earnings increased over the period from 11.2 to 21.6 per cent, thereby reducing the inequality in the per capita earnings of employees taken as a whole. The data also shows that there was a rise in the per capita earnings of workers as a percentage of that of the supervisory staff (from 32.3 to 41.5 per cent), further reinforcing the thesis of a secular trend towards reduction in inequality in both inter-personal and inter-industry earnings per employee.

Savings 9

The data available on savings have certain limitations. One set of time series is available from the CSO data on national accounts while another is available in RBI reports. Krishnamurthy and Saibaba[1] have pointed out that the net domestic savings rate, according to the RBI data, is generally higher than the savings rate according to the CSO data. Further, the average annual change in the CSO series is about three-quarters of the corresponding change in the RBI series. They also point out that the peaks and troughs of the two series broadly correspond with each other, and the variability of the two series, measured by the average absolute deviation from the trend, is about the same for both. They have confined their analysis to the RBI series and add 'we do not expect the conclusions drawn in this paper to be substantially altered by the use of CSO data'.

As this study is based on national accounts, we have used the CSO data on the subject. Table 9.1 gives the total net savings at current prices and their proportions to the NDP for the period 1950-51 to 1979-80.*

It is evident from Table 9.1 that while there has been a conspicuous rise in the rate of savings as a percentage of the NDP (from 6.82 per cent in 1950-51 to 19.54 per cent in 1979-80), there have been considerable fluctuations in its annual growth. These fluctuations show no correspondence to the annual growth of the NDP. Evidently, there is a time lag between changes in income and savings. However, if one takes the figures of savings and the NDP over five-year periods and the average share of savings in the NDP in these periods, we find a steady increase in the growth rate over the six five-year periods.

Table 9.2 certainly confirms the existence of a secular trend in the growth of the savings rate during the period under review; but the rate of increase is

* We have used the NDP instead of the NNP as is conventional. This is because a break down by sectors is not available for the NNP, while it is for the NDP. Also, the difference between the NDP and NNP is marginal in terms of percentages.

Table 9.1

Net Savings at Current Prices, 1950-80

Year	*Total Savings (in Rs Crores)*	*Total Savings as Per Cent of NDP*	*% Change in Total Savings*	*% Change in NDP*
1950-51	651	6.82	—	—
1951-52	646	6.47	−0.7680	4.6073
1952-53	417	4.24	−35.4489	−1.6016
1953-54	530	5.06	27.0983	6.6124
1954-55	625	6.50	17.9245	−8.3015
1955-56	982	9.84	57.1200	3.8502
1956-57	1113	9.85	13.3401	13.2265
1957-58	834	7.32	−25.0674	0.8850
1958-59	782	6.20	−6.2350	10.7018
1959-60	1104	8.51	41.1765	2.8526
1960-61	1327	9.95	20.1993	2.7350
1961-62	1281	9.12	−3.4665	5.6243
1962-63	1544	10.36	20.5308	5.8076
1963-64	1825	10.68	18.1995	14.6682
1964-65	2023	10.04	10.8493	17.9004
1965-66	2562	12.32	26.6436	3.2410
1966-67	3112	12.92	21.4676	15.7541
1967-68	2939	10.38	−5.5591	17.5845
1968-69	3011	10.43	2.4498	1.9426
1969-70	4129	12.95	37.1305	10.4463
1970-71	4566	13.23	10.5837	8.2881
1971-72	5099	13.83	11.6732	6.7934
1972-73	5100	12.57	0.0196	10.0586
1973-74	8369	16.49	64.0980	25.0838
1974-75	9127	15.28	9.0572	17.7107
1975-76	10800	17.33	18.3302	4.3306
1976-77	13207	19.62	22.2870	8.0098
1977-78	14224	18.67	7.7005	13.1499
1978-79	18035	22.22	26.7927	6.5382
1979-80	17034	19.54	−5.5503	7.4383

Table 9.2

Average Shares in NDP (Percentages)

Period	*Share*
1950-51 to 54-55	5.82
1955-56 to 59-60	8.34
1960-61 to 64-65	10.03
1965-66 to 69-70	11.80
1970-71 to 74-75	14.28
1975-76 to 79-80	19.48

much higher in the last quinquennial period as compared to the earlier ones. This sharp increase in the second half of the seventies is due largely to the increasing quantum of remittances from Indian nationals abroad which has resulted in the growth of bank deposits; and foodgrain procurement and stocking on a large scale by the government, leading to a sharp rise in the amount of currency held in the household sector. Table 9.3 gives the relevant data.

Table 9.3

Foreign Exchange Reserves and Foodgrain Procurement

Year	Foreign Exchange Reserves (Rs Crores)	Foodgrains (in Million Tons)	
		Procurement	Public Distribution
1970-71	438.12	6.71	8.84
1971-72	480.38	8.86	7.82
1972-73	478.90	7.67	10.49
1973-74	580.78	8.42	11.41
1974-75	610.50	5.65	10.79
1975-76	1491.70	9.56	11.25
1976-77	2862.99	12.85	9.17
1977-78	4499.75	9.94	11.74
1978-79	5219.86	11.09	10.18
1979-80	5163.66	13.84	11.66

It is, therefore, an open question as to how far we can take for granted the continuing increase in the rate of savings in the last quinquennial period and the establishment of a trend rate of growth which includes this period.* All the same, that the savings rate increased as a trend during the thirty years of economic development after 1950-51 is a fact which cannot be questioned.

Aggregate savings are drawn from three sources — the public sector, the private corporate sector, and the household sector. Table 9.4 gives the relevant data at current prices for the six quinquennial sub-periods in the period under review.

Of the total savings of Rs 136,998 crores during the whole period, household savings account for Rs 104,483 crores (76.26 per cent). Except for the first and third sub-periods, the quinquennial share has also been of the same order. It appears, therefore, that household savings will stabilise at about 75 per cent of total savings, unless the share of the public sector undergoes a further increase as a matter of policy.

* In this connection, it is of historical interest to note the very optimistic note struck by the then Planning Commission in their *Revised Draft Five Year Plan Report* (1978-1983) issued on 3 December, 1979, stating that 'In fact, our savings rate is comparable to the rate in middle income and even some high income industrialised countries and it is apparent that the country has achieved a high savings rate despite its low per capita income'. They expected the savings rate to increase to 25.8 per cent by 1982-83 and 'by the end of the current plan, it should begin to level off in India'. This was referred to in critical terms by the author in the Zakir Husain Memorial Lectures delivered at Aligarh (reproduced in *EPW*, 31 May, 1980, pp. 965 -77). Subsequently, the savings rates were revised and showed a downward trend.

Table 9.4

Composition of Savings: Quinquennial Averages (in Rs Crores)

Year	*HH Savings*			*Corporate Savings*			*Public Sector*		
	Amount	*% of Total Savings*	*% of NDP*	*Amount*	*% of Total Savings*	*% of NDP*	*Amount*	*% of Total Savings*	*% of NDP*
1950-51 to 54-55	2034	70.90	4.12	227	7.91	0.46	608	21.19	1.23
1955-56 to 59-60	3775	78.40	6.48	288	5.98	0.49	752	15.62	1.29
1960-61 to 64-65	5123	64.04	6.43	647	8.09	0.81	2230	27.88	2.80
1965-66 to 69-70	12732	80.82	9.51	500	3.17	0.37	2521	16.01	1.88
1970-71 to 74-75	24890	77.15	11.19	2014	6.24	0.91	5357	16.61	2.41
1975-76 to 79-80	55929	76.30	14.95	2391	3.26	0.64	14980	20.44	4.00
TOTAL	104483	76.26		6067	4.43		26448	19.31	

The public sector accounts for 19.31 per cent of total savings during the period, and has declined marginally from 21.19 per cent in the first sub-period to 20.44 per cent in the last. The corporate sector's share of the total is 4.43 per cent over the period as a whole, but it has fallen from 7.91 per cent in the first sub-period to 3.26 per cent in the last, and is the declining factor in the savings scene. As a proportion of the NDP, however, both household and public sector savings have shown a more or less steady increase over the different quinquennial periods, the former rising from 4.12 to 14.95 per cent, and the latter from 1.23 to 4.00 per cent. The private corporate sector has also shown an increase from 0.46 to 0.64 per cent, though its share in the total savings has declined between the two sub-periods. On the whole, the growth trend of the total savings as a percentage of the NDP has also been reflected in that of its components, though primarily in the public sector.

The performance of the corporate sector has been disappointing as far as its contribution to raising the Indian savings rate is concerned. Whereas in developed countries the corporate sector contributes significantly to national savings, it has not done so in India, in spite of the developments within the secondary and tertiary sectors of the economy and the significant increase in manufactured output. This is partly due to the massive increase in the use of loan capital in Indian industry and the fall in the share of profits in factor incomes which have been discussed in Chapter 8. It is also due to the continuing and significant position of the unincorporated private sector in Indian manufacturing and commerce, which is reflected in household savings. Another determining factor is our taxation policy which discourages the accumulation of undistributed profits in companies and corporations. Corporate profits, therefore, cannot be regarded as a factor of any significance in the rise that has taken place in the savings rate in India.

The public sector, however, has undoubtedly contributed to the growth of the savings rate in the country. It must be added, however, that this has been due not so much to non-departmental public enterprises as to profits from departmental enterprises and revenue surpluses (see Table 9.5).*

Table 9.5

Public Sector Savings — Annual Averages by Quinquennial Periods

Period	*Administrative Departments (Rs Crores)*	*Non-departmental Enterprises (Rs Crores)*	*Total (Rs Crores)*	*Share of Non-departmental Enterprises*
1950-51 to 54-55	108.2	31.2	139.4	22.38
1955-56 to 59-60	112.2	38.2	150.4	25.40
1960-61 to 64-65	436.6	9.4	446.0	2.11
1965-66 to 69-70	495.8	8.4	504.2	1.67
1970-71 to 74-75	933.4	138.0	1071.4	12.88
1975-76 to 79-80	2574.8	421.2	2996.0	14.06

The largest contributor to savings has been the household sector. Household savings are made up of two broad categories — one relating to financial savings and the other to what the CSO terms 'savings in physical assets'. Table 9.6 gives a break up of household savings for quinquennial periods by financial savings and physical assets.

Table 9.6

Composition of Household Savings

Period	*As Percentage of NDP*			*As Percentage of HH Savings*		
	Financial	*Physical*	*Total*	*Financial*	*Physical*	*Total*
1950-51 to 54-55	1.16	2.96	4.12	28.07	71.93	100.00
1955-56 to 59-60	3.17	3.31	6.48	48.95	51.05	100.00
1960-61 to 64-65	3.65	2.78	6.43	56.63	43.37	100.00
1965-66 to 69-70	3.37	6.14	9.51	35.46	64.54	100.00
1970-71 to 74-75	4.96	6.23	11.19	44.36	55.64	100.00
1975-76 to 79-80	7.48	7.47	14.95	50.05	49.95	100.00

While the data on financial savings are fairly accurate and obtained directly from the sub-sectors to which they pertain, the figure for savings in physical assets is derived from the difference between estimated total capital formation and capital formation in the public and private corporate sectors, obtained directly from the accounts available in these sectors. The figure of total capital formation is derived by the commodity flow approach of goods

* Savings from administrative departments is the difference between the total revenue receipts and income from entrepreneurship and property, and revenue expenditure. Additional taxation is largely responsible for this factor.

and services, and the estimated relations of such commodity inputs to physical capital formation. Savings in physical assets in household savings is thus a figure derived from estimated national capital formation and cannot have the same measure of reliability as financial savings.*

Household savings should obviously be connected with personal disposable income and private final consumption expenditure. Data on both these items are available at current prices in the national accounts for the period under review. There is a secular increase at current prices in the rate of household savings from disposable income which is confirmed if we take three-year periods of disposable income and savings (see Table 9.7).

Table 9.7

Savings and Disposable Income

Period	*Savings*	*Disposable Income*	*Per Cent Difference over Previous Periods*		*Average Rate of Savings from Disposable Income*
			Savings	*Disposable Income*	
1950-52	1151	28305	—	—	4.07
1953-55	1701	29177	47.78	3.08	5.83
1956-58	2092	44220	22.98	51.55	4.73
1959-61	2550	38660	21.89	−12.57	6.60
1962-64	3439	49187	34.86	27.22	6.99
1965-67	6983	70249	103.05	42.82	9.94
1968-70	9288	91410	33.01	30.12	10.16
1971-73	14967	123498	61.14	35.10	12.12
1974-76	24097	181660	61.00	47.10	13.26
1977-79	38216	237768	58.59	30.89	16.07

The average household savings rate has risen from 4.07 per cent in the first sub-period to 16.07 per cent in the last sub-period. But even over three-year periods, the percentage increase in savings does not show any correlation with that of disposable income. The lag relationship between incremental income and savings, therefore, cannot constitute a full explanation of the behaviour of savings over the period. In fact, while the abnormal increase in savings, as compared to the marginal increase in disposable income in the period 1953-55 over 1950-52, can be explained by the fall in the price level and the significant increase in disposable income at constant prices over that at current prices, it is difficult to explain the incremental rise in savings during 1965-67 (which contained two severe drought years) or the sharp fall in this increment during the next three-year period which had two more or less average years but also included one really good year. But if we look at the

* This would apply to actual figures under 'physical assets'. But the figures given in Table 9.6 for both 'physical assets' and 'financial assets' would both have some measure of unreliability as they are calculated on the basis of total household savings which includes physical assets.

average range of savings from disposable income during the successive three-year periods, we find that there was an increase in every period over the previous one (except for one period viz., 1953-55), which definitely supports the thesis of a secular increase in the rate of domestic savings.

The savings behaviour of the household sector seems to suggest several explanations in addition to that of a savings-income lag. It is possible that the period has seen a redistribution of money income in favour of savers as against non-savers. Among savers, it is in favour of those who respond less quickly in increasing their consumer expenditure than those who do, due to the different ways in which they look at incremental income — as being permanent or transitory. Money redistribution is also in favour of the high income groups whose marginal propensity to save is much higher irrespective of whether they regard the increase in income as permanent or transitory. In view of the fact that physical assets are treated as a part of household savings, the increase in the average rate may also be an indication of business-oriented savers putting their savings into physical assets rather than increasing their consumption expenditure. Financial assets are mostly held by the affluent and an increase in household savings in the form of financial assets may be another indication of the increase in money income favouring this class. All these possible explanations seem consistent with observed phenomena, and can give a reasonable explanation of the secular increase that has taken place in the average rate of household savings along with the existence of a large proportion of the population below the poverty line in both rural and urban areas.

Reference has been made in Chapter 2 to rural and urban household savings separately on the basis of estimates made in the RBI bulletins for the period 1950-62, and extrapolation of the same for the subsequent years on the basis of both a constant ratio and regression.

The RBI estimates give rural savings a share of 40.50 per cent of household savings in 1950-57 which goes down to 31.79 per cent in 1962-63. Extrapolation on the basis of constant ratio gives it a share of 31.97 per cent in 1979-80, while on the basis of regression it yields a lower figure of 26.81 per cent. The actual figure probably lies between the two, at about 29 per cent in 1979-80. But in view of the fact that these results are based on extrapolation for a major portion of the period rather than on firm estimates, all that can be said is that the rural share is definitely lower than the urban and that it has been falling during the later years of the period under review. Table 9.8 gives the results of this exercise.

This fall in the rural share of savings is confirmed by our earlier findings on the rise in rural per capita consumption expenditure as a percentage of the urban during this period.

It has been seen from Table 9.6 that the share of financial assets as part of household savings has been steadily increasing from 28.1 per cent in the first quinquennial sub-period to 50.1 per cent during the sixth sub-period. This rise in financial savings is the possible result of three factors. One is the conversion of hoarding in non-currency form, such as gold and jewellery, to

Table 9.8

Rural/Urban Savings, 1950-79 (in Rs Crores)

Year	Constant Ratio			Regression	
	Rural	Urban	Total	Rural	Urban
1950-51	196	288	484		
1951-52	220	139	359		
1952-53	165	143	308		
1953-54	169	249	418		
1954-55	111	355	466		
1955-56	157	660	817		
1956-57	196	681	877		
1957-58	182	451	633		
1958-59	162	420	582		
1959-60	219	647	866		
1960-61	206	695	901		
1961-62	201	582	783		
1962-63	240	755	995		
1963-64	363	774	1137	298	839
1964-65	418	889	1307	332	975
1965-66	598	1273	1871	384	1487
1966-67	832	1772	2604	535	2069
1967-68	832	1770	2602	534	2068
1968-69	810	1725	2535	521	2014
1969-70	1033	2197	3230	663	2567
1970-71	1131	2408	3539	727	2812
1971-72	1295	2756	4051	832	3219
1972-73	1314	2795	4109	844	3265
1973-74	2176	4631	6807	1398	5409
1974-75	2041	4343	6384	1311	5073
1975-76	2544	5416	7960	1633	6327
1976-77	3118	6635	9753	2017	7736
1977-78	3481	7410	10891	2289	8602
1978-79	4539	9659	14198	2838	11360
1979-80	4197	8930	13127	3519	9608

currency and bank deposits because of the growing commercialisation and monetisation of the economy. A second is the result of the increase that has taken place in household income due to economic development and the accompanying distribution and consumption factors referred to earlier. There can also be no doubt that the third, and perhaps the most crucial, factor is the expanded infrastructure of banking and other facilities for financial savings, which must have provided both motivation and access for an increase in the rate of financial savings. The significance of the third factor, especially during the 1970s, which saw a sharp rise in the quantum and share of financial savings in household saving (its compound growth rate from 1970-71 to 1979-80 being 20.02 per cent as against 9.44 per cent during the 1960s), is evident from the massive increase in the number of branch offices opened by banks. In June 1969 the number of branches was only 8,262 while they had gone up to 32,419 in June 1980, or four times, after bank nationalisation.

The number of rural bank offices rose at a faster rate — from 1,833 in June 1969 to 15,105 in June 1980, giving them a share of 46.6 per cent of total banking offices in 1980 as against 22.2 per cent in 1969. It is worth noting that whereas the share of rural branch deposits accounted for 11.9 per cent of all bank deposits in June 1980, their share in the addition of deposits accuring after bank nationalisation was 22.8 per cent. It is also relevant to point out that whereas credit constituted only 54.5 per cent of rural deposits in June 1980, the corresponding figure for non-rural deposits (semi-urban, urban, and metropolitan) was 68.9 per cent, giving the rural sector a larger share of net deposits to gross deposits than the non-rural sector, thus raising the rural percentage of financial savings held in the form of net bank deposits.

There can be no doubt that the aggressive policy of expanding rural bank offices, which followed bank nationalisation, did have a role in increasing the rural rate of financial savings in the form of bank deposits.[2] But the bulk of the increase in financial savings held in net book deposits still remains with the urban sector, which can be inferred from the fact that of the total bank deposits minus credit in June 1980, the share of the rural sector was only 19.8 per cent.

Financial savings are constituted not only of net bank deposits but also of a number of other items. Table 9.9 gives the break up of financial savings of households by quinquennial periods and their percentage share in total household savings.

It is seen from Table 9.9 that there has been a drastic change in the composition of financial savings in the last sub-period as compared to the first. While the share of currency has more than doubled (from 7.17 to 17.74 per cent) and that of net bank deposits increased by about eight times (from 5.42 to 40.69 per cent), that of shares and debentures fell from 28.32 to 3.67 per cent. The net claim on the government also fell from 13.29 to 2.89 per cent as also Life Insurance Funds (which declined from 18.18 to 10.01 per cent)and Provident funds (from 27.62 to 25.00 per cent). While the fall in the share of Provident funds is marginal, that of Life Insurance Funds is nearly half, while the fall in shares and debentures and net claims on the government are drastic, being one-seventh and one-fifth respectively. It is quite clear that, over the years, neither the private corporate sector nor the government have been able directly to channel financial savings into their investments, while it is the banking sector that has been able to secure the major share of the increase in financial savings. Though Life Insurance Funds and Provident funds have been able to obtain 35.01 per cent of the financial savings in the last sub-period (1975-76 to 1979-80), the share of direct mobilisation of financial savings by both the government and the private corporate sector was only 6.56 per cent. The private corporate sector has had access to the financial savings of the household sector via banks and other financial institutions; as also the government through banks, financial institutions and the investments of Life Insurance and Provident funds. Financial mediation has thus

Table 9.9

Financial Savings by Component Items (in Rs Crores)

Period	Currency		Net Deposits		Shares & Debentures		Net Claim on Government		Life Insurance Funds		Provident Funds		Total HH Sector Saving
	Amount	Percentage	Amount	Percentage	Amount	Percentage	Amount	Percentage	Amount	Percentage	Amount	Percentage	Amount
1950-51 to 54-55	41	7.17	31	5.42	162	28.32	76	13.29	104	18.18	158	27.62	572
1955-56 to 59-60	545	29.49	191	10.34	243	13.15	346	18.72	168	9.09	355	19.21	1848
1960-61 to 64-65	760	26.20	555	19.13	407	14.03	35	1.21	363	12.51	781	26.92	2901
1965-66 to 69-70	1145	25.36	1071	23.72	516	11.43	−339	−7.50	621	13.75	1501	33.24	4515
1970-71 to 74-75	2171	19.66	3889	35.23	362	3.28	−112	−1.01	1315	11.91	3415	30.93	11040
1975-76 to 79-80	4966	17.74	11390	40.69	1028	3.67	809	2.89	2803	10.01	6997	25.00	27993

played an essential role in the transfer of household financial savings into investment assets or capital formation. The saving public as such, whose funds are involved, have no direct connection and, therefore, no real interest or monitoring role in the utilisation of their financial savings for investment.

Since statutory obligations determine the investment pattern of the resources of both bank deposits and Provident funds and Insurance funds, it is clear that those who are actually making the financial savings have virtually no control over or say in the investment of their savings. This passive role of the household saver in the investment process has had inevitable effects on the efficiency of the utilisation of savings for the country's economic development. While households contribute directly to financial savings, it is the intermediaries who determine how they are invested; and they are influenced in their choice, either directly or indirectly, by government policy and the needs of public enterprises, or private corporate enterprises.

It is also doubtful if we can regard all financial savings as available for investment. Obviously, part of these savings really represent cash balances rather than savings. As cash balances are expressed in net form, it conceals the magnitude and change in financial transactions represented by borrowing and repayments which would be a significant factor in business transactions. In fact, the problem regarding the behaviour of household savings arises from the fact that households do not represent merely the consuming sector but also include business units in the form of either individual or unincorporated enterprises; and one does not know how far the financial assets given under household savings represent their share.

In this context Gothosker and Venkatachalam[3] have disaggregated the RBI estimates of financial savings for the period 1960-61 to 1975-76 and brought in trade debts and liabilities along with net physical assets for estimating the volume of net household savings. The disaggregated figures of financial assets by what they have called liquid, semi-liquid and ill-liquid assets give an interesting indication of the motivation behind and the real nature of household savings in financial assets. They also give figures of the element of trade debt in these assets and of the liabilities of the households to the banking system, which would mostly concern households engaged in business.

Who are these financial savers? There is no statistical way to answer this question except possibly in regard to Life Insurance and Provident funds. On the fairly reasonable assumption that they come largely from the employee class, both salaried and wage earners, we can say that one reason for their rise in absolute terms at current prices by about seven times over the period 1950-51 to 1979-80 is the large share that employee compensation has in factor incomes and also the rise in their share, as we have seen in Chapter 8. Table 9.10 gives data on the growth of employee compensation and savings in Life Insurance and Provident funds. The figures are given only for the period 1960-61 to 1979-80 due to the non-availability of data on factor incomes prior to 1960-61; and they are at current prices.

Table 9.10

Employee Compensation and Financial Savings in Provident Funds and Life Insurance Funds (in Rs Crores)

Period	Employee Compensation	Provident Funds	Life Insurance Funds	Total	Percentage of Employee Compensation		
					PF	LIC	Total
1960-61 to 64-65	27054	781	363	1144	2.89	1.34	4.23
1965-66 to 69-70	47001	1501	621	2122	3.19	1.32	4.51
1970-71 to 74-75	82792	3415	1315	4730	4.12	1.59	5.71
1975-76 to 79-80	147141	6997	2803	9800	4.76	1.90	6.66
1960-61	4497	126	50	176	2.80	1.11	3.91
1979-80	34988	1694	733	2427	4.84	2.09	6.93

Savings in the form of Provident funds are wholly attributable to the employee class.* They have risen from 2.89 per cent of employee compensation in the first sub-period to 4.76 per cent in the last sub-period, the rise between the initial and final years of the whole period being from 2.80 to 4.84 per cent. This increase is largely due to the extension of the Provident fund facility to a larger section of employees, and partly an increase in the rate of contribution. That a significant proportion of employees still do not have the advantage of this facility is clearly indicated by the fact that the average percentage of Provident fund to employee compensation is only 4.76 per cent (or 4.84 per cent if we take only the final year of the period), whereas the statutory contribution is one month's salary/wages or 8.25 per cent. There is, therefore, considerable scope for increasing the financial savings of households through Provident funds (with a matching contribution from employers) if it is made compulsory for all employees in both the public and private sectors and in the organised as well as unorganised segments of the latter.

As regards financial savings in the form of Life Insurance Funds, it cannot be entirely attributed to employee compensation; a major share must also come from other factor incomes as well as from the mixed income of the self-employed. That the percentage of the Life Insurance Fund to income, even if it is wholly attributed to employee compensation, is as low as 2 per cent is a matter for concern. If the income to which it is attributed covers other factor incomes and the mixed income of the self-employed, it will only form the negligible figure of 0.8 per cent. Here, again, there is great scope for increasing financial savings of households if Life Insurance could be extended to the vast number of income earners who are still not covered by it. Since

* Recently, a general Provident Fund Scheme has been introduced for the non-employee class (or those with fluctuating incomes) but their share in the total of Provident fund savings has been negligible so far.

financial savings in the form of Provident and Life Insurance funds mainly come from the less affluent sections of society, they constitute an ideal means for mobilising small savings and involving a large proportion of the population in the saving process. If some way could be found for establishing an observable and identifiable link between these savings and their investment, a large proportion of the popuiation would also get involved in the developmental process of savings and investment.

As regards savings in the form of physical assets which constitute such a large proportion of household savings, these figures exclude durable consumption goods purchased by households. They include, of course, residential construction, construction connected with use as productive capital, and other fixed capital like machinery and equipment. The data do not give any break up by agricultural and non-agricultural sectors among households nor between residential construction of households and productive physical assets formation, or between rural and urban household enterprises. It is also not possible to desegregate the productive capital of these physical assets between the agricultural households affected by the green revolution and the unincorporated small industries sector in urban areas. All this casts some doubt on the efficacy of basing our planning on such uncertain and mixed data as we have of such savings, and using projections of these figures for the future. All the same, there is no doubt that physical assets do constitute a major form of saving in the household sector and include a significant element in physical capital formation in the agricultural sector and in the unincorporated industrial and tertiary sectors.

It is difficult to reconcile the rising trend in the total savings rate with the continuance of roughly half the population under the poverty line, referred to in Annexure 1.12 to Chapter 1 of the *Sixth Plan Report (1980-85)* issued in 1981. On the basis of the limited analysis made so far of the growth of savings, several explanations can be offered for this paradoxical feature of aggregate savings behaviour in India. These are:

1. The declining share of the primary sector (mainly agriculture) in the NDP is because the marginal propensity to save on the part of the agricultural sector is lower than that of the secondary and tertiary sectors or the non-agricultural sector.
2. An increase in the inequality of income distribution leads to an increase in the share of high income groups with a larger marginal propensity to save than the other income groups.
3. A deliberate attempt on the part of the government to increase savings in the public sector by budgeting for revenue surpluses and profits from public enterprises.
4. The creation of incentives for increasing savings by increasing the return in the form of interest and by tax concessions.
5. An increase in the share of urban areas in the NDP because the propensity to save is higher in urban areas as compared to rural areas. This is linked with factor 1 above.

6. The growth of the corporate sector.
7. The fluctuating character of the annual NDP may also result in some increase in the rate of saving.
8. Whether inflation, which has been a feature of the Indian economy since the mid-sixties, has also helped to raise the rate of saving is a moot point, as it can have both positive and negative effects. On the positive side, towards an increase in saving is the inequality it promotes in income distribution in favour of upper income groups whose propensity to save is higher as also the motivation of the savers in general to keep up their desired or planned rate of savings in real terms. On the negative side is the increase it brings about in the money expenditure on consumption by savers and realisation on their part of the erosion in the real value of savings and fall in the real return received from a given rate of interest.

It would perhaps be correct to conclude that each of these factors contribute to an explanation of the rise in the savings rate in India in spite of its continuing low per capita income.

Savings constitute the base for non-inflationary capital formation, capital formation constituting a critical determinant of economic growth. So, apart from the exercises made on estimates of savings and their projections for the future, what is much more important is to formulate appropriate policies for increasing the rate of savings in the economy. Savings are a function of both income and current consumption. Increasing income and decreasing the proportion of income spent on consumption, are both ways to increase savings. In a country like ours, increasing consumption at certain levels and decreasing consumption at other levels may generate more savings by increasing income and therefore increasing savings.

It must also be remembered that savings involve postponement of current consumption or providing for future consumption or acquisition of durable consumption goods including residential accommodation or meeting other lumpsum liabilities expected to accrue in the future. There is a natural tendency to provide for the future. In regard to household savings, this is adversely affected not so much by a rising price level and a resulting fall in the purchasing power of the currency unit (of course within the limits of tolerance) as by security of the assets, the rate of return, capital appreciation (which is really another form of raising the rate of return), and the ease with which the instrument in which the saving is held can be converted into cash or into immediately usable purchasing power.

Increasing savings means increasing the average rate of saving as well as the marginal rate of saving. The latter need not necessarily mean the transfer of income to those who have a high marginal propensity to save because of their high income. The average rate of saving can be increased by raising the marginal rate of saving by a small measure for a larger number of people as against the smaller number who already have a high marginal rate of saving. To get the latter to increase their saving is not to increase their income but to restrict their expenditure on conspicuous or status consumption. To get the larger number to increase their savings is to increase their income both positively and by stabilising the prices of essential consumption goods, and to motivate them to effect a small rate of increase in their existing nil or low marginal savings. Such an approach would truly be a policy for savings with economic justice.

It is doubtful if the economic policy we are following today is one of savings with economic justice. In fact, it is the absence of this link that is the explanation behind the high rate of savings we are achieving along with the growth of the population below the poverty line. This is why the Planning Commission has been faced with the problem of how a low income country like India is apparently reaching levels of saving which are associated with medium and even some large income industrialised countries. Our apparently high current rates of saving should really make us think again about the savings policy we are pursuing rather than lead us to build an optimistic framework for future economic growth and then use it to deal with the problem of poverty and unequal distribution in India.

The problem with the savings policy in India is not limited to what we are doing to promote household savings. We are placing our trust in the government sector for obtaining the incremental savings required for economic development. In fact, every Planning Commission has placed in the forefront of its saving policy an increase, and a substantial one at that, in savings from the government sector. There may have been some justification for this policy when the rate of savings in the household sector was abysmally low and there was no guarantee that private savings would finance the investment that was necessary to give the country the economic infrastructure it needed for its development. Added to that was the fear that the unrestricted domination of private savings in investment would lead to a worsening of the inequality of incomes and wealth in the country. In actual fact, the savings policy we are following in the private household sector is adding to the inequality of wealth and incomes in the private sector. The policy of relying on the government sector for a crucial increase in savings has been accompanied by a policy of giving the public sector a major role in national investment and an increasing share of the NDP. This has not given the country a high rate of economic growth; nor has it improved the moral standards or enhanced the quality of life of the affluent let alone of the common man.

Our experience in regard to government sector savings should be taken note of here. During the four completed five year plans and the three annual plans between 1951-52 and 1969-74, the amount raised by the government from their own resources amounted only to 40.9 per cent of the plan outlay. Of this amount, the balance from current revenues at pre-plan rates of taxation amounted only to Rs 41 crores as against a projected figure of Rs 4,089 crores. Additional taxation raised Rs 9,389 crores against an estimate of Rs 6,818 crores. The surplus from public undertakings was Rs 2,557 crores against an estimate of Rs 3,688 crores. Deficit financing accounted for Rs 5,162 crores against an estimate of Rs 3,225 crores. External assistance was Rs 8,174 crores against an estimate of Rs 8,570 crores. These figures show that the realised current revenue surplus has fallen tremendously below estimates, and that the realised surplus from public undertakings has fallen significantly compared to the estimates, while deficit financing and additional taxation receipts have increased much above the estimates. It is only external assistance that has more or less retained parity between realised and estimated figures. Evidently, additional taxation and deficit financing have played a significant role in the financing of plan outlays during this period (1951-52 to 1975-76).

In the light of this experience, it is difficult to be optimistic about the Planning Commission's estimate of the budgetary resources of the central and state governments for financing the public sector plan during 1978-83, which was then identified with the Sixth Plan period. Their estimate of the current surplus during the period was Rs 9,038 crores, consisting of Rs 1,918 crores on the central account and Rs 7,120 crores on the state account. Additional tax measures were estimated at Rs 15,664 crores, with the centre's share at Rs 9,850 crores and the states' share at Rs 5,814 crores. While the estimates for the central sector were revised downwards from the first Sixth Draft Plan estimates, those for the states' sector underwent a sharp upward revision of Rs 2,385 crores in their revenue surplus and Rs 1,814 crores in their additional taxation receipts. The contribution from public enterprises (both central and state) was placed at Rs 8,602 crores with a downward revision of Rs 1,694 crores from the draft plan estimates. Deficit financing was placed at Rs 2,961 crores, which meant nil deficit financing for 1980-81 to 1982-83. In addition, prices have risen above the level at which these estimates were projected, with inevitable repercussions on the real cost of projected public sector investments.

While the possibilities of additional tax measures by the centre may be realised, it is very doubtful if the corresponding estimates for the state governments are likely to be. It is also doubtful whether the projected revenue surplus by the centre, and, certainly, by the states will be realised. Further, it was exceedingly unrealistic to think that there will be no deficit financing during 1980-81 to 1982-83. In fact these have all proved to be deficit budget years, with the deficit totalling Rs 1,700 crores in 1980-81, Rs 2,085 crores in 1981-82 and a budgeted deficit of Rs 1,365 crores for 1982-83.

In the light of these facts, it is a pity that the Sixth Plan (covering the period 1980-85) should also have relied to such an extent on public sector savings. The estimated figure is Rs 34,200 crores at 1979-80 prices, giving it a share of 23.8 per cent in the expanded total of domestic savings (Rs 143,647 crores) with budgetary surpluses accounting for 9.0 per cent and public enterprises for 13.9 per cent.

The moral injunctions that the Planning Commission have spelt out for implementing their projections merely reiterate what their predecessors had done. Their actual experience of the fiscal behaviour of both the central and state governments are well known. If the Planning Commission's estimate of budgetary resources for financing the plan fail to materialise, will there be further deficit financing, further additional taxation or further recourse to external assistance and borrowing from Euro-currency markets or will the plan targets again undergo a drastic downward revision? Only the future can give a correct answer.

It is time, therefore, for us to do some re-thinking on the subject and evolve a policy that will increase not only the common man's income but also his saving, thus ensuring a more durable basis for economic growth with social justice. If we have realised that economic growth by itself does not ensure economic justice, we must also understand that savings based either on inequalities of household income or the compulsion of savings through the government sector will not bring about economic justice either, nor perhaps even the desired measure of economic growth itself.

References

1. K. Krishnamurthy and P. Saibaba, 'Savings Behaviour in India,'*Occasional Papers,* New Series 6, Institute of Economic Growth, 1981, pp. 5 & 51-52.
2. *Banking Statistics,* Credit Planning Cell, RBI, June 1980.
3. S.P. Gothoskar and T.R. Venkatachalam, 'Household Saving and Investment in India,' *Margin,* October 1979.

Capital Formation and National Income 10

Capital is considered to be the crucial factor in determining economic growth, even though it is recognised that income generation also depends upon natural resources, human skills and organisational efficiency. The data on capital formation given in the NAS is not based on the functional concept of capital, as it includes residential construction which is a long-term durable consumption good. At the same time, it does not include durable consumption goods other than residential construction belonging to the household sector. Inventories are traditionally included under capital; but their functional role of generating income depends upon their composition by raw materials, semi-finished goods and finished goods, and by producer and consumer goods. Accumulation of inventories may take place on account of simple speculation to guard against a possible rise in the price of inputs or to secure an extra profit from a possible rise in the price of finished products. Details for these items are not available in the NAS.

The NAS gives the sectoral composition of capital formation by construction, machinery (including equipment) and changes in stocks; but construction and changes in stocks do not have the same functional role except where construction work is undertaken on projects like irrigation and roads and bridges, where the act of construction plays the same role as machinery in industrial undertakings. From a functional point of view, capital covers not only fixed capital formation but also working capital, including supplies of wage goods, and production inputs and short-term credit. In addition, while arriving at the net gross capital, there is also the question of gross and net capital formation, including repairs and maintenance (which is treated as current expenditure), and depreciation (which is treated as capital consumption). Further, it is significant that neither intangible non-human capital formation, such as is constituted by research and development expenditure, nor human capital creation in the form of skills and working efficiency by the expenditure incurred on education and health is treated as capital formation by the NAS; these are considered to be consumption expenditures.

The NAS do not give figures of capital stock. Without these data it is not possible to calculate average capital-output ratios. Incremental capital-output ratios do not serve the same purpose, as they do not take into account either past accumulation or differing gestation periods of capital formation given in annual terms. In spite of these limitations, the data on fixed capital formation given in the NAS represent the major production potential in the economy and, as such, constitute a crucial element in the analysis of economic growth as represented by the NDP or other national magnitudes of the output of goods and services.

It goes without saying that, in spite of the use made of capital-output ratios for making projections of future output, the magnitude of capital formation is not the only relevant factor. Apart from the effect on income generation by human capital formation, there are a number of factors which influence the impact of capital formation on the generation of income. Among them are labour inputs; working capital supplies; monetary and fiscal policies and the method of financing adopted for fixed capital formation; the assets in which the fixed capital is formed; its distribution by different management sectors like the public sector, the private corporate sector and households; the gestation periods involved; the degree of utilisation of capital when formed; and the efficiency of utilisation. It is only when the appropriate accompanying conditions are fulfilled that the best results are achieved by a given degree of capital formation. Unfortunately, the Planning Commission reports do not contain the necessary data or analysis that are relevant for judging the efficiency of fixed capital formation on the generation of income and the acceleration of economic growth.

Table 10.1 provides data for the gross domestic capital formation (GDCF) adjusted for errors and omissions at both current and constant (1960-61) prices for six quinquennial sub-periods over the period 1950-51 to 1979-80. The figures given are both actuals and in index form with 1960-61 = 100.

Table 10.1

GDP and GDCF at Current and Constant Prices (in Rs Crores)

Period	*GDP at Factor Cost*		*G D C F*		*GDCF Index Actuals: 1950 = 100*		*Rate of Increase over Previous Period of GDCF*		*Difference Between Rate of Increase of GDCF at Current over Constant Prices*
	Current	*1960-61 Prices*	*Current*	*1960-61 Prices*	*Current*	*Constant*	*Current*	*Constant*	
1950-54	10275	10253	979	1283	112	100	—	—	—
1955-59	12207	12290	1810	2099	209	158	84.9	63.6	21.3
1960-64	16831	15296	2980	2749	392	241	64.6	31.0	33.6
1965-69	28484	17690	5312	3696	659	300	78.3	34.4	43.9
1970-74	47255	20784	9662	4635	1395	368	81.9	25.4	56.5
1975-79	80050	25258	19422	5932	2547	473	101.1	28.0	73.1

The GDCF has increased at a faster rate than the GDF at both current and constant prices. The increase of the latter at constant prices is only 373 per cent, while at current prices it is 2447 per cent. It is the former that represents the real increase in capital formation.

In fact, columns 8 and 9 of Table 10.1 show that except during the first decade — which was, as pointed out in Chapter 3, a non-inflationary period — there is an increasing difference in the rates of growth of the GDCF over successive five-year periods at current and constant prices. The ever increasing expenditure which the economy has been incurring and the continuous rise in the rate of growth of the GDCF over successive five-year periods in the last two decades has been accompanied by a progressively smaller increase in real capital formation. Inflation has brought down the rate of growth in the country's real capital formation.

The role of capital in the generation of income (subject of course to the role played by other factors) is determined by capital stock. The NAS gives figures of annual additions to the capital stock from 1950-51 onwards but does not give an estimate of the initial capital stock in that year. Thus, with the statistics given by the NAS, only incremental capital-output ratios can be calculated for assessing the role played by capital in the growth of the NDP between 1950 and 1980. However, such a ratio does not serve the same purpose as the average capital-output ratio does, because it does not take into account either the differing gestation periods of additions nor the accumulated influence of capital stock. A number of estimates of capital stock for different years have been made by individual researchers. The estimates used in this study are the ones made by Uma Roy Choudhury for 1950-51.[1] The stock figures given by her have been used to generate annual estimates for the intervening years by using the CSO figures of annual additions.

Table 10.2 provides figures of gross capital stocks, annual gross increments to capital, GDP, and annual average and incremental capital-output ratios. The figures are at 1960-61 prices and represent, therefore, the relation between the growth of real capital and real output.

The annual figures of both GDP and incremental capital as well as the average and incremental capital ratios show wide fluctuations. These fluctuations are obviously due to various factors — such as, the influence of the monsoon on agricultural output (which forms a significant portion of the GDP); the extent of utilisation of the capacity of capital stock which varies from year to year; and the varying composition of capital stock, especially incremental capital, in terms of its ability to generate output and the varying periods for doing so. It is difficult, therefore, to trace a secular pattern in the average and incremental capital-output ratios through the annual figures. However, if we take five-yearly averages of these ratios, we can find a definite trend of change, as can be seen from Table 10.3.

While the incremental capital-output ratio shows fluctuations even in terms of quinquennial averages and seems to have improved during 1975-79, the average capital-output ratio shows a steady increase, the increase being

Table 10.2

Growth of Real GDP and GDCF (in Rs Crores)

Year	*Gross Capital Stock*	*Annual Addition to Gross Capital Stock*	*Gross Domestic Product*	*Capital-Output Ratio*	
				Average	*Incremental*
1950-51	24071	1328	9191	—	—
1951-52	25620	1549	9784	2.46	8.00
1952-53	26640	1020	10108	2.53	3.15
1953-54	27830	1190	10730	2.48	1.91
1954-55	29158	1328	11053	2.52	4.11
1955-56	31022	1864	11433	2.55	4.91
1956-57	33414	2392	12066	2.57	3.78
1957-58	35661	2247	11908	2.81	−14.22
1958-59	37562	1901	12881	2.77	1.95
1959-60	39654	2092	13160	2.85	7.50
1960-61	42198	2544	14071	2.82	2.79
1961-62	44547	2349	14609	2.89	4.37
1962-63	47279	2732	14990	2.97	7.17
1963-64	50194	2915	15797	2.99	3.61
1964-65	53400	3206	17013	2.95	2.64
1965-66	56937	3537	16265	3.28	−4.73
1966-67	60847	3910	16472	3.46	18.89
1967-68	64487	3640	17821	3.41	2.70
1968-69	67901	3414	18357	3.51	6.37
1969-70	71881	3980	19536	3.48	3.38
1970-71	76136	4255	20244	3.55	6.01
1971-72	80613	4477	20562	3.70	14.08
1972-73	84795	4182	20340	3.96	−18.84
1973-74	90172	5377	21296	3.98	5.62
1974-75	95058	4886	21480	4.20	26.55
1975-76	100103	5045	23510	4.04	2.49
1976-77	105530	5427	23811	4.20	18.03
1977-78	111258	5728	25870	4.08	2.78
1978-79	118437	7179	27225	4.09	5.30
1979-80	124718	6281	25872	4.58	−4.64

Table 10.3

Average and Incremental Capital-Output Ratios (5 Yearly Averages) at Constant Prices

Period	*Average Capital-Output Ratio*	*Incremental Capital-Output Ratio*
1950-54	2.50	3.51
1955-59	2.71	4.85
1960-64	2.92	3.28
1965-69	3.43	5.41
1970-74	3.88	11.48
1975-79	4.20	6.42

sharper during the latter half of the period under review.

Turning to the use-wise and industry-wise distribution of the GDCF during the period, it is to be noted that the data are not corrected for errors and omissions. Current prices have been used as they give a better picture of the distributional pattern; constant prices have the problem that the rate of deflation of the different components are not comparable. The relevant figures are given in Table 10.4 for quinquennial periods.

Table 10.4

GDCF by Type of Assets at Current Prices (Rs Crores) (Annual Averages)

Period	*Construction*	*Machinery*	*Changes in Stocks*	*Total GDCF*	*Percentage of GDCF*		
					Construction	*Machinery*	*Changes in Stocks*
1950-51 to 54-55	667	279	74	1020	65.39	27.35	7.26
1955-56 to 59-60	1017	617	185	1819	55.91	33.92	10.17
1960-61 to 64-65	1630	1178	375	3183	51.21	37.01	11.78
1965-66 to 69-70	3039	1979	475	5493	55.32	36.03	8.65
1970-71 to 74-75	4724	3557	1756	10037	47.07	35.44	17.49
1975-76 to 79-80	9394	7682	2940	20016	46.93	38.38	14.69

It is seen from Table 10.4 that machinery and equipment increased the most, followed by stocks and construction. The increase in machinery and equipment should have led to an increase in the productivity of incremental capital. The increase in stocks does not have the same functional role and its increase, therefore, may not have led to a significant increase in the productivity of capital. The fall in the percentage of construction should normally lead to an increase in the productivity of capital. On balance, therefore, there should have been some increase in incremental capital productivity, but this has not happened except during 1975-79 which has had some exceptionally good agricultural years as well as a low rate of inflation. Obviously the explanation lies in longer gestation periods for incremental capital and under-utilisation of capital brought into productive use. Both these explanations also fit the observed phenomena on the subject.

Regarding distribution of the GDCF by management, that is, between the public and private sectors, Table 10.5 provides figures for quinquennial periods. Table 10.5 shows that the public sector has increased its share quite significantly in the incremental gross capital formation. To the extent that the public sector management is less efficient than private sector management could be one of the reasons for the increase in the incremental capital-output ratio during the period.

The variation in the distribution by assets in capital formation between the public and private sectors could also provide some explanation for the rise in the capital-output ratio because of the differences in the productivity of the

Table 10.5

Distribution of GDCF Between Public and Private Sectors at Current Prices
(Rs Crores)

Period	Public	Private	Total	Share of Public Sector
1950-54	309	711	1020	30.29
1955-59	743	1077	1820	40.82
1960-64	1473	1710	3183	46.28
1965-69	2222	3272	5494	40.44
1970-74	4035	6003	10037	40.20
1975-79	9039	10977	20016	45.16

different types of assets, and the differences in the asset composition of capital formation between the public and private sectors. Table 10.6 consists of data compiled from the CSO white papers on national accounts which are at current prices.

Table 10.6 shows that the GDCF provided by construction activity has gone up faster in the public sector than in the private sector. To this extent, it may partially account for the rise in the incremental capital-output ratio. Construction in the public sector is generally more expensive, leakages are greater and not all construction is for productive purposes. Construction in irrigation helps in adding to the national agricultural output, but this is subject to the hazards of the monsoon. Moreover, irrigation projects have a long

Table 10.6

Composition of Public and Private Sector GDCF by Assets

Period	Construction		Machinery		Stocks	
	Public	Private	Public	Private	Public	Private
1950-54	235 (23.04)	433	63 (6.18)	216	11 (1.08)	62
1955-59	488 (26.81)	529	187 (10.27)	430	68 (3.74)	118
1960-64	946 (29.72)	684	426 (13.38)	752	101 (3.17)	274
1965-69	1348 (24.54)	1691	734 (13.36)	1246	140 (2.55)	335
1970-74	2191 (21.83)	2534	1256 (12.52)	2303	588 (5.86)	1162
1975-79	4411 (22.04)	4983	3374 (16.86)	4308	1254 (6.26)	1686

Note: Figures given in brackets are percentage shares of the public sector GDCF in the total GDCF.

gestation period and suffer from a considerable degree of under-utilisation. Roads and bridges do increase the income generating capacity of many sectors of industrial origin but do not give a direct return in terms of output.

The high rate of growth of stocks in the public sector's GDCF can also be a reason for the rise in the incremental capital-output ratio, not only because stocks do not have the same functional role as other components of capital, but also because their accumulation is determined more by national security and public policy than by economic returns. It is true that the crucial area of machinery and equipment has increased faster in the public sector, but the base from which it started was small and the rise that took place was higher during the last three sub-periods than in the earlier three. Moreover, the machinery and equipment used in the public sector has a longer gestation period, since it is concentrated in the fields of heavy and basic industries and in providing the infrastructure for transport and power. In addition, considerations of public policy governing welfare facilities as a model employer increase the unit costs of operation, while controlled prices come in the way of the public sector's ability to secure a better return. It is, therefore, clear that the higher growth of the GDCF in the public sector has contributed to the increase in the incremental capital-output ratio seen over the period.

It is interesting to note that the sectors in which investment has increased its share in the total are manufacturing, mining, construction and electricity, while the sectors in which they have fallen are real estate, agriculture, railways and public administration. In other sectors, the changes over the period are fairly marginal (see Table 10.7).

Table 10.7

Distribution of the GDCF at Current Prices

Industry	*1950-54*	*1955-59*	*1960-64*	*1965-69*	*1970-74*	*1975-79*
Agriculture	25.36	19.17	15.17	16.66	19.23	17.23
Forestry	0.16	0.26	0.32	0.29	0.29	0.34
Fishing	0.56	0.76	0.46	0.69	0.57	0.56
Mining & quarrying	1.19	0.59	2.14	1.66	1.95	3.84
Registered manufacturing	13.82	19.09	23.16	21.96	20.66	18.85
Unregistered manufacturing	1.85	2.26	2.56	5.11	8.18	6.94
Construction	1.40	2.35	3.00	2.56	1.77	1.90
Electricity	3.57	5.40	8.65	8.15	7.60	10.05
Railways	6.95	10.78	9.57	4.55	3.26	2.30
Other transport	4.42	4.86	6.11	5.89	6.97	5.70
Communication	0.95	0.71	1.04	0.98	1.12	1.29
Trade, hotels, etc.	5.83	4.29	3.27	3.40	7.95	8.63
Banking & insurance	0.36	0.31	0.33	0.43	0.45	0.54
Real estate	23.70	16.18	10.90	18.31	12.73	12.28
Public administration	7.55	10.28	10.50	6.87	7.74	5.85
Other services	2.33	2.71	2.82	2.49	1.53	1.70
TOTAL	100.00	100.00	100.00	100.00	100.00	100.00

The average industry-wise capital-output ratios can be determined by taking the distribution of the capital stock in 1950-51 by industrial origin given by Uma Roy Choudhury (*op. cit.*) and adding to it the annual increase by industrial origin given in the CSO *White Paper*. Table 10.8 lists the relevant figures only for the base years of the three decades under review and the final year in the third decade.

Table 10.8

Average Capital-Output Ratio at 1960-61 Prices

Sector	*1951-52*	*1961-62*	*1971-72*	*1979-80*
Agriculture	1.27	1.49	1.85	2.70
Mining & quarrying	1.62	2.07	4.06	7.51
Registered manufacturing	3.22	4.20	5.96	7.01
Unregistered manufacturing	1.85	1.56	2.37	3.53
Electricity	9.47	12.34	15.15	17.90
Railways	10.37	11.46	12.71	12.16
Other transport	6.21	5.92	7.07	7.23
Communication	3.22	3.63	4.45	5.46
Trade, hotels, etc.	2.51	2.08	1.87	2.70
Banking & insurance	1.03	0.77	0.76	0.77
Public administration	2.32	4.41	4.20	3.75
Real estate	16.08	17.79	16.88	18.62
Other services	—	0.90	2.71	2.33
TOTAL	2.46	2.89	3.70	4.58

It is interesting to note that the lowest capital-output ratios are found in agriculture, banking and insurance, and trade (including hotels and restaurants), while the highest capital-output ratios are in real estate, electricity, railways, other transport, mining and quarrying and registered manufacturing. All except real estate fall under the category of infrastructural facilities. The high capital-output ratio of real estate is explained by the restrictions on rent which limit returns, and the high cost of building materials which often have to be bought in the black market.

Of the other two components of the infrastructure — namely, communications and public administration — the former has a fairly high capital-output ratio, which is above the total capital-output ratio, while the latter does not show any specific tendency. Registered manufacturing also has a ratio which is higher than the average. Unregistered manufacturing has, on an average, less than half the capital-output ratio of the registered manufacturing sector and is well below the total capital-output ratio. Curiously, mining which also had a low capital-output ratio in 1951 and 1961, underwent a sharp increase from 2.07 in 1961-62 to 4.06 in 1971-72 and then to 7.51 in 1979-80, thus exceeding the capital-output ratio of registered manufacturing in the final year. Banking and insurance, on the other hand, has had no increase in its capital-output ratio, which is also the lowest among all the sectors of industrial origin. Also, the sectors with the lowest capital-output ratios have shown the lowest increase during the period, except unregistered manufacturing which has doubled its capital-output ratio. It is also worth noting that those sectors which are labour intensive have a lower capital-output ratio than those which are capital intensive. It may be rash to draw policy conclusions regarding investment policy from this analysis, but it does appear that a part of the explanation for the rise in the incremental capital-output ratio during the period may be the larger investments of incremental capital in sectors with a lower productivity of capital in terms of output.

The change that has taken place in the capital-output ratio in the factory sector under registered manufacturing is seen from the data given in the ISD Bulletin No. 8 referred to earlier. The ratio of gross value added at constant prices (base 1960 = 100) divided by fixed capital at constant prices and converted into indices for the different industrial groups in the factory sector is given in Table 10.9.

Table 10.9

Index of Capital-Output Ratio in the Factory Sector

Industries	*1960*	*1977*
Chemicals & chemical production	100	63
Cement	100	171
Iron & steel	100	69
Non-ferrous basic metals	100	18
Electric light & power	100	64
Machinery except electric	100	107
Electrical machinery & appliances	100	115
Ship-building & repairing	100	29
Railroad equipment	100	155
Motor vehicles	100	116
Repair of motor vehicles	100	183
Metal production except mechanical equipment	100	91
Rubber products	100	56
Petroleum refineries	100	127
Structural clay products	100	184
Spinning & weaving	100	96
Pulp, paper & products	100	144
Miscellaneous food products	100	110
Tobacco products	100	73
Sugar	100	64

Ten of the twenty industrial groups show a fall in the ratio of gross value added divided by fixed capital between the initial and final years of the period for which data are available. The fixed capital in 1960, that added between 1960 and 1977, and the fixed capital in 1977 are listed separately for these two categories of industries in the factory sector (see Table 10.10).

The second group, where the component industries have shown a rise in the capital-output ratio, accounts for about 87 per cent of the additional fixed capital formation during the period, and 86 per cent of the total fixed capital

Table 10.10

Fixed Capital in the Factory Sector

Industry	*Fixed Capital in Rs Lakhs*			*Percentage to Total*		
	1960	*1977*	*Addition over 1960-77*	*1960*	*1977*	*Addition over 1960-77*
Group I						
Cement	5226	19911	14685	4.01	1.11	0.88
Machinery except electric	4493	62514	58021	3.44	3.47	3.47
Electrical machinery	3559	49884	46325	2.73	2.77	2.77
Railroad equipment	4812	8016	3204	3.69	0.45	0.19
Motor vehicles	2994	25690	22696	2.30	1.43	1.36
Repairs to motor vehicles	1203	5806	4603	0.92	0.32	0.28
Petroleum refineries	4161	22330	18169	3.19	1.24	1.09
Pulp & paper	5014	35286	30272	3.84	1.96	1.81
Structural clay	1998	5384	3386	1.53	0.30	0.20
Miscellaneous food products	7992	20039	12047	6.13	1.11	0.72
TOTAL	41452	254860	213408	31.78	14.16	12.77
Group II						
Chemicals & products	11817	219652	207835	9.06	12.19	12.44
Iron & steel	21352	237435	216083	16.37	13.18	12.93
Non-ferrous basic metals	1727	41112	39385	1.32	2.28	2.36
Electric light & power	19192	849525	830333	14.71	47.16	49.69
Ship-building & repairing	709	12168	11459	0.54	0.68	0.69
Metal production except mechanical equipment	2548	17801	15253	1.95	0.99	0.91
Rubber products	1674	15787	14113	1.28	0.88	0.84
Spinning & weaving	22359	104275	81916	17.14	5.79	4.90
Tobacco products	808	3605	2797	0.62	0.20	0.17
Sugar	6789	45078	38289	5.21	2.50	2.30
TOTAL	88975	1546438	1457463	68.22	85.85	87.23
GRAND TOTAL	130427	1801298	1670871	100.00	100.00	100.00

stock in 1977 as compared to 68 per cent in 1960. It is also worth noting that the two industrial groups in the factory sector — chemicals and electric light and power — which have shown a sharp increase in their capital-output ratio, between them account for more than 62 per cent of the total additional capital formation during the period, and for nearly 60 per cent of the fixed capital stock in 1977. This obviously has an effect on the increase in the overall average and incremental capital-output ratios in the economy during the period.

This thesis is also supported by the pattern of investment during the period taken in conjunction with the percentage of increase in the GDCF in the period as a whole, the inverse of which is a possible indicator of the productivity of the incremental capital of the different industrial sectors over the period as a whole. If we examine the percentage difference in the GDCF and the GDP in terms of constant prices, by the different sectors of industrial origin, taking the total of the GDP and GDCF increments over the entire period of thirty years, we get the data in Table 10.11.

Table 10.11

Sector-wise Distribution of the GDCF and the GDP

Sector	*Percentage of GDCF*	*Percentage of GDP*
Agriculture	17.77	20.80
Forestry & logging	0.40	0.72
Fishing	0.34	0.55
Mining & quarrying	4.50	1.43
Registered manufacturing	25.36	14.97
Unregistered manufacturing	7.47	7.05
Construction	2.22	4.58
Electricity	13.93	2.63
Railways	2.32	2.42
Other transport	6.52	5.08
Communication	1.47	1.12
Trade, hotels, etc.	5.27	13.58
Banking & insurance	0.59	3.20
Real estate	3.59	3.94
Public administration	6.72	11.07
Other services	1.53	6.86
TOTAL	100.00	100.00

It is clear from our analysis that the policy we have followed for capital formation during this period, from the point of view of maximising productivity and the impact on growth, has been erroneous. The correct policy would be a detailed examination of capital formation by asset distribution, industrial sectors and management patterns; average incremental relations to output; the factors responsible for differences in total returns, both avoidable and unavoidable in technical terms; the extent to which marginal equality of return to capital in terms of the national product can be achieved in its different uses in a mixed economy like ours; and the role played by social and other policy objectives in diluting this classical economic objective.

It is important to note that this sombre thesis of increasing capital-output ratios leading to a reduction in the effectiveness of additional capital formation may be incorrect in view of certain considerations affecting the quantum of both the GDCF and the GDP between 1950-80, which have not been discussed so far. What goes against the thesis of the increasing capital-output ratio is the phenomenon of undeclared output which is not covered by the CSO figures of NDP growth. On the other hand, capital consumption is not fully covered by the depreciation figures given in the national accounts, as they do not include obsolescence, are based on historical costs and do not take into account the destruction of physical capital caused by natural disasters like cyclones, storms, earthquakes and floods and the fall-out they cause in the efficiency of some of the physical capital located in other areas. It requires a great deal of concerted study and the use of unpublished data before one can arrive at any statistical formulations of their magnitudes and the difference it would make to the capital-output ratios based on national accounts data.

What can be positively said is that the money values of capital formation, whether at current or constant prices, do not bring out the differential effect of the relative prices of capital goods and output in general on the capital-output ratio. In particular, during the later part of the period under review, this differential effect results in over-estimation of capital formation and, therefore, tends to exaggerate the magnitude of the capital-output ratio. The omission from capital formation of capital destruction due to natural factors also tends to exaggerate the capital-output ratio. The known presence of a significant degree of under-utilisation of created capital capacity and unrecorded increases in output would also tend to make for over-estimation in the currently used figures of capital-output ratio, which do not take this factor into account when quantifying the capital figures used for working out this ratio.

An acceptance of the validity of these four factors leads to the realisation that the rate of growth of capital formation, as seen through the national accounts data, tends to be an over-estimate. This would in turn imply that the weight of these factors would be in the direction of bringing in an element of over-estimation in the capital-output ratio based on this data. This conclusion would, however, be valid only on a macro basis or with reference to national aggregates. The fact that capital-output ratios have been rising even in individual sub-sectors of the manufacturing sector definitely supports the thesis advanced here of a secular rise in the capital-output ratio in the Indian economy. On the whole, there can be no doubt that the capital-output ratio has been rising, especially in the latter half of this period, though the extent of the rise may not be as much as implied by the use of capital and output data which exclude the factors mentioned above.

It has been indicated earlier that real tangible capital alone does not determine economic growth or lead to an increase in national income and productivity. There are other determinants of economic growth which have to be taken into account and which perhaps play a larger role in effecting increases in the national output of goods and services in a country like India. The most important of these is human capital formation. Capital, natural resources, labour, and management conjointly determine production; and of these labour is the most important. Labour becomes productive only when it is treated as human capital and all possible measures are taken to improve its productivity and to maintain the increase. This is why so many economists (beginning with Theodore Schultz and going on to John Kendrick) have emphasised human capital as a major instrument of economic growth. Schultz and Blaugh have placed stress on education; Shuz Mushkin on health; and Kendrick the cost of rearing children, creating internal migration facilities for enabling labour to find its most productive outlets, and research and development expenditure, besides covering the whole subject of investment in human capital and its role in production. Machlup has gone even further and has included 'intellectual' and 'spiritual' knowledge among the components of human capital creation.

There is a vast corpus of recent literature on human capital, but it has still to be accepted by both traditional and modern economists dealing with economic growth. As the constituents of human capital also contribute to human happiness, human capital contributes both to economic growth and human welfare, unlike non-human or physical capital which does not necessarily do both. Because of the dual purpose it serves, expenditure on human capital does not find a place in the data on capital formation in the national accounts; and because of the many intangible and non-quantifiable elements that go into human capital creation, even the literature on human capital does not cover all its manifold aspects. Nevertheless, human capital is as, if not more, important than physical capital; and it has to be given due weight in any analysis of capital formation and economic growth or national income. In a country like India, where labour constitutes the dominant element among the factors of production and there is scarcity of capital, human capital becomes even more significant in analysing economic growth.

Education and health are the most important components of human capital creation in terms of skills and physical efficiency. Expenditure on education and health is incurred from current revenues by central and state governments and from private final consumption expenditure by the private sector. Table 10.12 provides data for 1960-61 and 1979-80 at current prices along with figures for net domestic capital formation, adjusted for errors and omissions, also at current prices.

It will be seen that expenditure on education and health, or human capital creation expenditure, is roughly half of that incurred on non-human net domestic capital formation. Both the government and private sectors have stepped up their expenditure on human capital formation. In fact, it has increased 9.58 times, while the NDCF has increased 9.68 times. The government sector's expenditure has increased 12.08 times, while that of the private sector has increased 7.72 times. The government's share in the expenditure has increased 1.26 times; and government expenditure has increased from 42.78 per cent in 1960-61 to 53.92 per cent in 1979-80; while that of the private sector has gone down from 57.22 per cent to 46.08 per cent. Expenditure on education in the government sector also includes expenditure on scientific research.

The increase in the expenditure on education and health, which is about half of that incurred on adding to the NDCF, should have led to a reduction in the capital-output ratio and helped the productivity of both capital and labour to grow significantly. However, this has not happened. Part of the

Table 10.12

Expenditure on Education and Health at Current Prices
(Rs Crores)

Sector	1960-61 Education	Health	Total	NDCF
Centre	64.54	13.67	78.21	—
State	195.39	80.84	276.23	—
Total government	259.93	94.51	354.44	—
Private	269.00	205.00	474.00	—
GRAND TOTAL	528.93	299.51	828.44	1808.00
TOTAL CAPITAL FORMATION	—	—	—	2636.44
Sector	**1979-80 Education**	**Health**	**Total**	**NDCF**
Centre	450.6	83.5	534.1	—
State	2575.7	1171.6	3747.3	—
Total government	3026.3	1255.1	4281.4	—
Private	2092.0	1567.0	3659.0	—
GRAND TOTAL	5118.3	2822.1	7940.4	17495.0
TOTAL CAPITAL FORMATION				25435.4

explanation may lie in the inadequacy of this expenditure in terms of its volume; but more important is the inefficient management of this expenditure. Even more than the inefficiency accompanying the investment pattern of the NDCF and its utilisation is the pattern of the expenditure on education. The maldistribution of expenditure between primary, secondary and higher education, between general and vocational education, and between formal and non-formal education has led to a colossal wastage in terms of expected results, and made education perhaps the most unprofitable of all the sectors of industrial origin in the economy in relation to the investment made in it.

Primary education — which has a large share of the education expenditure, and which is all the education that the bulk of the children in the country get — has little relevance to the attitudes, skills or environmental knowledge required for development. This is particularly true of rural India.[2] The wastage and stagnation between those who enrol and those who complete their primary education is quite staggering and there is a drop-out rate of nearly 50 per cent. If we take into consideration that those who dropout never achieve literacy and that a large proportion of even those who have had four years of primary schooling do not retain their literacy skills for long, then education would have earned the epithet of a 'sick industry' if it was treated as an industry and was expected to achieve minimum norms of output and minimum returns on investment. Since education is not treated as an industry and the investment made in education is treated as consumption and not capital formation (human capital), this industry continues to remain sick and unable to make its expected contribution to national domestic productivity.

What is true of primary education is equally applicable to secondary and higher education. Many individuals who have completed secondary and higher education have obtained sizeable returns on the investment they have made in their education, but they constitute a minor portion of the total. Wastage, stagnation, detentions and failures are conspicuous at both these levels of education. Many of those who have completed their education do not find any productive outlet for the skills or training they have acquired, and join the ranks of the unemployed, making the products of higher education perhaps the most conspicuous example of under-utilised or unutilised productive capacity in the economy.

The number of educated applicants on the live register of employment exchanges has increased from 0.6 million in December 1961 to 7.7 million in June 1980, and their share in the total number of such applicants, including the uneducated, has gone up from 32.2 to 50.5 per cent.[3] Of this number, those who have matriculated increased from 0.464 million to 4.222 million (or nearly nine times), those with undergraduate qualifications from 70,000 to 1,982 million (or more than twenty-eight times), and those with a Masters degree or higher qualifications from 56,000 to 1,458 million (or twenty-six times). These figures are appalling. Even if 50 per cent of those registering themselves as job-seekers are already employed and are only seeking to better their current employment prospects, and even if a part of the increase is only statistical on account of the increase in the number of employment exchanges and in the tendency to enrol on the register of live applicants, the magnitude of the figures and their rapid growth over the years show how a large proportion of the investment made in secondary and higher education is unfruitful.

It is only investment in professional and technical education that has paid dividends in terms of its contribution to the increase in national output, but even here supply exceeds effective demand, and exports, or 'brain drain' as it is more popularly called, has become an increasingly acute problem in India. It is true that the country's foreign exchange resources are benefiting by the fact that technical and professional education is becoming an export industry, but against this is the loss sustained by the national economy and the growth of its domestic output on account of defects in planning, recruitment policies, bureaucratic hurdles and the stagnant social, political and cultural climate in the country. It is also doubtful if education has contributed to a betterment of the country's social and cultural climate if one takes into account the increasing state of discontent, agitation, violence and the deteriorating law and order situation in the country during the later years of the period under review. Altogether, education has failed to play its expected role in human capital formation and to increase national domestic output or even to bring about a better social and ethical climate in the country.

There has also been sizeable expenditure on health and family welfare, the total — including both the public and private sector — having increased from Rs 300 crores in 1960-61 to Rs 2,822 in 1979-80, or by more than 9.4 times at current prices. The share of the public sector has gone up from 31.6 per cent in 1960-61 to 44.5 per cent, the bulk of the increase being accounted for by family welfare (or, as it was earlier termed, family planning). While the increased expenditure on health has helped in reducing mortality rates and increasing longevity, physical efficiency in terms of good health and nutritional intake needed for the purpose has not undergone any material change for the better.[4] While there has been limited success in promoting contraception and sterilisation, there has been no significant reduction in the birth rate, especially among the low income groups who constitute the majority of the population, nor a reduction in the growth rate of the population during 1950-80. This relative lack of success in securing adequate returns on health is partly due to the inadequacy of expenditure, faulty planning and failure to provide enough concomitant health measures — such as, public hygiene in terms of drinking and bathing water, drainage, and sanitary facilities and mass education in private hygiene. Thus, we have largely failed to promote the formation of physical human capital which is needed for working efficiency, for the improvement of labour productivity and for a simultaneous improvement in the capital-output ratio.

Information and communication have an important role in human capital formation, both in terms of creating a scientific enviornment and in promoting social harmony. It is not necessary to expand on the failure to achieve these objectives during the period under review. In fact, we have recently moved even further away from realising these objectives. While this is especially true in regard to social harmony, we have even been largely unsuccessful in creating a scientific temper which is evident from the growth of obscurantism, irrationality and the growing popularity of astrology during recent years. It may not be possible to give a statistical formulation of the effect of this phenomenon on the growth of output or the capital-output ratio or labour productivity, but there can be no denying its existence nor any reason to underplay its significance for the growth of the net domestic product. The outlook for human capital formation is even more dismal than in the case of non-human capital formation; and is undoubtedly one of the major reasons for the slow rate of national economic growth and the increasing capital-output ratio. Here again more in-depth studies are required on the coverage, pace, content and relevance of the measures we are taking for human capital formation. Above all, we need deliberate and practical policies for changing motivations, expectations and attitudes to education. Equally vigorous efforts are required for improving health and nutrition and reducing birth rates and promoting the small family norm, as well as for expanding and improving our information and communication system. In fact, it is time that we re-examined our policies and expenditure patterns with regard to education, health, information and communication from the point of view of their impact on an effective and efficient creation of human capital and the maintenance and improvement of such efficiency.

Altogether, our progress in capital formation has not produced satisfactory results for either economic growth or human welfare. Many intangibles are involved. In addition to the factors mentioned earlier, there are others — such as, the curbs on the motivation to undertake entrepreneurial activities induced by populist slogans and bureaucratic rigidities; the increasing politicisation of economic decisions, as well as an increasing emphasis on regional, communal, lingual and casteist loyalties at the expense of not only national integrity but also economic growth; and the general mood of cynicism and frustration combined with the feeling that merit and reward are no longer related. All these factors are not quantifiable or subject to statistical calculations or populist remedies. Yet they are extremely important for economic growth. Though human capital formation cannot alone provide the answer, it also needs more study, analysis and attention than it has received so far as a determinant of economic growth and eventually national welfare. That is the only excuse offered for including what purists may regard as an irrelevant digression in a study on India's national income.

References

1. Uma Datta Roy Choudhury, 'Industrial Break-down of Capital Stock in India.' *Income and Wealth,* IARNIW, April 1977.
2. A vivid and well-argued account of the relation of education to rural development at the grass-roots level, based on participant observation in a Karnataka village, is given in Sudha V. Rao's unpublished thesis which has been awarded the Ph.D. degree by Sussex University.
3. *Statistical Outline of India,* Tata Services Ltd., 1982, Tables 137 & 138.
4. For a comprehensive review of the nutritional status of the population and the lack of a national policy on food, health and nutrition, see V.K.R.V. Rao, *Food, Nutrition and Poverty,* New Delhi, Vikas, 1982.

Productivity and Growth 11

It would be simple to analyse productivity and growth if it were possible to relate the economic growth which has taken place in India during the last thirty years to the increase in productivity in the different factors of production that have contributed to this growth. However, this is not possible. Even in the case of developed countries, which have greater, more detailed and more reliable data, research workers have found it difficult to break up productivity by individual factors of production; and the results of their work cannot be considered as sufficiently satisfactory. What will be done here, therefore, is to take the growth in the value of output per unit of input for each factor of production (overlooking the fact that the resulting figure is really a joint product of its contribution along with those of the inputs of other factors of production), using this to show its contribution in terms of increased productivity by proxy.

The factors of production we will consider are land, labour, capital and management. Table 11.1 gives the value at constant prices (1960-61) of the NDP in the initial and final years of the period under review and the volume or quantum of the first three of these factors of production.

It will be seen that while the NDP has increased at constant prices by 171.32 per cent in thirty years, the net area sown has increased by only 21.09 per cent, the number of workers by only 54.16 per cent, and the volume of capital stock by as much as 418.13 per cent. Evidently, a much larger volume of capital than labour, and of labour than land, has been required to bring about the increase of 171.32 per cent in the NDP. It also seems to indicate that, in terms of productivity per unit, land has played a more important role than either labour or capital, and labour more than capital. This impression is confirmed by Table 11.2 which gives the input-output ratios of these factors in terms of their proportion to the change in the NDP without segregating their individual contributions.

The negative change shown under capital (–47.63) is only a reflection of the increase in the capital-output ratio discussed in Chapter 10 and an indication

Table 11.1

Volume of NDP and Factors of Production

	1950-51	*1979-80*	*Percentage of Change 1950-80*
NDP (in crores — at 1960-61 prices)	9122	24750	171.32
No. of workers (million)	139.50	215.06	54.16
Net sown area (million)	118.75	143.80	21.09
Capital stock (Rs million)	240710	1247180	418.13

Note: The NDP figures are from the NAS converted into 1960-61 prices, of workers from the 1951 and 1981 census reports, and of net sown area from *Area, Yield and Production Estimates, 1981.*

Table 11.2

Output-Input Ratios of Factors of Production

	1950-51	*1979-80*	*Percentage of Change 1950-80*
NDP per worker (in Rs)	653.91	1150.85	76.00
NDP per hectare of net sown area (in Rs)	768.17	1721.14	124.06
NDP per rupee of capital stock (in Rs)	0.37896	0.19845	–47.63

of the larger volume of capital required to produce a given unit of NDP in 1979-80 as compared to 1950-51. The change under land (124.06) is partly due to the increased share of non-agriculture in the NDP of 1979-80 as compared to 1950-51. The figure shown under labour (76.00) only partially reflects the increase in the productivity of labour; the remaining part is due to the role played by the increased volume of land and capital associated with it. All the same, the figures do convey the impression that the rise in productivity has been higher in the case of land than of labour or capital, and, possibly, more so in the case of labour than of capital.

Identifying the NDP from agriculture and allied activities with the volume (or value at constant prices) of the output from land, we find that this has increased by 69.63 per cent — from Rs 4,936 crores in 1950-51 to Rs 8,373 crores in 1979-80. It has been indicated earlier that this has been accompanied by an increase in the NDP-land ratio of 124.06 per cent. Obviously this ratio is an over-statement of the increase effected in the NDP by land; the correct ratio would be that given by the increase in the NDP from agriculture to that in the NDP as a whole, or 22 per cent. This is as compared to the increase in the net sown area (21.09 per cent).

The obvious inference from this is that it is the increase in the quantum of land that has played a major role in the increased contribution of agriculture to the NDP, but this assumption is not correct. The index of productivity of the net sown area has gone up from 70.1 in 1950-51 to 132.7 in 1979-80, or by 89.3 per cent. This increase in productivity has been the result of the enhancement of the yield due to irrigation, the application of science and technology in the form of high yielding varieties of seeds, and the investment of capital in energy, credit, machinery, fertilisers and pesticides (see Table 11.3, which has been compiled from several issues of *Indian Agriculture in Brief*, a Government of India publication).

Table 11.3

Factors in Increasing Land Productivity

Item	*Unit*	*1950-51*	*1978-79*	*Percentage Change 1950-79*
Net sown area	Million hectares	118.75	143.80	21.09
Net irrigated area	Million hectares	20.85	39.09	87.48
Tractors	In lakhs	0.09	3.67	3977.78
Electrical pump sets	In lakhs	0.82	20.84	2441.46
Fertiliser consumption – nutrients	Million tonnes	0.07	5.12	7214.29
Consumption of power	KWH per hectare of GCA	1.50	57.20	3713.33
Cooperative credit	Rs crores	22.90	1023.45	4369.21
Bank credit	Rs crores	340.96*	2223.18	552.04
Stock of agricultural graduates	Thousands	15.11+	92.90	514.82
Villages electrified	Thousands	3.00	250.00	8233.33
Index of net sown area		86.8	103.8	19.59
Index of productivity of net sown area		70.1	132.7	89.30
Index of yield		96.0	122.4	27.50
Index of area under crops		78.2	108.0	38.11
Index of agricultural production		58.5	137.9	135.73
Index of cropping intensity		93.7	104.0	10.99
Index of cropping pattern		98.4	105.4	7.11

* Figures are for 1970-71.
+ Figures are for 1960-61.

The spectacular progress in the factors contributing to the increased productivity of land may broadly be clubbed together under the generic head of improvement in the quality of land and the green revolution. The fact that the index of productivity per hectare of net sown area has gone up by 89.3 per cent while the yield per hectare of gross crop area has gone up by only 27.5 per cent indicates that a lot of marginal and low quality land must have been brought under cultivation while extending the net sown area. In addition, an unidentified portion of the area already under cultivation in 1950-51 must have been of marginal quality.

There have been variations in the growth of the index of yield per hectare under the different groups of crops, which is illustrated in Table 11.4.

Table 11.4

Index of Yield by Major Groups of Crops

Crops	*1950-51*	*1979-80*	*Percentage Increase*
Cereals	69.2	110.2	59.25
Pulses	93.8	76.5	−18.44
Oilseeds	98.0	104.2	6.33
Fibres	76.7	126.1	64.41
Plantations	77.8	139.1	78.79
Fruits & vegetables	89.4	122.6	37.14
Condiments & spices	98.8	101.4	2.63
Others	83.6	101.0	20.81
Food	69.2	110.2	59.25
Non-food	87.2	110.2	26.38
All crops	76.0	107.8	41.84

The contribution of labour to the NDP is more complex. The census returns according to occupations provide the participation rate of the possible working force and the number of workers by industrial origin according to the classification used in the census. This total, which has been used in Table 11.1, indicates an increase of 54.16 per cent in the number of workers, or an addition of 75.56 million between 1979-80 and the 1950-51.

The Indian labour force includes both the self-employed and those working for wages or salaries; and it does not correspond to the total number of workers in standard terms (i.e., those working eight hours a day and 300 days in a year). The houre of work of the self-employed includes a large element of non-work — either chronic, seasonal or occasional — and is characterised as under-employment. In the case of those who offer themselves for work on wages or salaries, not all are able to get work; these are the unemployed. The degree of unemployment of these workers has not yet been statistically identified with a reasonable degree of accuracy. In fact, the census occupational totals do not really represent the total number of employed workers (whether working for themselves or on hire) in standard terms of working. To this extent, the value of the NDP per worker or change therein does not indicate the fully employed worker's contribution to the NDP. This is, of course, quite apart from the fact that an unidentified portion of this value is not attributable to labour productivity but is the result of the productivity of land and captial and the changes therein.

The NDP per worker has increased from Rs 654 in 1950-51 to Rs 1,151 in 1979-80 at constant prices (or by 76 per cent). This increase, to the extent that it is due to the individual role of labour as a factor of production, is not attributable to any increase in the number of working days or working hours in the case of employees; while in the case of the self-employed, the number of working days and hours is self-regulated and there is no reason to believe that it has undergone any increase. The increase in the per capita contribution of labour to the NDP or its productivity can, therefore, be rightly attributed to the improvement that has taken place in the quality (i.e., knowledge, organisation, skills, and working efficiency) of labour over the period. Table 11.5 provides relevant data.

Table 11.5

Educational Improvements

Item	*Unit*	*1950-51*	*1979-80*	*Percentage Increase*
Literates	Thousands	166.00		
Primary school students	Millions	22.30	90.90	307.6
Secondary school students	Millions	1.20	9.70	708.3
Teacher trainees	Thousands	75.65	170.43	125.3
Undergraduates in Arts & Science	Thousands	342.00	2832.00	728.1
Post-graduates in Arts & Science	Thousands			
Engineering college students	Thousands	13.27	351.43	2548.3
Engineering school students	Thousands	21.15	111.99	429.5
Vocational training students	Thousands	10.39	265.30	2453.4

The figures for student enrolment given in Table 11.5 are drawn from the Planning Commission's publication — *Basic Statistics Relating to the Indian Economy*. The percentage increase they show during the three decades are impressive. In addition, many staff-training institutions in different fields of productive activity have been set up during the period, and many training programmes, seminars, conferences and workshops relating to improvement in productivity have been organised. These should have brought about a significant improvement in the quality and efficiency of labour and increased its individual productivity and contribution to the NDP much above what seems to have been actually achieved.

The reason for this inadequate increase in labour productivity is largely due to the failure of our educational policy in building up the technical and other skills relevant for the economic development of our labour-abundant economy, as also the requisite work-ethic, entrepreneurial spirit, and the social harmony, collective working norm self-reliance and national identity so necessary for speeding up the development of a country like India with its continental dimensions. The tragic record of India's educational system, policy, and priorities is a whole subject by itself, which is outside the scope of this work. It requires a competent, objective, and in-depth study which is yet to be undertaken. What can be said here is that with all its inadequacy in relation to requirements, the massive investment made by the country in education and training during the period under review should have yielded better results in terms of labour productivity.

The occupational trends accompanying the country's economic developments, as well as inter-state variations in the labour force's response to attempts at improving its quality and its productivity, have also been responsible for the current situation.

Table 11.6 gives the value of the NDP per worker in agriculture and non-agriculture at constant prices between 1950 and 1980. This Table also includes figures for 1977-78, as the final year of the period under review in this study (1979-80) was a particularly bad agricultural year. Taking the initial and final years of the period, it is evident that the NDP per worker in agriculture has increased by only 14.64 per cent at constant prices, while that of workers in non-agricultural fields has increased by 118.09 per cent, or more than eight times that of those engaged in agriculture. The number of workers in non-agriculture (who constitute only about a third of the labour force) has increased only by 150 per cent during the period, while that in agriculture has actually increased by 48 per cent instead of diminishing as is common in development. This increase in the number of agricultural workers (with a much lower rate of increase in their per capita NDP) and the absence of a substantial increase in the number of non-agricultural workers (with their higher increase in per capita NDP) must have combined to keep the increase in the NDP per worker at a much lower level than if there had been a substantial change in the occupational distribution of the labour force between agriculture and non-agriculture.

Table 11.6

NDP Per Worker in Agriculture & Non-agriculture (Rs at Constant Prices)

Sector	1950-51	1977-78	1979-80	Per Cent Increase In 1977-78 over 1950-51	Per Cent Increase In 1979-80 over 1950-51
NDP per worker in agriculture	506.9	661.7	581.1	30.54	14.64
NDP per worker in non-agriculture	993.6	2134.2	2167.0	114.79	118.09
NDP per worker in total of agriculture and non-agriculture	653.9	1147.6	1150.9	75.49	76.00

Data are available only from 1960-61 to 1977-78 for inter-state variations in the NDP per worker and are presented in Table 11.7 at constant (1960-61) base prices. The states are arranged in descending order according to the magnitude of their per worker NDP in 1960-61.

The range of variation in the increase in per worker NDP is startlingly wide, from 5.03 per cent for Madhya Pradesh to 102.94 for Haryana. Among the states registering a large increase were Karnataka (96.03 per cent), Punjab (82.40 per cent), Rajasthan (60.76 per cent), Maharashtra (60.38 per cent), and Gujarat (52.87 per cent). Among the states registering a medium rise were Tamil Nadu (48.96 per cent), Andhra Pradesh (48.30 per cent), Orissa (45.15 per cent) and Kerala (41.08 per cent). Among the states showing a low increase were Bihar (20.49 per cent), Uttar Pradesh (18.43 per cent) and West Bengal (12.81 per cent).

Table 11.7

NDP Per Worker (Rs at Constant Prices)

State	*1960-61*	*1977-78*	*Percentage Increase*
Punjab	1166.61	2127.93	82.40
West Bengal	1157.17	1305.41	12.81
Gujarat	870.80	1331.16	52.87
Haryana	850.99	1727.02	102.94
Maharashtra	842.84	1351.72	60.38
Kerala	787.32	1110.76	41.08
Tamil Nadu	724.34	1079.00	48.96
Karnataka	645.17	1264.73	96.03
Uttar Pradesh	638.83	756.59	18.43
Rajasthan	583.27	937.66	60.76
Andhra Pradesh	526.71	781.11	48.30
Bihar	516.25	622.01	20.49
Madhya Pradesh	491.47	516.19	5.03
Orissa	488.13	708.53	45.15
Assam	NA	NA	NA
ALL INDIA	730.51	1147.55	57.09

The inter-state distribution of the labour force in 1960-61 as well as the increase in the labour force in 1977-78 is provided in Table 11.8. The rate of increase in the high-rise states (Group I) is greater than that of the medium-rise states, the growth of the medium-rise states is higher than that of the low-rise states. The first group constituted 31.3 per cent of the labour force in 1977-78, the second group 26.8 per cent, and the third group 41.9 per cent. This must have contributed to lowering the overall average of the rise in the per worker NDP (which is being used as a proxy for labour productivity) between 1960-61 and 1977-78.

The overall rise in per worker NDP of 57.1 per cent was constituted by a rise of 27.6 per cent in the per worker NDP from agriculture and 75.9 per cent of that from non-agriculture. These sectoral NDPs per worker were also marked by inter-state disparities. It is evident from Tables 11.9 and 11.10 that their range was wider in the case of the per worker NDP from agriculture than from non-agriculture. In both these tables the states are arranged in descending order of the magnitude of their per worker NDP in 1960-61, and are at constant prices.

The range of variation between the states of the per worker NDP from agriculture in its increase over the period 1960-78 is from –10.17 per cent (in the case of Kerala) to 106.08 per cent (in the case of Haryana); and in their comparative magnitude in 1977-78 from Rs 474.07 (in the case of Andhra Pradesh) to Rs 1,631.76 (in the case of Punjab). As regards per worker NDP from non-agriculture, the range in increase is from 36.07 per cent (in the case of West Bengal) to 136.66 per cent (in that of Karnataka); while in regard to the comparative position in 1977-78, the range was from 1123.48 (in the case of Kerala) to 2574.15 (in that of Punjab). Some states have a comparatively

Table 11.8

Distribution of Labour Force by States (in Millions)

States	*1960-61*	*1977-78*	*Per Cent Increase*
Group I			
Haryana	2.879	3.245	12.71
Karnataka	10.726	12.371	15.34
Punjab	3.466	4.509	30.09
Rajasthan	9.584	9.519	−0.68
Maharashtra	18.948	22.131	16.80
Gujarat	8.475	10.055	18.64
Total	54.078	61.830	14.33
Group II			
Tamil Nadu	15.352	17.403	13.37
Andhra Pradesh	18.663	20.955	12.28
Orissa	7.662	7.987	4.24
Kerala	5.630	6.563	16.57
Total	47.307	52.908	11.84
Group III			
Bihar	19.235	19.576	1.77
Uttar Pradesh	28.850	30.554	5.91
West Bengal	11.580	14.383	24.21
Madhya Pradesh	16.929	18.333	8.29
Total	76.594	82.846	8.16
TOTAL (ALL GROUPS)	177.979	197.584	11.02

Table 11.9

Per Worker NDP from Agriculture (Rs at 1960-61 Prices)

State	*1960-61*	*1977-78*	*Percentage Increase*
Punjab	1182.24	1631.76	38.02
Kerala	1071.43	962.48	−10.17
West Bengal	831.46	956.66	15.06
Haryana	751.11	1547.92	106.08
Tamil Nadu	607.37	614.32	1.14
Gujarat	531.97	730.82	37.38
Karnataka	523.26	899.92	71.99
Uttar Pradesh	501.64	631.62	25.91
Maharashtra	483.89	612.85	26.65
Andhra Pradesh	432.82	474.07	9.53
Rajasthan	414.82	756.98	82.48
Orissa	385.37	628.21	63.01
Madhya Pradesh	356.66	600.14	68.27
Assam	NA	NA	NA
Bihar	NA	NA	NA
ALL INDIA	518.60	661.70	27.59

Table 11.10

Per Worker NDP from Non-Agriculture (Rs at 1960-61 Prices)

State	1960-61	1977-78	Percentage Increase
Maharashtra	1676.90	2542.15	51.60
Gujarat	1593.94	2368.01	48.56
West Bengal	1536.45	2090.72	36.07
Rajasthan	1170.96	1962.79	67.62
Punjab	1144.54	2574.15	124.91
Haryana	1082.05	2373.87	119.39
Uttar Pradesh	1054.55	1727.86	63.85
Madhya Pradesh	1008.00	1708.44	69.49
Karnataka	937.01	2217.52	136.66
Tamil Nadu	903.55	1721.13	90.49
Orissa	778.06	1448.39	86.15
Andhra Pradesh	732.88	1461.05	99.36
Kerala	578.59	1123.48	94.18
Assam	NA	NA	NA
Bihar	NA	NA	NA
ALL INDIA	1213.60	2134.16	75.85

higher per worker NDP from both agriculture and non-agriculture; some have a better position in regard to the per worker NDP from agriculture than from non-agriculture and vice versa; while some others have a comparatively worse position in their per worker NDP from both agriculture and non-agriculture. In overall terms, the southern states have fared better in labour productivity in non-agriculture and worse in agriculture, with the exception of Karnataka which has also done well in agriculture. Punjab and Haryana have fared better than the national average in both. Table 11.11 compiled from Tables 11.9 and 11.10 indicates the comparative position and also gives the inter-state ranking in this respect.

It is worth noting the positions of Punjab and Haryana, which between them occupy the top three slots in per capita NDP from both agriculture and non-agriculture. Evidently, these two states are the success stories in labour productivity. Karnataka has maintained the fifth rank in both agriculture and non-agriculture; Uttar Pradesh has maintained the eighth rank, while Orissa, Madhya Pradesh, Andhra Pradesh and Tamil Nadu all figure among the lower rankings (nine and below) in both agriculture and non-agriculture. The remaining states have a mixed ranking in these two sectors.

As regards capital productivity, Table 11.2 indicated that the NDP per rupee of capital fell from 0.379 in 1950-51 to 0.198 in 1979-80 (or by 47.6 per cent), reflecting the increase that has taken place in the average capital-output ratio between those years. As already seen in Chapter 10, there are substantial variations in the average capital-output ratios by sectors of industrial origin as well as in their rates of increase over the period; when the investment pattern is at adverse variance with the productivity of capital, it leads to an increase in the overall capital ratio and to a consequent decrease

Table 11.11

Per Worker NDP from Agriculture and Non-Agriculture — 1977-78 (at 1960-61 Prices)

State	Amount in Rs		Ranking	
	Agriculture	Non-Agriculture	Agriculture	Non-Agriculture
Punjab	1631.76	2574.15	1	1
Haryana	1547.92	2373.87	2	3
Kerala	962.48	1123.48	3	13
West Bengal	956.66	2090.72	4	6
Karnataka	899.92	2217.52	5	5
Rajasthan	756.98	1962.79	6	7
Gujarat	730.82	2368.01	7	4
Uttar Pradesh	631.62	1727.86	8	8
Orissa	628.21	1448.39	9	12
Tamil Nadu	614.32	1721.13	10	9
Maharashtra	612.85	2542.15	11	2
Madhya Pradesh	600.14	1708.44	12	10
Andhra Pradesh	474.07	1461.05	13	11
ALL INDIA	661.70	2134.16		

in capital productivity. This is further illustrated in Table 11.12 which links the distribution of capital stock by industrial origin with that of the NDP by industrial origin during the same period.

Besides the investment pattern of capital stock with different capital-output ratios, there are many other factors which make for an increase in the overall capital-output ratio and decrease in capital productivity — such as, length of the gestation period, extent of unutilised capacity, inadequate and/or inefficient maintenance, lack of coordination in investment planning and consequent bottlenecks, and misdirected and unfruitful investment. In short, capital productivity suffers because of the lack of correspondence between the potential created and the results achieved in the production of goods and services for which capital is accumulated. This is what has been happening to the Indian economy during its thirty years of growth from 1950 to 1980.

The fourth factor of production is the management factor. My interpretation of this term is based on the relationship between the value of output and that of input, and the change in this relationship at constant prices over a period. If the ratio relating output to input increases over a period, it can be regarded as an improvement in managerial efficiency which would cover not only the volume of inputs used, but also their appropriateness, substitutability in terms of cost and technical efficiency, avoidance of waste, and coordination. The NAS data on inputs and outputs are given only for three sectors of industrial origin — agriculture and animal husbandry, mining, and registered manufacturing. Data are available at constant prices from 1950-51 to 1979-80 for the first two categories, while for registered manufacturing figures are available only from 1960-61 and that too only at current prices. To

Table 11.12

Percentage Increase (or Decrease) in Per Cent Shares of Capital Stock and NDP by Industrial Origin (1950-51 and 1979-80)

Sector	*NDP Per Cent Shares*		*Per Cent Shares Capital Stock*		*Per Cent Increase in Shares in NDP*	*% Rise or Fall in Share of Capital Stock*
	1950-51	*1979-80*	*1950-51*	*1979-80*		
Agriculture	54.11	33.83	27.06	19.16	−37.48	−29.19
Mining & quarrying	0.83	1.10	0.61	2.07	32.53	239.34
Registered manufacturing	6.30	11.34	8.38	18.28	80.00	118.14
Unregistered manufacturing	5.36	6.86	3.97	4.97	27.99	25.19
Electricity	0.26	1.55	1.34	7.17	496.15	435.07
Railways	1.66	2.12	8.18	5.82	27.71	−28.85
Other transport	1.61	3.43	4.72	6.12	113.04	29.66
Communications	0.37	0.85	0.48	1.02	129.73	112.50
Trade, hotel & restaurants	8.51	12.41	8.86	6.82	45.83	−23.02
Finance	0.84	2.51	0.34	0.40	198.81	17.65
Real estate	3.09	3.64	32.79	17.19	17.80	−47.58
Public adminstration	3.64	8.85	3.27	6.75	143.13	106.42
Others	13.42	11.51	NA	NA	−14.23	NA

convert these into constant 1960-61 prices, the wholesale index for manufactured commodities and industrial raw materials are used. These are obtained from the annual reports on currency and finance published by the Reserve Bank of India. Table 11.13 lists these figures for selected years.

Table 11.13

Output-Input Ratios at Constant Prices (1960-61)

Sector	*1960-61*	*1970-71*	*1975-76*	*1979-80*	*Percentage Rate of Change (1960-80)*
Agriculture & animal husbandry	4.6320	4.4936	4.2627	3.5906	−22.48
Mining	6.2442	5.1564	4.5635	4.3310	−30.64
Registered manufacturing	1.3978	1.3227	1.2855	1.2852	−8.06

The higher ratio of output to input in the case of mining and agriculture and animal husbandry is due to the large role played by land and natural resources, which are not taken into account in Table 11.13. The amazing fact revealed by this Table is the steady fall in the output-input ratio in the case of all three industrial sectors listed, though the fall has been considerably less in the case of registered manufacturing. The steep fall in the case of agriculture and animal husbandry and mining is particularly disquieting because of the cost-push effect they would have on the economy, as their output consists of either food or raw materials which enter into the cost of labour maintenance and industrial production. The fall in the output-input ratio of registered manufacturing, though less, is also a matter for concern as it belongs to the modern sector and enjoys the benefit of science and technology and the services of highly trained technical and managerial personnel. Data on the total material input expressed as a percentage of output for the twenty-one industries in the factory sector are available in *Bulletin No. ISD/8* of the CSO published in October 1981. The figures cover the period 1960-77. Table 11.14 gives the relevant data for 1960 and 1977 and the percentage change in 1977 over 1960.

It is evident from Table 11.14 that, except in the case of electric power and motor vehicles, the ratio of material input to output has increased in the case of the vast majority of industries, though at varying ratios. However, this does not indicate an improvement in efficiency in materials management.

In fact, both Tables 11.13 and 11.14 clearly reveal that India is developing into a high cost economy in spite of its comparatively low level of employee compensation. No doubt, there has been economic growth and a substantial increase in national output, but this is being achieved by increasing costs. The management factor in Indian economic development has not succeeded in reducing the unit cost in output even in real terms, after discounting the effects of an inflationary rise in prices.

Table 11.14

Total Material Input Expressed as Percentage of Output

Industry	*1960*	*1977*	*Percentage Change in 1977 over 1960*
Chemicals & products	0.66	0.76	+15.15
Cement	0.67	0.72	+7.46
Iron & steel	0.69	0.76	+10.14
Non-ferrous basic metals	0.77	0.78	+1.30
Electric light & power	0.56	0.52	−7.14
Machinery except electric	0.66	0.69	+4.55
Electric machinery & appliances	0.67	0.73	+8.96
Ship-building and repairing	0.52	0.59	+13.46
Railroad equipment	0.55	0.58	+5.45
Motor vehicles	0.73	0.68	−6.85
Repairing motor vehicles	0.58	0.71	+22.41
Metal products except machinery & equipment	0.71	0.75	+5.63
Rubber products	0.65	0.79	+21.54
Petroleum	0.60	0.89	+48.33
Structural clay products	0.50	0.62	+24.00
Spinning, weaving & finishing of textiles	0.66	0.75	+13.64
Pulp, paper & paper products	0.83	0.88	+6.02
Miscellaneous food products	0.66	0.69	+4.55
Tobacco products	0.79	0.85	+7.60
Sugar factories	0.76	0.83	+9.21

Altogether, there has not been much improvement in the operational management of the Indian economy or any considerable increase in national productivity in terms of either land, labour, capital or management, which could have been expected from the investments made or the resources created; or the scientific, technological or managerial or other relevant developmental skills built over the last thirty years of planning; or the significant increase in the role of the government and the public sector after independence in the country's economic development. This chapter clearly and unequivocally points to the conclusion that the major problem areas in the Indian economy are productivity and economic management. It is not simply an increase in output that affects national development. It is also the cost that accompanies the growth in output and the extent to which the potential created is converted into output.

That productivity is a major problem of the Indian economy is now recognised by the government. Early in 1982, the Prime Minister made a specific reference to this when announcing her revised 20-point economic programme. Though she was referring specifically to the working of public enterprises, what she said is equally applicable to private enterprise and the other areas of economic activity in the country. The new item she has included in the 20-point programme is to improve the working of public enterprises by increasing efficiency, capacity utilisation and generation of internal resources. Unfortunately, this is not being actually implemented in either the public or private management of the economy. Some of the items bearing on the subject of increased productivity are:

1. Full utilisation of fixed capital involving overhead costs in order to bring down the average cost per unit.
2. Similarly, full utilisation of working capital by suitable inventory control, and coordination in delivery, appropriateness and interlinking of inputs.
3. A flexible pricing policy based on a changing demand and supply situation, effecting well-tuned changes in prices, and suitable stock changes in final output accompanied by the regulation of distribution when necessary and practicable.
4. Avoiding break downs or other interruptions to production by:
   a) adequate attention to maintenance;
   b) sensitiveness to worker-feelings and early response to worker unrest by taking appropriate action to deal with legitimate grievances without waiting for a strike or a show of organised pressure by the workers to elicit such action;
   c) education of both workers and the public in regard to the specificity and reality of the problems faced by the management in operating the industry or area of economic activity.
5. Renovation of capital equipment with due regard to obsolescence and innovations.
6. Reorientation of production processes and marketing techniques in terms of modernisation by keeping abreast of what others are doing in this field. This was done by the countries of Western Europe under the Marshall Plan and enabled their industries to catch up with American efficiency, and in fact become a strong competitor in their foreign and domestic markets. This would involve periodic study tours by both executives and technicians both within and outside the country to get acquainted with the latest techniques relating to productivity, making suggestions for adapting such knowledge to their individual enterprises or fields of productive activity, and, more important, action on the part of the authorities concerned to give prompt consideration to such suggestions and take the needed follow-up action.
7. Creating incentives for increased efficiency on the part of managerial personnel at all levels by:
   a) continuity of tenure in key positions;
   b) promotional opportunities and internal growth;
   c) monetary or non-monetary recognition or public appreciation of good work; and
   d) promoting inter-industry and intra-industry competition by suitable public recognition on the basis of appropriate norms for recognition in managerial efficiency.

8. Identifying management with the needs of the national social environment by the avoidance of conspicuous consumption, and by taking the initiative to alleviate the social and environmental handicaps of their workers and neighbourhoods.
9. Inculcation in those responsible for the management of economic activity of a firm commitment to the extent practicable for the social, economic and environmental betterment of
   a) their locality and region;
   b) their rural hinterland;
   c) their workers;
   d) their salaried and managerial employees;
   e) the public, in terms of quality, cost and appropriateness of output for ensuring maximum benefit to them; and
   f) the industry in terms of internal surpluses and economic growth.

Above all, it is important that managers of economic activity should use their public relations organisations not for personal or institutional advertisement but in order to get to know the problems and needs of the public and to enlist their cooperation and participation to the extent possible in the developmental process.

Creating productivity consciousness and working for an increase in productivity, (whether of land, labour, capital or management), or of individual enterprises, (whether public or private, incorporated or household), is a major factor affecting economic growth with minimum costs and maximum returns, and the conversion of production potential into actual output. It is the establishment of this mutually reinforcing link between growth and productivity that makes for an increase in the rate of growth or the achievement of a high rate of economic growth. It constitutes a vital consideration when making extrapolations or projections for the future or undertaking perspective planning for economic growth. The presence or absence of such a link between productivity and growth can make all the difference to alternative scenarios for our economic future.

India's National Income, 2001 AD 12

Making projections for the future is an age-old habit which has of late become popular among thinkers and planners. It is difficult to resist the temptation of attempting such a forecast for India's national income, especially in a study like this which has interpreted growth and change in the Indian economy through an analysis of its national accounts data for a period of thirty years.*

There are several ways to approach this exercise in futurology. The normative approach formulates projections of national income on the basis of alternative assumptions regarding the extent to which national income should be increased over a defined period, doubled, trebled or quadrupled. Since it is the per capita NDP, rather than the NDP itself, which is significant for the welfare potential of the national population concerned, such projections are either based on a desired increase in the per capita NDP or accompany projections of the NDP with consequent projections for the per capita NDP. In this approach, the risk of failing to realise these projections increases, for then one is dealing not only with the future behaviour or growth of the national product but also of the population. This happens even when one is making projections using planned figures, which are based on targets and include policies, projects, programmes, resource mobilisation and administrative requirements for the realisation of these targets. The record of the Indian experiment in planned development contains ample evidence of the hazards underlying such macro-economic projections, whether on the growth of production of the NDP or a reduction in population growth which affects the per capita NDP.

A variant of the normative approach encompasses more norms (in addition to a desired growth in the per capita NDP) which have a deeper and more wide-spread bearing on welfare—such as, eliminating poverty, reducing un-

*Prof Austin Robinson first suggested that a chaper be included on India's national income in 2001 AD, on hearing about this study and after reading some parts of it in preliminary form in 1978.

employment or securing full employment, reducing inequalities in incomes and wealth, and combining social justice with economic growth. Here, again, India's experience with planned development provides ample proof of the complexities and pitfalls attending such an approach, and of the limitations of purely economic means for its implementation without taking into account and tackling the cultural, social, and political realities behind economic phenomena. The Indian experience has also shown that legislative, institutional or administrative reforms do not by themselves provide the answer.[1]

An alternative approach is to set out the desired target for the level of living by the year 2001 and then arrive at the projections of national development aggregates—such as, GDP, consumption, savings and investment and changes in the structure of the economy—to attain this target. This method has been used in *India 2001* which states:

> Our main findings . . . reveal that if we are to break the poverty barrier and achieve the targeted level of living by the year 2001, our GNP must grow at an annual compound rate of at least 13.8 per cent as in V3A. To achieve this our savings must grow at the rate of 17.4 per cent per annum and investment at the rate of 17.1 per cent per annum. Simultaneously, the total consumption expenditure must not be permitted to exceed a growth rate of 12.8 per cent per annum. With larger capital mobilisation from domestic and foreign resources, the national income could exceed the levels set in our target as is demonstrated in V3B and V3C. These findings are based on the assumption that India will achieve a breakthrough in checking the population growth rate and consequently the total population will be approximately 864 million by 2001.
>
> It is obvious that the annual growth rates of 3 to 5 per cent in GNP, as hitherto achieved, will have no tangible impact on the life and living standard of the people in India. Such growth rates will be unacceptable at both political and ethical levels.[2]

Another method of forecasting is to set out normative objectives but not utilise them individually to determine the projections. While one's head may be in the clouds, one's feet have to be very firmly on the ground. Resource constraints and past trends in growth are taken into account in this approach together with perceived possibilities of improvement; and it becomes a mixture of economic realism and ethical idealism in terms of social welfare. A study by Dr F.A. Metha which uses this approach was published in the *Second India Studies* sponsored by the Ford Foundation dealing with the second India that will be added after 2000 AD. This combination of economic realism and moral idealism is illustrated by the following excerpt .

> The central preoccupation of Indian technology, as indeed of the Indian economy itself, must, therefore, be with the fact that throughout the life-span of Second India, India will be a poor country, in absolute terms, if the current trend growth rate of 3 per cent continues, and in relative terms

even if the miraculous trend growth rate of 9 per cent is achieved . . . . Even if, by a miracle of miracles, India were to 'out-Japan' Japan by scoring an average annual growth rate of 9 per cent over the 27 years from 1973-74 to 2000 AD, she would not have a per capita GDP of more than 600 dollars by 2000 AD; that is, she will never have, *on the basis of current models of economic growth and on the current capital-cum-energy intensivity of modern technology,* the capacity to assure the masses of her people the three essentials of a decent quality of life — the provision of the basic amenities of life, the creation of a sense of security, and the access to communal services, like education, housing, basic medical facilities. The biggest single challenge to India is, therefore, to evolve a strategy of economic growth and, with it, innovation in technology, such as will enable India, *even at a low level of per capita income,* to satisfy the basic needs of her masses and at the same time to generate employment on a mass scale.[3]

The minimum growth rate that he considers necessary is a compound annual one of 5 per cent over the period 1973-74 to 2000-01 AD, adding, at the same time that 'this is a rate which India has often aspired to in her plans but never achieved'. His two alternatives are based on growth rates of 7 per cent and 9 per cent which he regards as 'optimistic rates'. While he has not stated that any single rate is feasible or fulfils his ethical norms, it appears from his study (including the comparisons that he has drawn from Chenery's work[4] on growth and structural change) that if he had advanced any single rate of growth as ideal for a desired and yet feasible projection, it would lie between 5 and 7 per cent, and nearer 5 than 7.

This study has dealt with the growth of India's national income during the thirty years between 1950-51 to 1979-80 and the changes which have accompanied it in the composition of the NDP, its pattern of consumption, factor shares, inter-state distribution, savings generated, and capital formation achieved with the help of both domestic savings and foreign capital. This growth in national income has been translated in terms of productivity of land, labour and capital. It has been found that the overall compound rate of growth over the period has been 3.6 per cent per annum, the actual rate from year to year showing wide fluctuations. Even the rate for quinquennial years have varied over the six periods constituting the thirty years under review. The trend rate for the first half of the period — 1950-51 to 1964-65 — has been a little higher than that for the whole period, while that for the later years — 1968-69 to 1979-80 (excluding the intermediate three years from 1965 to 1967) — has been a little lower. The growth rate during the last sub-period (1975-76 to 1979-80) has been higher than the trend rate for the whole period and of the two parts of the latter half of the period. Is it possible to make projections into the future on the basis of these past trends and project the national income of the country twenty years hence, i.e., in 2001 AD?

All projections have their limitations. Trends traceable from the past and extrapolated into the future need not necessarily yield an accurate picture in the light of the position that agriculture occupies in the Indian NDP and its continuing dependence on weather fluctuations in spite of the green revolution. It is even more difficult to establish long terms trends for the share of the non-agricultural sector, where there is a sizeable gap between planned and achieved output because of unutilised capacity, inadequate maintenance, and break downs due to industrial and political unrest; where public policy attempts to regulate the working of the economy are met with differences between objectives and achievements; and where inadequate attention is paid to the non-economic factors which affect the achievements of the targeted economic outputs.

In spite of these limitations, I have gone ahead with my projections for the NDP in 2001 AD. In this study, projections of the NDP are made on the basis of extrapolating the actual trend-growth rates during the period 1968-69 to 1979-80 at 1960-61 prices. This, of course, is based on the asssumption that the same trend growth rate will continue between 1979-80 and 2000-01 AD in spite of the factors mentioned above.

Several methods have been used to calculate the trend-growth rate. One method considers the NDP as a whole. An alternative is to add up the trend-growth rates of the NDP from each item of industrial origin to arrive at the total NDP. A third method arrives at the total NDP by adding up the trend-growth rates of the state domestic products (SDPs).* A fourth alternative is to apply the highest SDP trend-growth rate to all the SDPs and total these figures to give the overall NDP. A fifth alternative is to take the more modest course of applying the NDP trend-growth rate to all the SDPs which are below this rate and to add up these figures to arrive at the NDP as a whole.

These rates, based on growth at 1960-61 prices during 1968-79, are applied to the NDP figure in 1979-80 at current prices and projected to 2000-01 (hereafter referred to as 2001 AD) at 1979-80 prices. This will not only make the absolute figures in the projections more meaningful in terms of current purchasing power, but can also be compared with the projections made by the Planning Commission in its Sixth Plan Report. Table 12.1 gives five alternative NDPs in 2001 AD based on the five methods discussed earlier.

It is seen from Table 12.1 that the trend-growth rates on which these alternative projections are made vary from 3.6 per cent to 5.3 per cent. The lowest growth rate is the one which is derived from the growth of the NDP as a whole at constant prices during the period 1968-69 to 1979-80. The rate compares with the minimum rate of 5 per cent postulated by F.A. Mehta for the period 1973-74 to 2001 AD and the 5.2 per cent growth projected by the Planning Commission for the period 1979-80 to 1984-85 and 5.5 per cent for the subsequent ten years.

The second figure is calculated on the basis of the observed trend-growth rates of each sector of industrial origin in the NDP and gives a higher growth

***The SDP figures used in this chapter have been obtained directly from the CSO and may not always correspond with the figures taken from the Reserve Bank bulletins which have been used in Chapter 7 while discussing the regional mix of the NDP.**

Table 12.1

Alternative Projections of the NDP in 2001 AD (Figures in Rs Crores and at 1979-80 Prices)

Alternative	*1979-80*	*1984-85*	*1989-90*	*1994-95*	*1999-2000*	*2000-01 AD*	*Growth Rate 1979 to 2001*
1	87184	104048	124175	148195	176861	183228	3.6
2	87184	105601	129169	159593	199191	208473	4.2
3	87184	109328	133548	166899	207268	216647	4.5
4	87184	115671	148334	190220	243930	256373	5.3
5	87184	111984	139732	177287	223383	234081	4.8

rate of 4.2 per cent for the NDP as a whole. Table 12.2 gives industry-wise projections based on this alternative and the total NDP for the period 1979-80 to 2000-01 AD at 1979-80 prices.

Table 12.2

Projections of NDP by Sectors of Industrial Origin (Figures in Rs Crores and at 1979-80 Prices)

	1979-80	*1984-85*	*1989-90*	*1994-95*	*1999-2000*	*2000-2001*
Agriculture	30738	34104	37838	41982	46579	47557
Forestry & logging	1153	1224	1299	1379	1464	1481
Fishing	670	769	883	1014	1164	1196
Mining & quarrying	1308	1546	1827	2160	2553	2640
Registered manufacturing	9600	12369	15938	20536	26460	27836
Unregistered manufacturing	5898	7315	9072	11252	13955	14569
Construction	4402	4884	5419	6012	6671	6811
Electricity, gas & water supply	1338	1975	2916	4304	6353	6868
Railways	968	1166	1406	1694	2041	2118
Other transport & storage	3122	4379	6141	8614	12081	12927
Communication	698	930	1238	1649	2197	2326
Trade, hotels & restaurants	12729	16246	20734	26463	33774	35463
Banking & insurance	2817	4158	6138	9061	13375	14459
Real estate	2277	2976	3889	5083	6644	7009
Public administration	4572	6442	9078	12792	18026	19306
Other services	4894	5118	5353	5598	5854	5907
TOTAL	87184	105601	129169	159593	199191	208473

The growth of the different sectors of industrial origin at their actual trend-growth rates between 1968-79 brings about a significant change in the sectoral structure of the NDP in 2001 AD as compared to that in 1979-80. Table 12.3 provides the relevant figures.

It is evident from Table 12.3 that while the share of the primary sector in the NDP will decline from 37.35 to 24.09 per cent, the share of the tertiary

Table 12.3

Sectoral Structure of NDP in 1979-80 (Actual) and in 2001 AD (Projected) — Figures in Percentages

	Per Cent of NDP	
	1979-80	*2000-01*
Primary Sector		
Agriculture	35.26	22.81
Forestry & logging	1.32	0.71
Fishing	0.77	0.57
Secondary Sector		
Mining & quarrying	1.50	1.27
Registered manufacturing	11.01	13.35
Unregistered manufacturing	6.77	6.99
Construction	5.05	3.27
Electricity, gas & water supply	1.53	3.29
Tertiary Sector		
Railways	1.11	1.02
Other transport & storage	3.58	6.20
Communication	0.80	1.12
Trade, hotels & restaurants	14.60	17.01
Banking & insurance	3.23	6.94
Real estate	2.61	3.36
Public administration & defence	5.24	9.26
Other services	5.62	2.83

sector will increase from 36.79 to 47.74 per cent. The share of the secondary sector will register a modest increase from 25.86 to 28.17 per cent.

The third alternative is to apply the individual SDP trend-growth rates in 1968-79 to the SDPs in 1979-80 in order to make projections up to 2001 AD at 1979-80 prices and arrive at the NDP by totalling them. Table 12.4 lists the relevant figures.

Table 12.4 shows wide variations in the trend-growth rates of the SDPs during the period 1968-79. Excluding Delhi and 'other states', Haryana has the highest growth rate with 5.1 per cent, while Madhya Pradesh has the lowest growth rate (1.4 per cent). Many SDPs have a growth below that of the undifferentiated NDP rate of 3.6 per cent. These are Kerala (2.1 per cent), Orissa (1.7 per cent), Uttar Pradesh (2.3 per cent), West Bengal (2.4 per cent), Assam (3.4 per cent), Manipur (3.3 per cent), Bihar (2.0 per cent) and Himachal Pradesh (2.8 per cent). These are the states which need special attention in respect of their growth rate during 1980-2000.

The fourth alternative is to apply to all the SDPs the highest growth rate among them to obtain projections for 2001 AD and then total these figures to get the NDP. Excluding Delhi and 'other states', the highest growth rate is that of Haryana (5.1 per cent). Applying this rate to all the SDPs (other than Delhi and 'other states'), the results obtained are given in Table 12.5.

Table 12.4

Projection of SDPs and NDP in 2001 AD by Applying SDP Growth Rates for 1968-79
(Figures in Rs Crores and at 1979-80 Prices)

States	*Growth Rate 1968-79*	*1979-80*	*1984-85*	*1989-90*	*1994-95*	*1999-2000*	*2000-2001*
Andhra Pradesh	3.7	5910	7087	8499	10192	12223	12675
Gujarat	3.9	5210	6308	7638	9248	11198	11635
Karnataka	4.7	4321	5436	6840	8606	10827	11336
Kerala	2.1	2704	3063	3399	3771	4184	4271
Madhya Pradesh	1.4	4262	4569	4898	5250	5628	5707
Orissa	1.7	2156	2346	2552	2776	3020	3072
Tamil Nadu	3.7	6022	7222	8660	10385	12454	12915
Uttar Pradesh	2.3	10257	11491	12875	14757	16534	16914
West Bengal	2.4	7077	7967	8970	10099	11371	11644
Rajasthan	4.2	3225	3962	4866	5978	7343	7652
Jammu & Kashmir	4.5	718	895	1115	1390	1732	1810
Maharashtra	4.8	12200	15422	19496	24646	31157	32652
Assam	3.4	2037	2408	2846	3364	3976	4111
Punjab	4.6	3643	4562	5712	7152	8956	9368
Haryana	5.1	2312	2965	3802	4876	6252	6571
Manipur	3.3	115	135	159	187	220	227
Delhi	5.5	1453	1899	2482	3244	4240	4473
Bihar	2.0	5274	5823	6429	7098	7837	7994
Himachal Pradesh	2.8	542	622	714	820	942	968
Tripura	3.8	167	209	252	303	365	379
Other states	7.4	7579	14937	21344	32757	46809	50273
NDP		87184	109328	133548	166899	207268	216647

Whether it is possible to raise the growth rate of all the SDPs to that of the highest among them is doubtful in view of the differences in their natural resource endowments. However, to the extent that the highest SDP growth rate is the result of labour, capital and management factors, which are presumably capable of duplication elsewhere, it becomes a matter of appropriate policy measures and their effective implementation.

The fifth alternative is to apply the NDP (3.6 per cent) to all the SDPs whose growth rate is below that of the undifferentiated growth rate, which may be a more feasible proposition than the fourth alternative. We have seen earlier that the states with a higher growth rate are Orissa, Kerala, Uttar Pradesh, Bihar, West Bengal, Manipur, Himachal Pradesh and Assam. The figures that emerge by this method are given in Table 12.6.

All these five alternative projections of the NDP are listed in Table 12.1, details of which have been given subsequently (Tables 12.2 and 12.6), based on actual trend-growth rates during 1968-79. Any improvement effected in the different trend-growth rates will have the effect of raising the magnitudes of these projections and the rate of growth of the NDP projected for 2001 AD.

Table 12.5

Projections of SDPs and NDP in 2001 AD by Applying the Highest SDP Growth Rate to all the Other SDPs (Figures in Rs Crores and at 1979-80 Prices)

States	1979-80	1984-85	1989-90	1994-95	1999-2000	2000-2001
Andhra Pradesh	5910	7579	9719	12463	15982	16797
Gujarat	5210	6681	8568	10987	14089	14808
Karnataka	4321	5541	7106	9112	11685	12281
Kerala	2704	3644	4673	5993	7685	8077
Madhya Pradesh	4262	5465	7009	8988	11526	12114
Orissa	2156	2765	3545	4547	5830	6128
Tamil Nadu	6022	7722	9903	12699	16285	17116
Uttar Pradesh	10257	13152	16866	21628	27735	29150
West Bengal	7077	9074	11636	14922	19136	20112
Rajasthan	3225	4136	5303	6801	8721	9166
Jammu & Kashmir	718	921	1181	1514	1942	2041
Maharashtra	12200	15644	20061	25726	32990	34672
Assam	2037	2612	3350	4296	5509	5790
Punjab	3643	4672	5991	7682	9852	10354
Haryana	2312	2965	3802	4876	6252	6571
Manipur	115	147	189	243	311	327
Delhi	1453	1863	2389	3064	3929	4130
Bihar	5274	6763	8673	11122	14262	14990
Himachal Pradesh	542	695	891	1143	1466	1540
Tripura	167	225	289	370	475	499
Other states	7579	13405	17190	22044	28268	29710
NDP (Sum of SDPs)	87184	115671	148334	190220	243930	256373

Let us now examine F.A. Mehta's projections for 2001 AD on the basis of 3, 5, 7 and 9 per cent compound growth rates respectively over the period 1973-74 to 2001 AD. As his figures are at 1973-74 prices, they have been converted into 1979-80 prices by linking the price levels of these two years. Table 12.7 gives Mehta's alternative projections at 1979-80 prices.

Mehta's projections and my projections are not comparable because his projections are from 1973-74, whereas mine are from 1979-80. Of Mehta's four alternative projections, the one that come nearest to mine is the one made on the basis of a 5 per cent compound annual growth which is Rs 296708 crores of the GDP as against an NDP of Rs 256373 crores in my fourth alternative, which is calculated by applying to all the SDPs the highest SDP trend-growth rate during 1968-79.

It is also of interest to look at the changes in the sectoral structure of the NDP visualised by his four alternative projections. Table 12.8 gives the relevant figures.

With a rise in the growth rate from 3 to 5 per cent, Mehta's projections indicate a steep fall in the share of the primary sector (from 36.2 to 21.9 per cent) and an equally steep rise in the share of the secondary sector (from 26.8 to 38.8 per cent), while the share of the tertiary sector records only a margi-

Table 12.6

Projections of SDPs and NDP in 2001 AD by Applying the NDP Growth Rate to all the SDPs Below this Rate (Figures in Rs Crores and at 1979-80 Prices)

States	*1979-80*	*1984-85*	*1989-90*	*1994-95*	*1999-2000*	*2000-2001*
Andhra Pradesh	5910	7087	8499	10192	12223	12675
Gujarat	5210	6308	7638	9248	11198	11635
Karnataka	4321	5436	6840	8606	10827	11336
Kerala	2704	3227	3851	4596	5485	5683
Madhya Pradesh	4262	5086	6070	7245	8646	8957
Orissa	2156	2573	3071	3665	4374	4531
Tamil Nadu	6022	7222	8660	10385	12454	12915
Uttar Pradesh	10257	12240	14607	17433	20805	21554
West Bengal	7077	8445	10078	12028	14354	14871
Rajasthan	3225	3962	4866	5978	7343	7652
Jammu & Kashmir	718	895	1115	1390	1732	1810
Maharashtra	12200	15422	19496	24646	31157	32652
Assam	2037	2431	2901	3462	4132	4281
Punjab	3643	4562	5712	7152	8956	9368
Haryana	2312	2965	3802	4876	6252	6571
Manipur	115	137	164	195	233	242
Delhi	1453	1899	2482	3244	4240	4473
Bihar	5274	6294	7512	8965	10699	11084
Himachal Pradesh	542	647	772	921	1099	1139
Tripura	167	209	252	303	365	379
Other states	7579	14937	21344	32757	46809	50273
NDP (Sum of SDPs)	87184	111984	139732	177287	223383	234081

Table 12.7

F.A. Mehta's Projections of the GDP in 2001 AD (Figures in Rs Crores and at 1979-80 Prices)

Growth Rate Assumed (Per Cent)	*GDP*				
	1979-80	*1985-86*	*1990-91*	*1995-96*	*2000-01*
3	93983	110920	129840	152275	184034
5	93983	125881	162623	215884	296708
7	93983	137049	193421	279724	426546
9	93983	142302	221623	367132	680951

nal rise (from 37.1 to 39.3 per cent). In other words, the main area of growth when the rate goes up from 3 to 5 per cent would be the secondary sector. The same applies if the growth rate goes up to 7 per cent, but will cease to be the case if it goes up to 9 per cent, the lead position now being held by the tertiary sector. In all cases, there is a steep decline in the share of the primary sector. The consequent change in the occupational structure and the problems it would create for inter-sectoral per capita GDPs and rural/urban per capita GDPs are not indicated in Mehta's study.

Table 12.8

Sectoral Structure of GDP in 2001 AD Visualised by Mehta's Projections
(Figures in Percentages and at 1979-80 Prices)

Assumed Rate of Growth Annual Compound (Per cent)	1979-80			2001-01 AD		
	Primary	Secondary	Tertiary	Primary	Secondary	Tertiary
3	36.17	26.78	37.05	32.72	28.78	38.50
5	36.17	26.78	37.05	21.90	38.82	39.28
7	36.17	26.78	37.05	20.44	39.73	39.83
9	36.17	26.78	37.05	17.18	37.38	45.44

The Planning Commission has made projections for the GDP in 1994-95 on an assumed growth rate of 5.2 per cent during 1979-84 and of 5.5 per cent during 1985-95.[5] These have been brought up to 2001 AD by assuming that the growth rate of 5.5 will continue during 1995-2001. Table 12.9 provides the figures.

Table 12.9

Planning Commission's Projections of GDP at 1979-80 Prices

Year	Amount (in Rs Crores)	Growth Rate
1979-80	97051	—
1984-85	125050	5.2
1990-91	169501	5.5
1994-95	213600	5.5
2000-01	281414	5.5

The Planning Commission's projection of a GDP of Rs 281414 crores in 2001 AD is quite close to that of Mehta's figure assumed on a 5 per cent growth rate (Rs 296708 crores). It is also fairly close to the figure (Rs 256373 crores) of my fourth alternative projection.

Table 12.10 gives the sectoral structure of the GDP envisaged by the Planning Commission for 1994-95 and extended to 2001 AD on the assumption made in the foregoing.[6]

Table 12.10

Projected Sectoral Structure of the GDP in 2001 AD at 1979-80 Prices (Figures in Percentages)

Sector	1979-80	2000-01
Primary	35.13	25.93
Secondary	26.37	34.79
Tertiary	38.50	39.28

There is a sharp difference between the sector structure of the GDP projected for 2001 AD by Mehta and by the Planning Commission. Mehta's estimates give a higher percentage for the secondary sector (38.8) as compared to the Planning Commission (34.8), and a much lower percentage for the primary sector (21.9) as against the Planning Commission (25.9), with no difference between their projections for the tertiary sector (39.3 per cent in both cases). While Mehta's projections give a dominant role to the secondary sector in the envisaged growth of the GDP, the Planning Commission's figures appear to give it less significance. Mehta envisages a dwindling role for the primary sector whereas the Planning Commission appears to give it a larger continuing role, though with a lower share of the GDP. In any case, both the projections attribute a larger share of the GDP in 2001 AD to the secondary sector and a smaller share to the primary sector, leaving unresolved the question raised by me earlier regarding changes in the occupational structure.

The per capita GDP projections made by both Mehta and the Planning Commission are based on projections of population growth which have not been borne out by the 1981 census results, while the medium term projections made by Ambannavar[7] for 1981 in his volume entitled *Population* in the *Second India Studies* series brings his estimate very close to the figure actually revealed by the census (683 million and 684 million respectively). The change this can make to the per capita GDP projections can be seen from the fact that whereas Mehta envisages a population of 865 million in 1995-96, and the Planning Commission estimates it at 864 million in the same year, the medium term projection made by Ambannavar for that year is 921 million; and Ambannavar's figures are supported by the actual figures revealed by the 1981 census. Therefore, to talk in terms of doubling or trebling the per capita income is far more hazardous, as it faces the double risk of not fulfilling both the GDP projections and population projections. It is difficult to implement planned increases in production; it is even more difficult to implement planned decreases in the rate of population growth. In short, it is a matter of grave doubt whether it is really worthwhile putting forward perspective estimates of per capita GDP or NDP for 20001 AD or for 1994-95 AD, or even for 1990-91 AD.

I have made no attempt to put forward projections of my own for the NDP or its sectoral structure in 2001 AD. I have only given alternative estimates on the basis of alternative growth rates, all based on perceived trend-growth rates at constant prices during the period 1968-79. There are only two comments I can make on India's national income in 2001 AD. One is the near consensus on the possible and feasible annual compound growth rate of between 5 and 6 per cent during the closing two decades of this century. This is far higher than the trend-growth rate of 3.6 per cent of the NDP seen during 1968-79, but it is not beyond the bounds of feasibility. If the actual trend-growth rate of the individual sectors of industrial origin during 1968-79 are extrapolated to cover the remaining years before 2001 AD — on the assumption that the past behaviour of production variables will continue unchanged over the next twenty years — the NDP growth rate obtained is 3.6 per cent. If, however, the highest trend-growth rate among the SDPs during 1968-79 can also become the growth rate of the other SDPs during the remaining years of the century — assuming that what one state in India can achieve in production can also be achieved by the other states — then the NDP growth rate obtained is 5.1 per cent. If a further and not unreasonable assumption can be made that some new factors contributing to an increase in productivity will emerge during the next two decades, then an annual compound growth rate of between 5 and 6 per cent does not appear unattainable.

The realisation of a growth rate of between 5 and 6 per cent, however, depends entirely on what is done to rectify the deficiencies fully known to those in charge of economic management in the country, whether in the public or private sector. Remedial action has to be taken during the early years of this decade rather than later if it is to have an effect on the growth rate in the last two decades of this century. Remedial action cannot, however, be confined to the economic sphere or to technical problems of production. It has to be extended to the political, sociological, educational, cultural, and demographic spheres of national activity, official policies, and their implementation. Without establishing a feeling of national identity and commitment, social harmony, educational relevance, cultural rationalisation and family planning on a mass scale, no economic measures or policies can bring about the desired increase in the growth rate or lead to social justice along with economic growth. It would also help if national consciousness is created on productivity and economic growth, and people's positive cooperation and participation enlisted in the developmental process. This study of India's national income over a period of thirty years from 1950 to 1980 shows that what has been achieved is far below the potential and that there is a great deal that can still be achieved in various sectors of the economy and regions of the country. The second India that will emerge at the end of this century can certainly present a far more satisfactory picture than today's India, if only the country and those who can lead or influence it in its various spheres of activity learn from the past and accordingly mould their action in the future.

Before concluding it is necessary to emphasise some of the policy implications of the development which follow from the projections of India's national income in 2001 AD, and from the experience of its growth and change during the thirty years covered by this study. This has necessarily to be in the form of a summary, as it may otherwise result in another book!

1. India will continue to be one of the poorest countries in the world in terms of its per capita product, though some of its citizens may enjoy a standard of living on par with those living in the richest countries. This duality in Indian society, which has been growing over the last thirty years, has to be arrested if an explosive situation is to be avoided. Policies relating to an increase in production, composition of the product mix, conspicuous consumption, mobilisation of savings, pattern of

Appendix 1
Net Factor Income from Abroad

Table A 1.1 gives the quinquennial totals of the net factor income from abroad at current prices as given in the NAS, and their percentage to the corresponding NDP totals.

Table A 1.1

Net Factor Income from Abroad and its Proportion to the NDP
(Figures in Rs Crores)

Period	*NDP*	*Net Factor Income from Abroad*	*Percentage of Col.3 to Col.2*
1950-54	45320	−149	−0.33
1955-59	55198	−139	−0.25
1960-64	79560	−537	−0.67
1965-69	133930	−1178	−0.88
1970-74	222441	−1493	−0.67
1975-79	374140	−808	−0.22

Table A 1.1 shows that the country does not have any net factor income from abroad. On the contrary, it has been remitting a part of its NDP abroad. In terms of the proportion of the NDP, however, this has been less than 1 per cent. In fact, it reached a peak of 0.88 per cent in the quinquennial total of 1965-69, after which it has started declining, reaching 0.22 per cent in the total of the last quinquennium during the period under review. It has become a positive figure in the final year of this quinquennium — the country received a net factor income of Rs 69 crores (or 0.08 per cent of the NDP) in 1979-80.

However, overall external assistance constituted a significant amount during this thirty year period (1950-51 to 1979-80), totalling Rs 24,759 crores at current prices or 2.7 per cent of the total NDP during the period.* But the external assistance actually utilised was only 2.2 per cent of the total NDP period. Table A 1.2 gives the relevant figures of authorised and utilised external assistance during the period.

Table A 1.2

Authorised and Utilised External Assistance
(Figures in Rs Crores)

Period	*Authorisation (Amt.)*	*Utilisation (Amt.)*	*Per Cent of Amount Utilised to Amount Authorised*	*Share of Grants in Amount Utilised (Amt.)*	*Per Cent of Grants to Amount Utilised*
Upto end of 3rd Plan	5711.6	4508.8	78.94	336.9	7.47
1966-67	1506.5	1131.4	75.10	97.1	8.58
1967-68	718.5	1195.6	166.40	60.7	5.08
1968-69	946.8	902.6	95.33	65.2	7.22
1969-70	634.3	856.3	135.00	26.1	3.05
1970-71	761.9	791.4	103.87	43.5	5.50
1971-72	929.2	834.1	89.77	50.5	6.05
1972-73	676.2	662.2	97.93	12.0	1.81
1973-74	1170.6	1035.7	88.48	20.7	2.00
1974-75	1671.2	1314.3	78.64	93.9	7.14
1975-76	2653.5	1840.5	69.36	283.3	15.39
1976-77	1286.4	1598.9	124.29	245.8	15.37
1977-78	1897.0	1290.0	68.00	260.6	20.20
1978-79	2335.7	1265.8	54.19	273.4	21.60
1979-80	1859.5	1367.0	73.51	304.5	22.28
TOTAL	24758.9	20594.6	83.18	2174.2	10.56

It is evident from Table A 1.2 that of the total external assistance authorised during the period (Rs 24,759 crores), the amount utilised was only 83.2 per cent. Grants constituted 10.56 per cent of the external assistance which was utilised. While the share of the amount utilised to that authorised fell steadily during the latter part of the seventies, the share of grants recorded a sharp increase.

The *Economic Survey of 1980-81* also gives figures for the gross and net inflow of external assistance since 1970-71. The data are given in Table A 1.3.

The Survey also provides figures of external debt servicing for the thirty years under review in this study (see Table A 1.4). External debt servicing charges during the period increased from Rs 23.8 crores during the First Plan period to Rs 884.0 crores in 1979-80.

The steady increase in debt servicing charges is a matter for concern to the future of the Indian economy. The further rise that this will undergo with the

* *Economic Survey, 1980-81*, Table 7.1.

Table A 1.3

Inflow of External Assistance — Gross and Net
(Amount in Rs Crores)

Year	*Gross Disbursement*	*Debt Relief as Part of Gross Disbursement*	*Debt Servicing*	*Net Inflow of Assistance*
1970-71	791	77	450	341
1971-72	834	61	479	355
1972-73	666	106	507	159
1973-74	1036	117	596	440
1974-75	1314	116	626	688
1975-76	1841	133	687	1154
1976-77	1599	102	755	844
1977-78	1290	28	821	469
1978-79	1266	7	882	384
1979-80	1367	11	884	483

Table A 1.4

External Debt Servicing
(Rs Crores)

Period	*Amortisation*	*Interest Payment*	*Total Debt Servicing*
First Plan	10.5	13.3	23.8
Second Plan	55.2	64.2	119.4
Third Plan	305.6	237.0	542.6
1966-67	159.7	114.8	274.5
1967-68	210.7	122.3	333.0
1968-69	236.2	138.8	375.0
1969-70	268.5	144.0	412.5
1970-71	289.5	160.5	450.0
1971-72	299.3	180.0	479.3
1972-73	327.0	180.4	507.4
1973-74	399.9	195.9	595.8
1974-75	411.0	215.0	626.0
1975-76	462.7	224.2	686.9
1976-77	507.4	247.3	754.7
1977-78	560.6	260.1	820.7
1978-79	593.7	288.4	882.1
1979-80	570.1	313.9	884.0

recent massive loan that India has taken from the IMF and her increased dependence on commercial loans will make the situation worse. However, this falls outside the period under review in this study.

Appendix 2
Capital Consumption

Table A 2.1, compiled from the NAS, gives data on capital consumption during the thirty years under review and their proportion to the annual additions under gross capital formation.

Table A 2.1 indicates a steady increase in capital consumption every year with the annual additions to the GDCF. It also reveals remarkable variations in the proportion of capital consumption to the annual GDCF. This is natural because capital consumption is related to capital stock, and the figures given in this Table would, therefore, include capital consumption from capital stock in existence in 1950-51. Capital consumption figures would also show a larger proportion to the GDCF in earlier years than in later years because there would be less capital consumption or depreciation in the case of more recent additions to the capital stock than earlier additions. But as the GDCF during the period under review is several times that of the capital stock in 1950-51 (see Table 10.2 in Chapter 10), it is quite legitimate to use the percentage of annual capital consumption to annual GDCF to indicate the magnitude and change in capital consumption as a factor in the GDCF. However, if the annual figures are converted into quinquennial totals, one finds the behaviour of capital consumption more comprehensible as can be seen from Table A 2.2.

It appears from Table A 2.2 that about 30 per cent of the GDCF goes into meeting capital consumption requirements. This is why the GDCF is more relevant as a determinant of economic growth than the GDCF, though it is also true that to neglect capital consumption replacement would result in a lowering of the growth rate over a period. In fact, it is the actual consumption of capital (and involuntary destruction, as has been seen in Chapter 10) that is of crucial relevance in linking the growth rate with either the GDCF or the NDCF. However, data on capital consumption is based on depreciation, which is based on accounting and income-tax procedures; and it may not coincide with the conceptual contents behind capital consumption. This is why the national accounts data in recent years use the GDP and the GDCF

Table A 2.1

Capital Consumption at Current Prices
(Amount in Rs Crores)

Year	*GDCF*	*NDCF*	*Capital Consumption*	*Percentage of Capital Consumption to GDCF*
1950-51	954	630	324	33.96
1951-52	1188	829	359	30.22
1952-53	772	383	389	50.39
1953-54	909	517	392	43.12
1954-55	1070	641	429	40.09
1955-56	1469	1021	448	30.50
1956-57	1959	1473	486	24.81
1957-58	1843	1307	536	29.08
1958-59	1785	1158	627	35.13
1959-60	1996	1335	661	33.12
1960-61	2544	1808	736	28.93
1961-62	2438	1626	812	33.31
1962-63	2916	1984	932	31.96
1963-64	3266	2265	1001	30.65
1964-65	3735	2623	1112	29.77
1965-66	4390	3161	1229	28.00
1966-67	5437	4035	1402	25.79
1967-68	5334	3776	1558	29.21
1968-69	5113	3427	1686	32.97
1969-70	6285	4370	1915	30.47
1970-71	7177	4960	2217	30.89
1971-72	7976	5577	2399	30.08
1972-73	8066	5397	2669	33.09
1973-74	11784	8761	3023	25.65
1974-75	13306	9780	3526	26.50
1975-76	14729	10683	4046	27.47
1976-77	16390	11898	4492	27.41
1977-78	17770	12759	5011	28.20
1978-79	23925	18163	5762	24.08
1979-80	24294	17495	6799	27.99

rather than the NDP and the NDCF to determine capital-output ratios and the contribution of capital formation to economic growth. This is also subject to the limitation that capital consumption data do not include involuntary capital destruction or unidentified depreciation in the productive content of permanent natural resources like land. The data could also be subject to an even more serious limitation of the variability of the proportion of recorded capital consumption to changing capital stock, but this does not seem to hold in actual practice, considering the near stability in secular terms of this ratio over fairly long periods.

Altogether, the whole subject of capital consumption bristles with both conceptual and estimational difficulties and continues to remain a largely unresolved problem in the literature on national income and accounts.

Table A 2.2

Capital Consumption by Quinquennial Totals
(Amount in Rs Crores)

Period	*GDCF*	*NDCF*	*Capital Consumption*	*Percentage of Capital Consumption to GDCF*
1950-54	4893	3000	1893	38.69
1955-59	9052	6294	2758	30.47
1960-64	14899	10306	4593	30.83
1965-69	26559	18769	7790	29.33
1970-74	48309	34475	13834	28.64
1975-79	97108	70998	26110	26.89

Index